PENGUIN PLA
WESKER: LADY O
AND OTHER

Arnold Wesker, FRSL, Litt. D. (Hons.), was born in Stepney in
1932 and educated at Upton House School in Hackney. From 1948
to 1958 he pursued many trades from furniture maker to pastry
cook. His career as a playwright began when Lindsay Anderson,
who had read *The Kitchen* and *Chicken Soup with Barley*, brought
Wesker to the attention of George Devine at the Royal Court
Theatre; Devine sent *Chicken Soup with Barley* to the Belgrade
Theatre in Coventry, where it was first produced in 1958, under the
direction of John Dexter. A year later, having been turned down by
the Royal Court, *Roots* was directed by Dexter, again at the
Belgrade, Coventry, and in the following months he directed *The
Kitchen* at the Court for two Sunday Night experimental perform-
ances 'without décor'. *I'm Talking About Jerusalem* was added to
Chicken Soup with Barley and *Roots* to make up *The Wesker Trilogy*,
which created an enormous impact when produced in its entirety at
the Royal Court in 1960 and again at the Shaw Theatre in 1978. In
1979 the National Film Development Board commissioned a film
script of the three plays which, because Wesker made many cuts
and additions, is a new work – *The Trilogy* twenty years on!

His other plays include *Their Very Own and Golden City* (1965;
winner of the Italian Premio Matzotto Drama Award in 1964), *The
Four Seasons* (1965), *The Wedding Feast* (1974), *The Journalists*
(1975), *Shylock* (previously *The Merchant*, 1975), *One More Ride on
the Merry-go-round* (1978), *Caritas* (1980), *Four Portraits* (1982),
Annie Wobbler (1983), *Bluey* (1984), *Yardsale* (1985), *Sullied Hand*
(1985), *Whatever Happened to Betty Lemon?* (1986), *When God
Wanted a Son* (1986), *Boddenheim 1939*, adapted from a novel by
Aharon Appelfeld (1987), *Shoeshine* and *Little Old Lady*, one-act
plays for young people (1987), *Lady Othello* (1987), *Beorhtel's Hill*
(1988) and *The Mistress* (1988). In addition to plays, Arnold
Wesker has written poems, short stories and numerous articles.
Among these are a collection of articles and fragments, *Fears of
Fragmentation* (1970); *Six Sundays in January* (1971), including two
stories; a diary; the libretto for a documentary, *The Nottingham
Captain*; a TV play, *Menace*; a volume of short stories, *Love Letters
on Blue Paper* (1974), the title story of which he adapted for his play
of the same name; and a book of primitive paintings by

John Allin, *Say Goodbye You May Never See Them Again* (1974). He has also written an essay on education, *Words as Definitions of Experience* (1977); a personal account of a brief stay in *The Sunday Times*, *Journey into Journalism* (1977); a further collection of short stories, *Said the Old Man to the Young Man* (1978); a book for children, *Fatlips* (1978); a libretto for an opera of Caritas music, *Robert Saxton* (1988); a collection of essays, *Distinctions* (1984). Penguin has published five other volumes of his plays and a collection of short stories, *Love Letters on Blue Paper*.

Arnold Wesker was artistic director of Centre 42, a cultural movement for popularizing the arts, primarily through trade-union support and participation, from 1961 to 1970. He lives with his wife and one of his three children in North London.

ARNOLD WESKER

LADY OTHELLO AND OTHER PLAYS

One More Ride on the Merry-go-round
Caritas
When God Wanted a Son
Lady Othello
Bluey

VOLUME 6

PENGUIN BOOKS

PENGUIN BOOKS

Published by the Penguin Group
27 Wrights Lane, London W8 5TZ, England
Viking Penguin Inc., 40 West 23rd Street, New York, New York 10010, USA
Penguin Books Australia Ltd, Ringwood, Victoria, Australia
Penguin Books Canada Ltd, 2801 John Street, Markham,
Ontario, Canada L3R 1B4
Penguin Books (NZ) Ltd, 182–190 Wairau Road, Auckland 10, New Zealand

Penguin Books Ltd, Registered Offices: Harmondsworth, Middlesex, England

One More Ride on the Merry-go-round first published 1990
Caritas first published by Jonathan Cape 1981
This revised version published 1990
When God Wanted a Son first published 1990
Lady Othello first published 1990
Bluey first published in *Words* magazine August 1985
This collection first published 1990

1 3 5 7 9 10 8 6 4 2
Copyright © Arnold Wesker, 1981, 1984, 1985, 1990
All rights reserved

All rights whatsoever are reserved, and application for performance, etc.,
should be made in writing to Ian Amos, Duncan Heath Associates,
162 Wardour Street, London W1

Made and printed in Great Britain by
Cox and Wyman Ltd, Reading, Berks.

Filmset in Linotron Goudy by
Rowland Phototypesetting Ltd, Bury St Edmunds, Suffolk

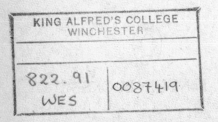

CONTENTS

ONE MORE RIDE
ON THE MERRY-GO-ROUND

CHARACTERS

JASON   fifty, Professor of Philosophy at Cambridge

MONICA   twenty-seven, Lecturer in History, New Yorker, Jason's
girlfriend

CECILIA
MONTGOMERY   } Cambridge Professors
ANTHONY

NITA   forty-nine, Jason's ex-wife

MAT   twenty-eight, young printer, Nita's lover

CHRIS   twenty-four, daughter of Jason and Nita, a drop-out

ECKHARDT   twenty-six, Jason's illegitimate son, a magician

One More Ride on the Merry-go-round was first performed at the Phoenix Theatre, Leicester, on 25 April 1985. The cast was as follows:

JASON	Ian Hogg
MONICA	Janene Possell
CECILIA	Yvonne Bonnamy
MONTGOMERY	John Hart Dyke
ANTHONY	David Ryder-Futcher
NITA	Pauline Yates
MAT	Mark Greenstreet
CHRIS	Julia Lloyd
ECKHARDT	Dursley McLinden
Director	Graham Watkins
Designer	Anthony Dean

ACT ONE

Scene I

Joyous music of Jane Oliver singing 'One More Ride on the Merry-go-round' (Columbia PC 34274). House-lights down to darkness.

Two people are making love. SHE, *twenty-seven, can speak her ecstasy.* HE, *on the verge of fifty, appears to have his mouth full. Music continues softly.*

PHASE ONE

SHE: Oh yes! There! There! Don't stop, please don't stop. Oh, your tongue! Your tongue! Oh my God! I'll die, just die! Don't stop! Oh my God! There, there! Don't stop! Oh, oh, ohhhhh . . . .
(Orgasm. Sighs. Music fades out. Long silence. The darkness continues.)

HE: It makes one so thirsty!

SHE: *(Contentedly)* Mmm!

HE: Breaks your back and makes you thirsty.

SHE: Mmm!

HE: I must be mad with my cancer of the spine.

SHE: And you said you were too old for it.

HE: Not too old, too intellectual. To a mind which contemplates infinity, sixty-nine is simply a number divisible by three.

SHE: You just needed the right woman.

HE: Or twenty-three.

SHE: I'll take ten years off you.

HE: But will you find me a job?

SHE: With ten years off you everyone will be offering you jobs.

HE: As a stud!

SHE: I'd pimp for you. Fifty pounds a throw, three throws a night, six nights a week?

HE: I'd be dead within the year.

SHE: With two months' holiday that's £36,000 tax-free, plus what you'd get from the dole.

HE: This is an immoral conversation.

SHE: (*Seductively*) Want to stop talking?

(*Sound of movement in bed. Continuing dark.*)

HE: Ouch! No, don't do that, you know I bruise easily. No, don't! Not there, please. I've suspected appendix. No, not there either, the umbilical cord was clumsily cut. No, no! Especially not *there*. I won't make it. It's three in the morning, I won't rise to the occasion. I won't! I promise you I just woooooooon't! (*Orgasm. Sighs.*) Oh ye gods and little fishes, who'd have known?

(*Long silence.*)

SHE: You're holding your breath again. Breathe!

(*Pause.*)

HE: That's how I'll die. A heart attack. One night you'll come and I'll go!

(*Sounds of morning.*)

SHE: Ah, sweet innocence. With all your intellect.

(*Music returns.*)

PHASE TWO

A slow, slow dawn comes up to reveal two naked bodies crazily entwined, asleep on a bed, centre, which is just being revolved around out of sight leaving –

– the study, lounge, dining room/kitchen of, believe it or not, a very tidy academic: full of personality, lived in. A central decorative feature is a painter's easel upon which is propped an unmounted original print, one of Matisse's 'paper cut-outs'. Strewn around are fascinating bric-à-brac, but – an order is there. The only disorder is that of female clothing flung all over the place. The lady seems to have undressed en route to the bedroom. Through the door from the bedroom emerges a man. He's short, dark, not handsome but – despite his black, sardonic humour he's life-loving and driven by an intellectual energy. He's about to become fifty. Dressed in an elegant if faded Edwardian dressing gown, he appears a wreck, surveys the scene of the night before. Here and there he finds scraps of paper at which he

6

glances, then screws up. He looks in a mirror, shudders. His name is
JASON.

JASON: I need mirrors to make sure I'm there! (*Picks out a piece of paper stuck in the mirror's corner.*) And I must stop writing poetry.

SHE: (*From the bedroom*) Especially if it's bad poetry.

JASON: You're cruel.

SHE: Not cruel, just honest. You're a philosopher, you shouldn't be misusing language. Bring me my clothes, please.

(*He begins to collect them but absent-mindedly abandons the task halfway.*)

JASON: The Victorians were right, no one should be seen before midday.

SHE: It *is* midday! A gorgeous spring midday.

JASON: What I say is: If spring comes, can *winter* be far behind? (*Pause; pulling himself up*) On the other hand my position is enviable. I have not resigned a job and a wife, I've gained my freedom.

SHE: My clothes, Jason, please!

JASON: More or less. (*Picks up the clothes but abandons them because a new idea strikes him: to make an omelette.*) And freedom presents problems. The first, obviously, is: did I want it? Or (*in one breath, as he's prone to do*) am I a victim, if victim is the right word, of the demise of the wife and work ethic for, as the twentieth century draws to its end, both ethics beg the question: does one need to work and wive quite so hard, so long or so fruitlessly in order to find one's true self, which, now that I'm free, will I like when I find? Whew! Long sentences, they'll be the death of me! Or, to put it simply: am I embarked upon an odyssey or a nightmare?

SHE: Please bring me my clothes.

(*Now he's distracted by mail on the passage floor.*)

JASON: (*Reading*) It looks as if only the dreaded triumvirate are coming to my party. *They'll* tell me if it's odyssey or nightmare.

SHE: Jason, listen to me. You don't need the dreaded triumvirate to tell you why you should continue working.

JASON: My one ally since undergraduate days writes –

SHE: Read Chekhov! 'In work is salvation!'

JASON: (*Reading*) 'I will not join you since it does not appear to be a birthday celebration, rather a wake for the death of your intelligence. If you want me to offer thoughts on your dilemma to work or not to work, I will, endlessly, but not in the company of the three-headed monster known as Anthony Cecilia Montgomery. You have opted for the very three heads which would not have been better than even none! Affectionately, Barney.'

SHE: Who is 100 per cent correct.

JASON: (*Reading another card*) My ex-wife's style is even more to the point. 'Pig! Your daughter returns from a year of kibbutz life. Don't think even the Jews have saved her from sloth. Be a father! Yours – Unchained!' Only Nita would mention pigs and Jews in the space of a two-lined postcard. 'PS I believe in a society where you help your neighbour because you love him.' Crass statement!

SHE: My clothes, please.

JASON: Did you know my ex-wife's declared quest in life? To find a handful of words which would encapsulate a total philosophy for living. I'd find sentences scrawled on bits of paper all over the place. 'I believe in equal opportunity but not that all people are equal!' 'I believe in the aristocratic spirit but not in aristocracy!' Things like that. I'd find them. All over the house. Scrawled on a serviette before eating, or a piece of lavatory paper before –

SHE: Please! My clothes!

PHASE THREE

JASON: (*Ignoring request, calls:*) Coffee? Tea? Cocktails? Andrews Liver Salts? I have a nice line in mineral waters – French, Italian, Romanian. (*Goes to cupboard for crockery.*) How about some Earl Grey tea and lemon, in my favourite-unmarked-so-we-don't-know-what-they-are tea cups. The only set of blue and white I insisted on keeping, and now that my wife the gauleiter is no longer here to pursue her possessive watch on the Rhine we can *use* the beautiful things instead of keeping them stacked and stored for a future which looks as if it'll always be insecure so why bother. Whew! I really must try giving up long sentences. As if there weren't enough things to die of.

(*He reaches for a pack of cards. He is about to try something he has obviously attempted many times: he shuffles hopefully, then bends the pack in, hoping to squeeze and stretch the cards from one hand to the other. He fails again. They scatter. He returns to making an omelette.)*

France! Italy! Romania! Ah! Centres of Roman civilization! Travel! That's what I really want to do. Samarkand, Mississippi, São Paulo, Quezaltenango . . . No one should be allowed into university who hasn't travelled for two years. Tehuantepec, San Francisco, Tahiti, Sumatra . . . Perhaps we're moving from the age of work ethic to the age of the travel ethic. Borneo, Venice, Cairo, Alexandria . . . The problem is, (*over to his books*) now that I've resigned my job and the philosophy department has lost its least boring pedagogue, so you can imagine what the others were like and why this country hasn't produced an original philosophical work since Wittgenstein and he was Viennese so doesn't count – (*finds another poem in the Wittgenstein book.*) Yeach! When did I write that? – not that anyone would care or even understand since we're none too happy as a nation when confronted with abstract ideas which is at once our strength and downfall because – now where the hell did that sentence begin?

SHE: 'Now that I've resigned my job –'

JASON: Ah! Now that I've resigned my job – but what was I going to say after that?

SHE: Go back to the sentence before, might give you a clue.

JASON: How on earth do you expect me to remember so far back?

SHE: Something about travel. You think we're moving from work ethic to travel ethic, but the problem is, now that –

JASON: (*Saying it with her*) – now that I've resigned my job can I afford to travel? Whew! Nearly didn't make it. No one realizes how dangerously philosophers live.

PHASE FOUR

MONICA *comes in. She's a beautiful New Yorker, nubile and naked, who confronts him boldly, brazenly, hands on hips.*

JASON: Monica, *please!* My system can't take such shocks.

MONICA: If you won't bring my clothes to me, me has to come to my clothes.

(*She stretches over him for her panties. He flinches.*)

JASON: Don't *do* that! Isn't it bad enough you nearly gave me a stroke last night?

MONICA: One good stroke deserves another, I always say.

(*Panties on, she gathers strewn clothes into one pile.*)

JASON: Did you know my wife was a health-food freak? I had no ailments at all until we married. She'd name them, I'd develop the symptoms! (*Beat.*) Before I met her I was tall, blond and blue-eyed.

MONICA: Jason, do you think that for once we could have breakfast with you *out* of your dressing gown?

JASON: You're beginning to sound like her.

MONICA: Wives are either what their husbands bring them to or what their husbands deserve. Did you walk around like that in front of her?

JASON: Of course not. I was presentable because that's what she liked about me.

MONICA: You knew exactly what she liked about you?

JASON: She put up with it for twenty-five years.

MONICA: 'Put up with it' is perhaps just what she did. Doesn't mean it's what she liked.

JASON: Nita was dowdy, dull and depressing. I could see it in everyone's eyes.

MONICA: While you were warm, witty and winning?

JASON: And could see it in everyone's eyes.

MONICA: And now?

(*He gathers the playing cards for another try.*)

JASON: Now? Well – poor Nita. 'I believe in a society where you help your neighbour because you love him.' I ask you! She's probably found what she's always wanted, as people do when they're released from their first mistake, someone meek, mild and mediocre who doesn't make too many personal or physical demands on her and leaves her to her wild social projects for improving the Third World.

MONICA: While you with *your* freedom have found –

JASON: – someone vivid, vital and voluptuous –

(*She provocatively slips on her bra. He retreats on his knees.*)

MONICA: – who *does* make too many personal and physical demands.

JASON: Don't *do* that! My God! Every morning brings its dangers.

MONICA: And every night its delights.
　　(*She bends to him for a long kiss.*)
JASON: You take neither my resignation nor my frailty seriously enough.
　　(MONICA, *only half clothed, attempts a few physical exercises.*)
MONICA: You're holding your breath again.
JASON: Oh, you're so oppressively fit.
MONICA: Swimming. Try it.
JASON: Too dangerous. All that water. To quote Dr Johnson: 'A sea voyage is like being in prison with the added danger that one can drown.'
　　(JASON *shuffles the pack; attempts his 'flourish'. Fails. Which brings her brief exercises to an end.*)

PHASE FIVE

MONICA: Jason, you're a mess. You may have 'found' yourself in bed but you've lost yourself in the world. Look at you! You need a shave.
JASON: You're turned on by my intellect, what need to shave?
　　(*She continues dressing.*)
MONICA: Your bright brain may turn me on but your grey stubble turns me right off again.
JASON: It's not grey!
MONICA: Your beard's grey, your eyes are bloodshot, and tiny blood vessels have burst around your nose.
JASON: (*Mock New York accent*) From the strain of it, the strain of it, goddammit!
MONICA: Don't best with me, because I'm a New Yorker and I'm your match.
JASON: (*Moving to her*) I'm not besting with you. 'Besting' is getting the best and last word over a partner you don't really love, and you I love. I only bested with my wife else she'd have bored me into the ground. But you, you are a beautiful history lecturer . . .
　　(*From behind he kisses her neck and cups her breasts. She picks up a cushion and bangs away at him.*)
MONICA: I will not have my qualities reduced to tits and bums. My lectures are full because my erudition is sound and primary and my

11

references reach out to literature and art. I may be a good fuck but I'm also a good scholar.

JASON: Does that make you a fucking good scholar or a good scholarly fuck! (*Under blows*) Ouch! My lumbago! I give in, give in, give in!

MONICA: You're vain, pompous, bumptious, pretentious, condescending, hubristical, and you don't deserve me.

(*She stops raining blows.*)

JASON: Of that I'm certain.

MONICA: Self-pity as well! *Argumentum ad misericordum.*

JASON: It's *misericord—iam.*

MONICA: *Don't* correct me!

JASON: I was merely bantering.

MONICA: You're not so hot on Latin that *you* can correct *me*.

JASON: You're a minefield!

(*In anger she goes off to the bedroom to collect something.*)

Jesus! Who invented this world?

(*While she's gone he finds a white sheet of paper, a thick felt pen and writes large:* PAX. I LOVE YOU. *She returns with cosmetics and a hand mirror. She's going to make up her face. As she returns he swings the notice in front of her. She ignores it and begins to make up. He pours out tea.*)

MONICA: Do you realize you never apologize?

JASON: Because it's always *you* who cause a quarrel.

MONICA: He can't hear himself! That's just not possible! It takes two to make a fight. Two!

JASON: (*The philosopher*) Not sure I can accept that. It may take two to become *involved* in a fight but only one is needed to *cause* it.

MONICA: But without the other one being there, there'd be nothing.

JASON: Right! *That's* my guilt, to have been there, *that* I accept, I stood in the line of fire.

MONICA: Instead of running away, you mean?

JASON: Now follows the accusation about cowardice, I suppose.

MONICA: You always run away.

JASON: I want to travel, not the same thing.

MONICA: And if you think I'm going to hitchhike round the world with you –

JASON: (*Trying to calm her, approaching with cup of tea*) Samarkand, Mississippi, São Paulo, Quezaltenango . . .

MONICA: I don't think you respect anyone or anything . . .

JASON: . . . Tehuantepec, San Francisco, Tahiti, Sumatra . . .

MONICA: . . . not me, not your emotions . . .

JASON: . . . Borneo, Venice, Cairo, Alexandria . . .

MONICA: . . . no wonder your wife left you!

JASON: We left each other.

PHASE FIVE A

JASON: I placed my goodbye note in the kitchen and she placed hers in the study. On the same day. But in rebellion against the stations allotted us in life we decided not to enter either place. And so a month passed before we knew what we'd done to one another. At which she giggled and I became furious.

(*He goes on to fry the omelette.*)

MONICA: The more I hear about her the more she sounds my kind of woman.

JASON: Now comes the ganging-up sequence. 'We were both fools to love him.'

MONICA: No woman leaves without cause.

JASON: Oh yes, defend her! You're right. She's defendable. Defendable and dependable. But mad! Quite mad! 'A week's wage for the Third World!' Every family in Europe to give up one week's wage for training expertise, education, machinery!

MONICA: Sounds very worthy to me.

JASON: Worthy but – hare-brained! Committees all over Europe, experts working out what the money could be spent on, debates in the press, on radio, TV. Not charity but self-help! And – and this is her genius – she's doing it in two stages, getting pledges first so that when people give up their one week's wage, which they can pay in instalments, they won't feel it's done in isolation. Not *one* pledge to be called upon unless there's a 55 per cent response, it must be a majority wish also!

(*He proudly presents her with the finished omelette.*)

MONICA: (*Referring to Nita's plan*) Brilliant! Eccentric but practical. Not dull and dowdy at all.

JASON: But you didn't have to sleep with her! (*Pause.*) Yes, that sounds outrageously frivolous, doesn't it? Outlining a socially responsible project and then following it up with complaints about sexual inadequacy. Confronted by such a worthy woman, thoughts of fucking her seem sacrilegious, contemptible, decadent! And yet, the day she came to me and outlined her . . . her . . . megalo-maniacal project –

MONICA: – megalomaniac project –

JASON: – you can use both – was the day I knew we had to separate. And I was right. She didn't simply accept the suggestion, she leapt at it. Feeding the needy Third World was more important than physically feeding needy me! And so it should be! By any standards whatsoever she'd got her priorities right. But I had to flee.

Those nights, oh those nights when I'd go to bed angry, my teeth clenched. Everything she *was* made *me* feel unworthy. Everything *I* wanted *she* made me feel was ignoble. So, defend her, as long as you understand the difference between you. *She* numbed me, with *you* each sense is heightened. She was *dutiful*, you *demand*. She was *silent*, you *tell* me your pleasure. With her I only wanted to complain about my bumptious colleagues and illiterate students, with you I want to walk through the streets of Paris, dance in New York, ski in the Alps; attend opera in Milan, theatre in London, ballet in Moscow; go yachting in the Mediterranean, trekking across the Kalahari, shopping in Samarkand – slumming it across the world! (*Beat.*) To her I was predictable, you – I have energies to surprise. (*Beat.*) You're not impressed?

MONICA: No one's ever talked to me that way.

JASON: No one's ever loved you like I do.

PHASE SIX

JASON: (*Jumping up to break the mood*) Pah pom! What can I do today while you're forcing history into heads that would sooner be forcing their heads into you?

MONICA: (*Hurt to be jolted from a sweet moment*) Your wife left you because your humour's perverse, you know that?

JASON: Wrong! My humour is different. *I* use irony, *she* used mockery mistaken for irony. My humour has pity and laughs thankfully to God that there but for his grace go I; most of my colleagues' humour is loud and vulgar and full of pleasure in man's fall. Mockery. The English disease.

(*Fade in joyous sound of Jane Oliver singing.*)

MONICA: Jason, I beg you, for your own dignity, listen to Barney and don't submit yourself to this ordeal with your mocking colleagues.

JASON: (*Looking through his address book*) Montgomery has agreed.

MONICA: Celebrate your fiftieth birthday with friends who *love* you.

JASON: Cecilia has agreed.

MONICA: It's humiliating to be told by others why you should continue working.

JASON: Anthony has agreed.

MONICA: A man should answer such questions himself.

JASON: This address book is filled with the dead, the missing and the forgotten! (*Beat.*) Mmmm! No one else, I think. I must face them alone.

MONICA: The three most vituperative minds in the college!

(JASON *gathers the cards for another try.* MONICA *helps him, both bending up and down.*)

JASON: Yes, we'll begin with your crab pâté and a '69 Mersault. Then I'll make a fillet de boeuf en cochonailles with an earthy Château Haut Brion '61 which I bought five years ago – don't gasp – £37 a bottle specially for my fiftieth, and which is now selling at – don't gasp – £182 per bottle plus VAT.

MONICA: Now if anything's immoral, drinking wine at that price is.

JASON: Drinking good wine at any price is never immoral. Might be sacrilegious serving it to the dreaded triumvirate.

MONICA: Listen to me! Give me one hour and I'll provide moral, historical, pragmatic and private reasons to justify a person working.

JASON: We won't bake a dessert, we'll buy one. Ice-cream and marrons glacés with the last of my 1945 Sauterne.

MONICA: You stubborn idiot, you!

JASON: And we'll serve them in my favourite Victorian-unmarked-so-we-don't-know-what-they-are blue-and-white dinner set.

MONICA: Where's your self-respect?

JASON: It is decided.

MONICA: I should leave you.

JASON: (*Sweet sadness*) You will one day, and all too soon. I'm surprised we've lasted six months. Who's got six months' worth of anything to give anybody?

(*He attempts his 'flourish' with the cards. Fails. Looks at her. Shrugs. 'And that's life.' Blackout. Jane Oliver up.*)

Scene II

Jane Oliver until JASON *speaks.*

Present are the 'dreaded triumvirate', ex-colleagues ANTHONY, CECILIA *and* MONTGOMERY. *They've been fed, brandies in hand.* JASON, *though in shirt and trousers, is still in his dressing gown.* MONICA *is clearing away. She has little patience with them.*

PHASE SEVEN

JASON: So there it is! We simply don't need as many people as we once did in order to run a nation of 60 million. Terrible! But it seems to be a fact. Technology has drained the need for labour and with it has drained away the work ethic. And if I were younger I'd seek out my fellow men and think up new work for us to do, gaily, together. But I'm not younger. I'm not old but I'm older than I'm younger, and though I love life I'm not too impressed with the living. Man's goodness cheers me too little to remain untormented by his stupidity. So, turn to the travel ethic, Jason, I say. Men have built cities other than Birmingham, developed customs other than the pub, evolved communications systems richer than mockery. Go! Know thy neighbour! Tarry not too long to become disenchanted, but pick up your roots and go! Now, watch.

(JASON *is going to attempt another 'trick'. The cutting-the-rope trick. He pulls a length from his dressing-gown pocket, shows its wholeness to them.*)

We take a rope, sir. We take one end of the rope and make a loop. We take another end of the rope and make a loop. We take a pair of scissors, sir. We cut one loop. We cut another loop. (*To* MONTGOMERY) Blow, sir. (*To* ANTHONY) Blow, sir.

(JASON *himself blows.*)

Now, shazam!

(*He dangles it. The rope falls in three pieces. Failure!*)

CECILIA: You're a good cook, Jason, but a fool.

MONTGOMERY: Not a fool but a fraud.

ANTHONY: More a slob, I'd say. Don't you *ever* emerge from that dressing gown?

JASON: (*To* MONICA) Do you sometimes feel you've been talking nonsense all day?

(*He tries to work out what went wrong with the rope trick.*)

MONICA: I warned you.

CECILIA: It's such a fatuous question, 'Why should a person work?' Like the simplest of truths it's self-evident. To eat!

MONTGOMERY: (*Of* CECILIA) No amount of scholarship will lift the utilitarian mentality from the female psyche it seems.

CECILIA: Don't be a twerp, Montgomery, that kind of comment was paling with Wilde.

MONTGOMERY: Don't involve Wilde, Cecilia, only undergraduates do that.

ANTHONY: I'd discuss the question seriously with him if only he'd dress. The style of his declination –

MONTGOMERY: Of his what?

CECILIA: Don't be a pedant, either.

ANTHONY: – the style of his declination leads me to think it's clinical rather than intellectual.

CECILIA: Don't be an ass, Anthony, the one is father to the other.

MONICA: But the which to which?

(CECILIA *contemptuously ignores her.*)

CECILIA: Have you got a private income?

MONICA: More brandy then?

CECILIA: (*Accepting it*) Of course not! Do you have goods you can sell off? Of course not! An original Matisse print, some quirky bric-à-brac, but hardly inexhaustible! Do you have someone who'll keep you? (*Looking at* MONICA) For a few years, perhaps, till the old sword melts or outwears its sheath, or the heart's too conscious of its ageing, and expires, defeated by time, or in middle age she discovers her sweet second childhood, so –

MONTGOMERY: All right, all right, Cecilia. Vivid but laboured.

CECILIA: So, food, from whence? Rent, from whence? New dressing gowns, from whence? It's not even worth asking.

ANTHONY: Oh, it's worth asking all right, and he wouldn't be the first to ask it. Greater minds have.

CECILIA: You, for example?

ANTHONY: Me, for example. I remember well, it was my second year as an undergraduate –

CECILIA: – the right age!

ANTHONY: Halfway through university studies, I stopped, took a bike out of Cambridge and pedalled, with a small haversack, due north to Hadrian's Wall, along which I took a slow walk for fourteen days there and back asking myself: why? for what purpose? to what end? to seek what? to have what? to impress whom? to fulfil which need? to answer which call? to –

MONTGOMERY: All right, all right, Anthony. The litanies of life *are* long, we know, but don't drown us.

CECILIA: What's a litany to do with his questions, you ass?

MONICA: To say nothing of mixed metaphors.

JASON: Besides, he's the twerp, Anthony's the ass.

ANTHONY: (*Ignoring all that*) And the questions were very real. I nearly had a nervous breakdown.

JASON: (*To* MONICA) All that fresh air.

ANTHONY: And what answers do you think I came up with? The old Judaeo-Christian one: that to be sustained by the blood of others is a good existence for gnats and jellyfish but not for men –

MONICA: – 'that neither days nor lives can be made holy, or noble by doing nothing in them . . .' Those aren't your answers, they're Ruskin's.

CECILIA: *You're* the fraud, Anthony, always thought you were.

ANTHONY: The confusion between what we've read in our youth and what we've come to think of as our own is not uncommon, Cecilia, as your own lectures often prove!

CECILIA: I'd believe in your confusion if you'd merely paraphrased, but word-for-word recitation is calculated intellectual fraud. You're the fraud, and Jason here is seeding before our very eyes.

MONTGOMERY: Our 'what' eyes?

CECILIA: Do stop being pedantic.

MONTGOMERY: Pedants wouldn't need to be pedantic if English ill-users didn't ill-use English.

MONICA: Wanna bet?

MONTGOMERY: I trust she's more amusing in bed, Jason.

18

(MONICA *swiftly dives her hand between his legs. He yowls. She hangs on.*)

MONICA: Why don't you come and find out? I'd show you parts of yourself you didn't know existed.

MONTGOMERY: (*When she lets go*) A night with you would be hard labour, you have a fist like a hammer.

MONICA: Needed to break rocks!

CECILIA: Now then, children. We've other problems to crack. Our friend and colleague here has lost sight of the work ethic. Some people lose appetites for food, some for social intercourse, others for political action, some lose love of country, love of family, some lose God, some –

MONICA: – lose heart!

CECILIA: Jason, having resigned his job, has now resigned all reason for the work ethic which went with that job. A monstrous problem. But work, the justification for work is, like truth in the American Declaration of Independence, self-evident: there's no alternative way of paying for our food and creature comforts.

MONTGOMERY: Nonsense! And what of those with private incomes? One works because it's an immutable law of human nature, the very essence of existence. All your justifications moral or pragmatic are merely dished up for the mob, the accrued cant which organized society has to lay upon its idle members.

(MONICA *feigns another attack between* MONTGOMERY's *legs.*)

MONICA: *Idle* members?

MONTGOMERY: Keep away!

MONICA: Well, there you have them, Jason. Three theoretical reasons for work. Moral, pragmatic, endogenous. And I must confess that my intellectual honesty rises above private nausea, and each one makes sense. Choose!

JASON: Let's have the cake first.

PHASE EIGHT

JASON *emerges from the kitchen with his own birthday cake lit with one tall, elegant candle.*

JASON: A little something to finish which my ex-wife baked for us.

(JASON *cuts.* MONICA *serves.*)

19

CECILIA: Not too much for me. I'm over-stuffed.

MONICA: Uh-uh! No boasting now.

MONTGOMERY: You're still friends then?

JASON: It's not that we're friends, but that we're not enemies.

ANTHONY: Do you see each other?

JASON: Not if we can help it. I have appetites she felt inadequate for not satisfying, she has reproaches for my infidelities which stir guilts – we make an uncomfortable couple, even divorced.

CECILIA: How pretty this blue-and-white set is.

(JASON *finds a rolled piece of paper in the cake.*)

JASON: A fortune cookie!

MONICA: It's his favourite Victorian-unmarked-so-he-doesn't-know-what-they-are blue and white.

JASON: Oh, good grief! 'I believe in a society where you help your neighbour because you love him' – we've had that one – 'and leave him alone because you respect him.' It's growing!

MONTGOMERY: Nita still trying to explain existence in a word or two?

JASON: 'Fraid so. She lives an utterly responsible, social and domestic life, pursuing her incredible two-year project to feed the Third World, and keeping a home for our wayward work-shy daughter who's just returned from a failed kibbutz life in Israel – who can be enemies with such a woman?

CECILIA: Especially if she bakes cakes like this. Very good, very good indeed. Light.

ANTHONY: And not that heavy butter cream. Fresh cream. The real thing.

MONTGOMERY: Bit too much vanilla essence, or something bitter. Sticks to the top of the palate.

CECILIA: And these blue-and-white plates, the colour! Do you know I think I could eat another slice.

ANTHONY: It *is* a bit more-ish.

MONTGOMERY: Quite something.

(*They each help themselves.* JASON *thinks he's conquered the rope trick. Calls them to watch. Delivers his patter. Does it again. Fails. Pieces of rope drop to the floor.*)

PHASE NINE

CECILIA: Come, Jason, be sensible. You're too old for magic. Respond to us. We've given three theoretical reasons why you must work.

JASON: My friends, I've misled you. Not intentionally, but from insouciance.

MONTGOMERY: He means carelessness.

CECILIA: Pedant!

MONICA: Wasn't he the ass?

CECILIA: No, Anthony was the ass.

MONICA: I thought he was the twerp.

CECILIA: No, that was Monty.

MONICA: I thought he was the pedant.

CECILIA: Twerp *and* pedant.

MONICA: Sounds like an opera by Borodin.

CECILIA: That's *Poet and Peasant*. And it's an overture by Suppé. Are you all right?

MONICA: (*Perplexed, as though a sickness approached*) I'm not sure.

JASON: You see, my question shouldn't have been, 'Why should I work?' but, 'Why, at the age of fifty, should I *continue* working?'

ANTHONY: Bravo! Bravo!

(*He seems surprised at his exclamation.*)

CECILIA: (*Referring to the 'bravo'*) What did he say that for?

JASON: Work, like books or people or social actions, should belong to a certain age in one. (*In one breath*) D. H. Lawrence when you're eighteen but not when you're thirty-five, Sibelius at seventeen, the Schubert quartets when you're thirty, at fifteen you hate your sister, at twenty-nine she swims back into your affections, political or social actions between twenty and thirty-seven, after which your family is more important. (*Breathing deeply*) But work! Work is considered right for an entire lifetime. Sixty for women, sixty-five for men. Madness! And I haven't the slightest wish to contribute further to my society at the tender age of *fifty*! Disturbing, isn't it? Yet what can I do? I've given my life to the study and teaching of moral philosophy and now – awful discovery: I find that, to paraphrase our teacher, Ruskin, whenever I'm selfish – doing, travelling, reading what *I* like – I'm at my happiest, but when I deny

21

myself – give my money away, work at what seems useful, dutiful – I get miserable and unwell. Upsets one's moral principles, and mine are going I dare not think where, yet driven am I no more.

MONTGOMERY: But you can't lie still, like Oblomov, and do nothing.

JASON: Right! And so, in place of work I've developed instead this enormous appetite to wander and fuck my way round the world.

ANTHONY: Bravo! Bravo! (*Pause.*) I wish I knew why I kept saying that.

PHASE TEN

CECILIA: Do you know this blue and white really is quite extraordinary. The blue jumps out at you. I've only just noticed.

MONICA: No one's heard a thing.

(*Now strange things begin to happen.* MONTGOMERY *has been slowly backing away from the company and is backed up, tense, to the wall, as though trying to control something in himself. He bursts into, and abruptly checks, strange giggles.* CECILIA *is taking off her boots, her stockings, and soon will be taking off more.* ANTHONY *just chatters, to himself for all he cares, using a huge felt pen on the back of the Matisse print to illustrate his maths.*)

ANTHONY: I think I'll have another slice of cake. Delicious cake. Only a few slices left. But sufficient to divide into six, which is what they call a 'perfect' number.

JASON: What on earth is happening here?

ANTHONY: All 'perfect' numbers are equal to their true divisions. For example, six can be divided by one, two and three which, when you add them up, also make six.

$$6 = \frac{\begin{array}{r} 1 \\ 2 \\ 3 \end{array}}{6}$$

Beautiful! Twenty-eight is another perfect number. You can divide twenty-eight by one, two, four, seven and fourteen, add those numbers and they also make twenty-eight!

$$28 = \begin{array}{r} 1 \\ 2 \\ 4 \\ 7 \\ \underline{14} \\ 28 \end{array}$$

Beautiful! But most beautiful are 'friendly' numbers, numbers which when you add their true divisions equal each other. Isn't that satisfying? Take two hundred and eighty-four and two hundred and twenty. Two hundred and eighty-four is divisible by one, two, four, seventy-one and one hundred and forty-two. Add those together and you've got – why, two hundred and twenty!

$$284 \, \& \, 220$$
$$284 = \begin{array}{r} 1 \\ 2 \\ 4 \\ 71 \\ \underline{142} \\ 220 \end{array}$$

Like human relationships! Different people match because the true divisions of one totals up to the other! Mathematics, like black and Jewish and small, is beautiful!

(*In between which* MONICA, *who, having pondered long, announces:*)

MONICA: Jason, you won't believe this, but I think they're high.

JASON: You mean drunk?

MONICA: No, I mean high. I feel it myself.

JASON: On what?

MONICA: On hash!

JASON: On hash? From where?

MONICA: The cake.

JASON: Nita's cake?

MONICA: Nita's cake.

JASON: Nita's birthday cake?

MONICA: Nita's birthday cake. Baked with love, hash and the meaning of existence in a word or two.

JASON: Good God! Nita! Has she gone mad?

MONICA: Perhaps she was always mad but you just didn't appreciate it.

(JASON *watches the unfolding scene before him.* MONICA *hovers between reflection and the goings-on around her.* CECILIA *turns to* MONTGOMERY *and indicates she wants to play a game – of throwing the blue-and-white tea plates to each other – simultaneously! He catches on. They throw the plates to one another, catch them. Do it again, the discs passing dangerously in mid-air.*)

JASON: Monica! Don't leave me now.

MONICA: You can't say I didn't warn you.

JASON: Monica! I need your sanity.

MONICA: But you ignored me.

(JASON *is mesmerized.*)

Jason, stop holding your breath.

(*The plates fly across three times.*)

JASON: Monica, Monica, Monica!

(*On the fourth they collide and smash in mid-air.*)

CECILIA: Oh dear. But unmarked you said?

(CECILIA *now clambers on to a table and slowly strips, uttering little 'gone' cries of 'whoop! whoop!' The lights will go out before she's too naked.* MONTGOMERY *hugs the wall with his back, every muscle clenched tight.*)

MONICA: (*To herself*) It must mean something.

MONTGOMERY: You think you're the only one who wants to wander and fuck his way around the world? So do I!

(*Joyous sounds of Jane Oliver singing in the background.*)

CECILIA: I think I hear voices.

MONICA: You're that much nearer to God, perhaps?

CECILIA: There's someone else in the room.

MONTGOMERY: Now you all listen to me! Listen, listen, listen to me. (*Beat.*) Only I've forgotten what I wanted to say.

CECILIA: Jason's father? There's a voice telling me it's Jason's father.

JASON: My father?

MONICA: She's hallucinating. Let her have fun. Won't ever happen again.

JASON: (*Not yet believing it*) But if she *is* in touch with my father there's a lot I want to know.

24

MONTGOMERY: Keep forgetting what I wanted to say. And it was so important.

CECILIA: (*Listens.*) What? A lemon drop?

JASON: It's him!

MONTGOMERY: *So* important.

JASON: My father was a lemon-drop addict!

CECILIA: No, I *don't* carry lemon drops around with me.

JASON: My chance!

CECILIA: Stupid question!

JASON: Ask him – am I right to give up work for travel?

CECILIA: Lemon drops!

JASON: Will I survive in some sort of modest, pleasant manner? Unrepentant? Ask him, Cecilia, while you're still mad.

MONICA: Gone.

JASON: Gone.

CECILIA: (*Calling*) Your son wants to know what it's like up there.

JASON: She's going to blow it.

MONTGOMERY: I mean if the truth must be told then this is the truth. This – is – it!

CECILIA: Oh my, oh, oh! Don't. Don't do that!

MONTGOMERY: But where the hell does it keep going?

CECILIA: Like father, like son, Jason. He's randy. Giving me goose pimples all over.

MONICA: She'll get her stuffing one way or another.

JASON: (*Calling out*) For Christ's sake, Dad, what kind of father are you? The first time you could get in touch and you lech! Help me!

CECILIA: (*Stern, but quite enjoying the presence*) Now be serious, your son needs you.

JASON: I want to give up work! I want to see the world before I die. All those civilizations you told me about. Christ almighty, Dad, I'm a philosopher and I've never been to Greece!

CECILIA: No! Don't go! Please! Damnation! Your questions have frightened him off.

JASON: Dad! Don't desert me. You're my own flesh and blood!

MONICA: Not sure you can make a case for that now, Jason.

MONTGOMERY: The truth is you all think I'm dry, bloodless and unfeeling. Well, I'm bursting with passion! When I make love it's necessary to close the windows.

MONICA: What on earth does he mean?

CECILIA: (*Referring to the presence*) Gone!

JASON: Gone?

MONICA: 'When I make love it's necessary to close the windows'??? Why?

JASON: (*Sinking away in a corner, out of it now*) My only chance of a reliable answer.

MONICA: I mean, what on earth can be happening when he makes love?

CECILIA: He was beginning to interest me.

MONICA: Open them, yes, to cool off, but –

MONTGOMERY: I will not lose control.

MONICA: What a curious thing to have said.

ANTHONY: (*Waking up*) We created the numerical system but now it has life and laws of its own.

MONTGOMERY: Hold fast. Hold steady. You're going to cry. Don't cry.

(CECILIA *begins slow yoga-type ballet.*)

MONICA: (*Referring to the behaviour of the dreaded triumvirate*) Jason! I understand! I now understand why *you're* right and *they're* wrong.

JASON: (*Calling across the city*) Neee–ta!

MONICA: Choice!

ANTHONY: We have no power over it, this numerical system.

JASON: (*Ignoring her*) Neee–ta!

MONICA: (*More to herself*) Personal choice!

ANTHONY: It's grown characteristics of its own.

MONICA: No dogma chains you; no narcotic drives you.

JASON: Nita, I'm coming to murder you!

MONICA: You were *born* high.

ANTHONY: We have no power over it but it continues to explain the universe.

MONICA: But not this lot.

MONTGOMERY: Don't cry! Don't give in! Don't ever give in!

JASON: You think you've bested me but I'm coming to tear you limb from limb!

MONICA: (*Contemptuously*) There they go over the top to they know not where.

MONTGOMERY: Never, never, never give in. Tight! Hold tight!

MONICA: Farewell.
MONTGOMERY: Never give in, never, never, never . . .
MONICA: (*Through cupped hands, echo-y*) Fareweeelll . . .
    (*Loud and joyous singing of Jane Oliver. Lights down.*)

ACT TWO

Scene I

Darkness. Jane Oliver singing.

Two people are making love. SHE, *about forty-eight, can speak her ecstasy.* HE, *about twenty-eight, appears to have his mouth full. Not the same couple!*

PHASE ELEVEN

SHE: Chrrristopher Coluuumbus! What a discovery! Oh my lordee, lordee! Yes! Yes! How can I bear it! How can it be borne! Go on, on, on! Yes, there. There! You've no idea. I feel so exposed. So open. To everything! Oh! Oh! Oh! I'm coming, I'm coming, here I come. Ohhhh!

(*Orgasm, sighs. Fade music.*)

Who would believe it? Whoever on this earth of misery and pain would believe such a wondrous thing? Oh lordee, lordee, Oh Jesus! Such happiness. Thank you.

HE: Exactly which one of us are you thanking?

(*Long silence.*)

It just ages one so!

SHE: Tired? A young man like you?

HE: Youth's not what it used to be.

SHE: My youth was never like this. A nibbled neck was all I got from silly boys who shoved tongues down my poor battered throat. (*Pause.*) Want me to make you something to eat?

HE: I'm not hungry.

SHE: You don't have to be hungry to eat.

HE: (*After a pause*) Well, West Ham won their match.

SHE: Were they playing anyone?

HE: No soul.

28

SHE: Bed after love is neither the time nor the place to read me the football results.

HE: Don't complain or I'll take my favours elsewhere.

SHE: You move out of my life and I'll break every bone in your body.

HE: You're scary, you know that?

SHE: Oh, shut up.

HE: You burn so fiercely.

SHE: Get back to work.

HE: Your husband must have left you with third-degree burns.

SHE: We're wasting time. Forty-nine approaches, my end is drawing close, got to catch up.

HE: Did *nothing* ever happen between you?

SHE: You're procrastinating.

HE: The poetry of youth?

SHE: Crawling through a bedroom scene with my husband Jason was like crawling through the desert and slaking your thirst in a sandbank. He would propound moral philosophy while performing. What you might call a *lay preacher*!

HE: A kind of sermon after the mount?

SHE: Stop procrastinating and work!

HE: You'll give me a heart attack, I'm too young to die.

SHE: Work!

HE: My father died of a heart attack.

SHE: Work!

HE: Collapsed in the lavatory, as though wanting to flush himself out before going.

SHE: Work!

(*Joyous singing of Jane Oliver as a slow, slow dawn comes up to reveal two naked bodies crazily entwined on a bed which is just being revolved out of sight, leaving –*)

PHASE TWELVE

– *a room not unlike Jason's study, but in total chaos. The house of a woman who's decided house-working days are over and all time spent on tidying up is time wasted from living. It's also a flat in the midst of a campaign, posters on the wall, filing cabinets, paper-filled trays on the desk, etc.*
NITA, *clad in a dressing gown, comes in from the bedroom, handsome,*

vital, voluptuously plump, a woman glad to be alive. She changes the record to Gladys Knight and the Pips (Budah Records BDS 5612), the joyful 'I Feel a Song'. She dances to it. A male voice is heard calling in the background. She can't hear it. Finally MAT *appears from the bedroom and turns down the sound. He's virile, young blood, intelligent, urbane and – naked.*

NITA: My God! A naked man!

MAT: Wrong! An angry man.

NITA: Are you going to rape me?

MAT: I've been shouting my head off in there for my clothes.

(He lunges for his pants. She grabs them first.)

NITA: What do you need clothes for if you're going to rape me?

MAT: Don't make jokes about rape.

NITA: I live a serious, responsible life – let me make jokes about rape.

(She throws his pants past him. He puts them on, and his trousers.)

MAT: 'Let you'? What powers do I have to let or not let?

NITA: *(Helping him on with his shirt)* What 'powers' do you have? You? You? Oh, you! Dance with me.

(By the time he's more or less dressed the second number should have been reached: 'Love Finds Its Own Way'. It's slower, sweeter. They dance. After a while –)

MAT: You know, you're working so hard to become young I think you might even make it.

NITA: I don't know if I'm in love with you, or you with me, or whether it'll last or where it'll go or what it means, and I don't care. But I know these things: you make me feel a good person, joyful, confident, wise, passionate, proud to be a woman – and infinitely sad to have so little time left.

(The phone rings.)

Let it ring. It can only be Jason.

(They dance on. The ringing continues.)

Probably wants advice about his new girlfriend.

(The ringing continues.)

Some dowdy old lecturer in philology –

(The ringing continues.)

– whose hobby is free-style wrestling.

(The ringing stops.)

It's probably hash-judgement day!
(*They dance on – suddenly – *)

PHASE THIRTEEN

NITA: God in heaven! My daughter! What time is it?

MAT: Eight fifteen. Her plane from Tel Aviv –

NITA: – arrives at nine forty-five. I'll miss it. She'll never forgive me. It'll be what she expected but she'll never forgive me. Make some coffee.

(NITA *rushes back into the bedroom from where she continues the conversation. The music very low in the background.*)

MAT: Bacon and eggs?

NITA: I'm not hungry.

MAT: You don't have to be hungry to eat!

NITA: Oh, he learns! My God, what a find, he learns!

MAT: Have you told Jason about us?

NITA: Why should I?

MAT: Ashamed of me?

NITA: No! Anxious! He may talk you out of me.

MAT: No faith in your lover?

NITA: No faith in your mistress. My ex-husband is my ex-bester. The beastly king of besting.

MAT: What's besting?

NITA: (*Briefly appearing*) 'Besting' is when two people can't stop trying to floor one another with words. Everything gets said, and regretted.

MAT: You quarrelled?

NITA: It's not that we quarrelled; to quarrel you must have something to disagree over. We didn't disagree, we agreed! To hate!

MAT: So?

NITA: So – to tell him about you would be to invite a 'besting' match. I don't feel up to it. (*She disappears again.*)

MAT: You just told me I gave you confidence.

NITA: That was bravado, inspired by the music.

MAT: Ah, the music! Beware of music. 'It seems to me that I feel what I do not really feel, that I understand what I do not understand, that I can do what I cannot do.' (*Pause.*) Tolstoy.

31

NITA: And he's literate! A lover who can intoxicate me *and* read!

MAT: Surprise! Surprise! And me a mere printer.

NITA: Nothing 'mere' about a printer who owns the machines which print.

MAT: How about a slice of toast?

NITA: The only thing I want right now is you and I can't, dammit! My daughter's interfering with my life again.

MAT: You make her sound monstrous.

NITA: I love her. Beauty, intelligence – all wasted. She makes me weep. Says it's my fault. My personality swamped her.

(*She returns, gorgeously dressed and made up.*)

Alibis! Children are full of alibis. If I'd been quiet and retreating she'd have accused me of not challenging her. Parents never win. Until they're dead. Well, I'm not waiting that long. If Israel didn't win the battle to save her for a useful life *I'm* going to have one last try.

MAT: You look very beautiful.

NITA: You. Only because of you. Nothing else. Simply that. Kiss me.

(*Joyous music of Jane Oliver singing. He does so, long and tenderly. She becomes weak, staggers to the door.*)

Oh Jesus! This is absurd. I won't live through it. Beyond this door is the edge of the world.

MAT: I simply don't believe your response to me. What do I do for God's sake? I don't know what I do to cause such –

NITA: Ecstasy? (*Still clinging to the door*) Oh Jesus, those lips. Look at those lips.

MAT: I mean I'm just a straightforward, ordinary –

NITA: – tender, imaginative, considerate, sweet, exhilarating, powerful, patient, demanding, sensual, endlessly loving, consummate lover –

MAT: – who reads!

NITA: Who f–

(*She draws in her breath, holding back the word and, eyes closed, she slides out of sight. The phone rings. MAT picks it up. Angry voice of JASON comes through. MAT holds the receiver away from himself, listens, then replaces it.*)

MAT: Hash-judgement day!

(*Loud singing of Jane Oliver. Lights down.*)

PHASE FOURTEEN

Sound of aeroplane landing takes over from music; it taxis to a slow halt, engines off, whirr to silence. Lights up. Door bangs. NITA *enters, hugging suitcase. She's followed by* CHRIS, *her daughter, beautiful, morose, about twenty-four, who immediately collapses into a chair.* NITA *at once busies herself unpacking, closely watching her daughter meanwhile. They've obviously either tried to converse and done so disastrously, or failed altogether. The daughter seems paralysed by the mother's spirit. Finally –*

NITA: And there's nothing more draining than relentless melancholy. You have that air about you that makes everyone else feel guilty for bothering to live. (*Pause.*) Despair is habit-forming! (*Pause.*) What an offspring you gave me, lordee. (*Listening*) What's that? I've too much energy? Well, I'm not going to apologize to her for that, Lord. It's not even true. If anything I didn't have energy enough. All day administrating stupid, oafish, female-resisting male civil servants, and in the evenings – flopped out, with her father complaining about his bumptious colleagues and illiterate students. Alibis! She's got an endless fund of alibis, haven't you? (*Pause.*) You see, I've got this young lover, Lord, and I couldn't tear myself away after one of the most extraordinary nights you ever did witness, which, Lord, I suppose you did, very embarrassing, but you must be used to it by now, so, I was late, couldn't make the airport in time, and the lady superior here, fresh from a nunnery I think though they told me she was going to the Holy Land – anyway, this head nun here thinks it's all vaguely disgusting. Mothers shouldn't make love, let alone allow it to make them late for meeting a daughter at the airport. Terrible, dark significance in all that, of course. And isn't she making me suffer! Making me suffer well and truly, aren't you? (*Pause.*) At least tell me that your twelve months working on a kibbutz was not wasted. (*Pause.*) Did you meet any nice Jewish boys? Tell me what it was like being a Gentile among all those Jews? Although with your capacity for reproach and guilt-making they probably mistook you for one of their own. (*Pause.*) At least smile at my wit. You're *never* going to smile are you, or talk, or get married? Might risk giving birth to a daughter who'd have a mother like me, eh? What about if it was a son with a mother like *you*?

CHRIS: At least –

NITA: She's speaking to me!

CHRIS: Not if *you* can bloody help it, it seems.

NITA: The shock. I'm sorry. Forgive me. Go on – 'At least –'

CHRIS: At least he'd be certain of a hearing.

NITA: No, he wouldn't. If he talked for longer than a minute you'd accuse him of being like me!

CHRIS: Here comes round two.

NITA: You'd say, 'You're like your grandmother, just like your grandmother. *She* used to want to talk and explain things and ask questions and tell stories about work, and discuss the book she'd read, the film she'd seen, the news item that worried her, the hopes she had, the fears, regrets, frustrations, the dreams she'd dreamt.' Which reminds me –

CHRIS *and* NITA: (*Together*) I had this extraordinary dream last night.

CHRIS: Of glaring significance.

NITA: Glaring!

CHRIS: In between fucking.

NITA: Don't be crude, it doesn't suit you.

CHRIS: Whereas it suits you perfectly?

NITA: With age comes glorious licence. All ego spent! No need, and certainly no time, for making impressions. Just a few minutes left for work and pleasure and –

CHRIS: – and dreams.

NITA: Dreams. It was about some youngsters, they were smashing up my flat. And they were full of contempt. Every dream has an overwhelming mood – sadness, elation, nostalgia, fear. In this one it was contempt, the contempt of youth.

CHRIS: Guilts. You feel guilty for pretending to be the age you're not.

NITA: (*Angry, defiant*) I feel guilty for nothing and I pretend nothing! Pretending I was happy with your father was *my* last pretence!

PHASE FIFTEEN

CHRIS: How *is* Daddy?

NITA: See for yourself.

CHRIS: Don't sulk, I've only just returned.

NITA: And within seconds you've got to me. Bloody children. Who'll protect parents from children, lordee?

CHRIS: Does he still hold his breath?

NITA: The Lord's been holding his breath since the first day of creation.

CHRIS: I'm talking about *my* father not yours. Well?

NITA: (*Silent, sulky*) Well, what?

CHRIS: Does he? Does Daddy still hold his breath?

NITA: Probably. Only never long enough.

CHRIS: Oh Mother, stop it.

NITA: Well, how should I know? I hardly ever see him. (*Pause*) He's got a new girlfriend.

CHRIS: Who?

NITA: Oh, some dowdy old lecturer in philology. The kind of woman he's always wanted, cerebral, suppliant and somnambulistic. Someone who doesn't make too many personal or physical demands. (*Pause*.) Sent him a birthday cake this year.

CHRIS: Damn! Forgot his birthday!

NITA: With hash in it!

CHRIS: Hash? You?

NITA: Hash and one of my notes.

CHRIS: Still trying to sum up life in a word or two?

NITA: And I'm getting there.

CHRIS: Hash!

NITA: 'I believe in a society where you help your neighbour because you love him, and leave him alone because you respect him.' (*Beat.*) Responsibility and privacy. Essential balance.

CHRIS: (*Not really having heard*) Hash!

NITA: Just needs a last round-off something. But I'm getting there. (*Reflects, giggles.*) A birthday cake with hash in it!

CHRIS: (*Giggling despite herself*) You're cruel and criminal.

NITA: Not at all. He was having round three of his most unfavourite associates to give him good reasons why he should bother to continue working – your father's also got problems. I was doing him a favour. Just wish I'd been there.

CHRIS: What could've happened?

NITA: Mmm! Taxes the imagination. No doubt he'll come storming round if catastrophe's struck. You two should get together soon, you have a philosophy in common now.

CHRIS: Here comes round three.

NITA: 'Work is for mugs.'

CHRIS: I don't *say* work is for mugs, I just can't decide what work I'm cut out for.

NITA: You're a photographer. Take photographs.

CHRIS: The whole world takes photographs and half of them are better at it than I am.

NITA: *There's* your problem, always your problem, you had to be excellent or nothing, and because you never took the trouble to be excellent you remained nothing.

CHRIS: Who could be excellent suffering as your victim?

NITA: There-are-no-victims-in-this-world; there are only those who *elect* to suffer.

CHRIS: Bullshit!

NITA: That's not bullshit.

CHRIS: That's bullshit and ignorance and stupidity and pig-headedness.

NITA: You're pig-headed! Pig-headed, lazy, cowardly, self-pitying like your father. I may have failed to prevent *him* stagnating but I won't fail with you, I will not! You could begin again, and again, and again, and take a degree.

CHRIS: It's too late you cliché-ridden old harridan, you. To begin again at anything it's too late and I don't have the degree-type brain, besides.

NITA: That's nonsense.

CHRIS: Not nonsense – realistic! I face reality.

NITA: Imagined reality.

CHRIS: Proven reality.

NITA: Nothing can be proven at the age of twenty-four.

CHRIS: Give me a child till seven, said the Jesuits.

NITA: Fuck the Jesuits!

CHRIS: No, you! You're the one seems hot enough to take on hordes!

PHASE FIFTEEN A

Long silence. Tempers cool.

CHRIS: Good God, I had the last word.

NITA: A bester! Your father's daughter!

CHRIS: Oh Mother!

NITA: But I'm not dead yet.

CHRIS: Why do you get at me as soon as I'm back? I'm not the brilliant academic you wanted me to be, so what? What's wrong with having no ambition?

NITA: The very question resounds with its own answer.

CHRIS: You wanted me to read? I read! And I learnt – about man and his seasons of madness.

NITA: *And* his sweetness and light!

CHRIS: Sometimes. But madness mostly.

NITA: But –

CHRIS: Don't tell me! Some are more exhilarated by the sweetness and light, I know, but not me! I belong to those who are more depressed by the madness, and there it is! We are who we are. I am who I am. I'm not cruel or morbid, I don't inflict unhappiness on my neighbour, I even find small pleasures here and there, but I have no expectations of him or life, and so nothing, nothing, nothing drives me sufficiently to get up and do.

PHASE SIXTEEN

CHRIS: Now, enough of me, what have *you* been doing with yourself?

NITA: Having a breast off.

CHRIS: Oh Ma!

NITA: What's in a breast? I've got another one.

CHRIS: Oh Ma! That's awful. I should've been told.

NITA: What for? To worry you? You were your own problem enough. Besides, it's not terminal.

CHRIS: Does Daddy know?

NITA: Probably not, he never got around to counting them!

CHRIS: *Be serious!*

NITA: (*Sheepishly*) I'm having a new one stitched on.

CHRIS: Oh Ma!

NITA: Stop 'Oh Ma-ing'. They're very efficient. It's a new material bunged up with this, this jelly or gristle or foam or something, and the material grows into your skin and takes on your body temperature. Clever stuff. And even if some heavy-handed eager Salvation Army box-collector pins a poppy through the puffed up boob it doesn't deflate – SSSsss! Great! Took infinite care, measuring and weighing the one that's left to get the right shape. All those stunningly handsome student doctors, and they each had to have their guesses. (*Cups her breast and flaps it up and down.*) 'Eight ounces!' 'Twelve ounces!' 'Thirty-two and a half ounces!' I hit that one.

CHRIS: Oh Ma!

NITA: No, don't worry. They weighed it properly.

(*She bends forward to a table and flops the breast on to it as though on to a weighing machine.*)

Fifteen and two-thirds ounces precisely.

CHRIS: How can you be so, so, so –

NITA: Irreverent? I don't have a solemn temperament. I've discovered myself. I may have lost a breast but I've found my body, and the body's beautiful.

(*They embrace.*)

Now enough of me –

PHASE SEVENTEEN

NITA: Back to you.

CHRIS: Bloody hell, round four?

NITA: The kibbutz. Israel. Did you take any photographs?

(CHRIS *reaches for an Arab shoulder bag and empties it over the floor, dozens upon dozens of exposed undeveloped films in their boxes.*)

You've developed *none* of them? Not one reel? Typical! The story of your life – undeveloped film!

(*The phone rings. She's surprised.*)

Why is the phone ringing? I asked service to put all calls through to the office.

CHRIS: I was wondering how you could be in the middle of such a huge campaign and not be constantly on the phone.

NITA: I decided to give my day over to you, except for fifteen minutes to sign letters.

CHRIS: A twenty-four-hour token of maternal love?

NITA: There are other people in this world aside from one's own children.

CHRIS: Yes, other people's children. Always easier to know how to handle them. Aren't you going to answer the phone?

NITA: It shouldn't be ringing.

CHRIS: Perhaps it's an emergency. Daddy. He's ill.

NITA: (*Cheered at the thought*) Or dead! (*Gleefully picking up the phone*) Yes? (*To* CHRIS) Alive! (*To phone*) Jason. Of course I made it myself, which baker do *you* know makes hash birthday cakes? (*Pause.*) I thought it would amuse and defuse the dreaded triumvirate. (*Pause.*) They're suing you? For what, loss of inhibitions?

(*She giggles with* CHRIS.)

For food poisoning? But hash isn't poisonous, it must be a joke to frighten you. (*Pause.*) No, you can't come over! I'm spending the day with your daughter. (*Pause.*) Of course she's here, how could I spend the day with her otherwise! (*To* CHRIS) Have you noticed what crass conversations one has on the phone? (*Into the phone*) But she's here for good.

(CHRIS *points energetically at her mouth.* NITA *gets the hint.*)

Take her out to dinner, act like a real father for once. (*Pause.*) Well, if you come you come alone. I don't want to meet your girlfriend; it's not fair on her and you should be considerate in such matters. (*Pause.*) You'll take the risk? Huh! Typical male! He'll take the risk on her behalf. Now listen – he's gone.

(*She puts down the phone.*)

CHRIS: Will you two never have a reconciliation?

NITA: We've bought a plot in the cemetery – we'll be *buried* together!

CHRIS: You sounded friendly enough on the phone.

NITA: On the phone we don't have to look at one another. When we look at one another *I* feel guilty for wanting more than he could give, and *he* feels guilty for having been inadequate. We make an uncomfortable couple, even divorced.

CHRIS: I never understood. After twenty-five years! What can be so awful in a marriage that's lasted twenty-five years? It's never made sense to me.

39

NITA: It's never made sense to you because no one talks about these things. I wanted to scream all the time. Walk around and scream and not stop. Aaaa!

(*She utters what's known as a long, primal scream.*)

Even doing it *now* makes me feel good, not doing it *then*, keeping it in *then* was like allowing the spirit to become slowly toxic. I wanted to be taken and – and – and – oh – yes, fucked! No, don't be embarrassed, you want to understand. He was a good man, even competent, but there was no – no – no urgency, no passion! I'm not talking about intenseness but about – oh – a wild gaiety, that's what I craved, an abandoned, relentless, intoxicated, wild gaiety. I wanted to be seduced, slowly wound up, to play games of exposure and innocence, to be ravished with his eyes, to be tongued, pursued, challenged, overwhelmed. I wanted everything to be possible and permissible, because what could be done in bed might, only might, then be done in life. For us it was done in neither place. We'd lie side by side, in the dark, make tiny signs to one another, crawl here, crawl there, a little of this, a little of that, meagre gestures of love-play, then do it – once – sigh, roll apart, and sleep. For another two weeks! And do you know how often it happens with Mat? Twice a day! And I don't come once but I come and I come and I come and I come and I come and I come! Within the space of an hour. Who ever believed it could happen? A fantasy! But it did, to me. (*Pause.*) I was once at a party and a young smart-arse came up to me and brazenly asked me to share his bed. A little thing in mind and spirit. And when I declined he leaned over and said with his damp arrogance, 'Pity'! And he pointed his finger up and continued, 'Because you see that ceiling? I could've taken you straight through there'! He couldn't have lifted me high enough to get a sheet beneath. But with Mat? He lifted me through the ceiling and among the stars like a female sputnik, and I haven't been down since. Reconciliation? To *what*? An academic phallus that could only rise after a two-hour reading of *Paradise Lost* by which time paradise *was* lost?

CHRIS: What contradictions you do have in your life.

NITA: *What* contradictions?

CHRIS: Well, your social work and your night life. Your campaign for the starving masses and your, your –

NITA: My fantastic, inventive, insatiable sex life?

CHRIS: Yes, that!

NITA: I have a motto. (*Jubilant*) Feed the hungry, fuck the healthy – hallelujah!

PHASE EIGHTEEN

MAT: (*From out of sight*) Anybody home?

NITA: And here comes the embodiment of them both.

(*Having let himself in,* MAT *enters, shopping bag in his arms. He wears a long overcoat, pockets bulging with something, a different image from the ardent young man of the earlier scene, suggesting his own brand of eccentricity.*)

Mat, my daughter Christine. Chris, this is Mat, my – my – my – er –

CHRIS: Yes, how *do* you describe him? It does sound silly at your age to talk about 'my boyfriend' especially when the friend *is* a boy.

MAT: (*Shaking hands*) Charmed. What a beautiful daughter you have, Nita. I don't know why but I imagined she'd be, well, lumpy.

NITA: 'Lethargic' was the word I used.

CHRIS: Have you been complaining to him about me, is that how you earned his shoulder?

NITA: I earned his shoulder and sundry other parts of his body with sundry other parts of *my* body – those that are left!

(MAT *plonks shopping bag in* CHRIS's *arms. Moves to clear up film cartridges. A tidy young man.*)

MAT: I'm also quite studious.

CHRIS: Coming from the verb 'to stud'.

MAT: She sounds more lethal than lethargic.

(CHRIS *snatches the Arab bag from his hands. She'll do her own clearing up.*)

CHRIS: Thank you! It's just that I can't find the enthusiasm to take up a profession and it offends her.

NITA: I don't like the way you two are getting on so well so quickly.

CHRIS: Haven't you got to go off and sign letters?

NITA: Don't know I can risk it.

CHRIS: (*Pointedly*) And don't forget *Daddy*'s coming!

NITA: (*Going*) A confrontation devoutly *not* to be missed! Hash-

41

judgement day! What *did* his poor old dowdy lecturer in philology say? (*Exits. Returns.*) I better warn you, this house is bugged. (*Exits.*)

PHASE NINETEEN

CHRIS: And tell me, young man, *are* your intentions honourable?

MAT: I'm not sure your mother wants them to be.

CHRIS: My mother is too old, too desperate and too vulnerable to know her own mind. Do you have a profession?

MAT: Am I being vetted for acceptability?

CHRIS: (*Tired of banter*) Don't let's. Please. Your profession?

MAT: Printer.

CHRIS: I see no ink stains on fingers.

MAT: New methods, new machines, no ink.

CHRIS: Who do you work for?

MAT: A firm called Time & Tide.

CHRIS: Why aren't you at work now?

MAT: I only work three days a week.

CHRIS: Short of orders?

MAT: No.

CHRIS: You ill?

MAT: No.

CHRIS: You're on strike?

MAT: No.

CHRIS: Stop making me work so hard. I hate talking. You can't be a printer, you're too articulate, confident –

MAT: Print workers would be very upset to hear you be so patronizing.

CHRIS: Ah! You *own* a print factory. What inverted snobbery to mislead me.

MAT: True. But I must be allowed my guilts. I happen to be super-efficient. The factory only needs me three days a week.

CHRIS: What do you do the rest of the time?

MAT: Read books. It's an illness. Developed it at the age of six. My pockets bulge with Penguins. Some people hang on to old blankets for security, or graduate to cigarettes. I need a book. Can't be without one. If I haven't started a new book I panic, become nervous, irritable, unreliable.

CHRIS: Any special kind of book?

MAT: Everything. Anything. *Mathematics for the Millions, The Age of Revolution, From Shakespeare to Osborne* – that sort of thing, nothing too intellectually demanding but just enough to keep my mind oiled, my imagination alert, my soul sensitive, my heart primed – (*begins to take books out of his pocket, each one gives him his new line, throws them in her lap*) – historical perspective enlarged, wit tickled, values challenged, judgements tempered, understanding deepened, my choices widened –

CHRIS: My God, take her! You're made for one another!

(*The doorbell rings.* CHRIS *goes to open it.* MAT *becomes absorbed in a book.*)

PHASE TWENTY

CHRIS: (*Off*) Hello?

YOUNG MAN'S VOICE: (*Off*) Is this the home of the Cornwalls?

CHRIS: It used to be three years ago. Now it's the home of only one Cornwall, and a – (*Calls back.*) – a who?

MAT: I don't *live* here.

CHRIS: Well, it can hardly be described as your reading room! (*To* VISITOR) Are you expected?

YOUNG MAN'S VOICE: No, I am not expected, I am a sort of relative.

CHRIS: Oh, come in, come in.

(*Both enter. The young man is very handsome, gentle, romantic-looking; his name is* ECKHARDT.)

But you're from the Continent.

ECKHARDT: Yes, from Germany.

CHRIS: I didn't know we had German cousins. *Are* you a cousin?

(*He hesitates.*)

Who are you?

ECKHARDT: (*Anxious, taking his time*) Well, if you are Christine, I am your half-brother, Eckhardt.

(*A long, long, stunned, paralysed silence. Then –*)

CHRIS: On whose side, mother's or father's?

ECKHARDT: Father's.

CHRIS: Father's?

ECKHARDT: I am sorry, it had to be known sooner or later.

MAT: But not without warning, announcement, preparation – something.

(ECKHARDT, *not knowing who addresses him, is uncertain how to reply.*)

CHRIS: This is my mother's – er –

(*She gives up, absorbed.*)

MAT: (*Offering his hand*) Matthew Cunningham.

ECKHARDT: (*Taking it*) I wanted a meeting desperately. The thought that it would be refused was unbearable to me.

(*More silence. The implications are racing through* CHRIS's *mind.*)

CHRIS: My God! I'm no longer an only child! (*Pause.*) Does my mother know?

ECKHARDT: I think not, but I am not sure. I did not know they were separated.

(*Awkward silence.*)

Forgive me. I am slow getting used to new situations. In my imagination this was all worked out. I would arrive, he would be here, he would greet me, we would be friends . . .

MAT: . . . he would explain you to his wife, she would be understanding . . .

ECKHARDT: Yes. I am not very clever. (*Referring to* CHRIS's *state*) I can see it.

CHRIS: Oh, bloody hell! Round five! Poor Daddy. What *will* he say, having to cope with age *and* the past catching up with him?

MAT: It's Nita *I'm* worried about. What will *she* say?

CHRIS: 'I didn't think he had it in him.'

MAT: 'He found *his Sturm und Drang* then!'

CHRIS: 'The second coming!'

ECKHARDT: (*Who's been forgotten*) Perhaps she will say: 'Welcome, and are you hungry and would you like something to drink and won't you sit down and you must be tired and tell me about yourself . . .'

(*They are reminded of their rudeness and prompted into over-exuberant hospitality.*)

CHRIS: Oh, how unforgivable, I'm sorry, but I've just got off the plane myself.

(*They imitate his German accent.*)

MAT: Welcome.

44

ECKHARDT: Thank you.

CHRIS: Are you hungry?

ECKHARDT: Yes.

MAT: Would you like something to drink?

ECKHARDT: Yes, please.

CHRIS: Won't you sit down, you must be tired.

ECKHARDT: Thank you.

MAT: Tell us about yourself.

ECKHARDT: I am a magician.

(*He produces a cane from nowhere.*)

CHRIS: (*Enthralled*) A magician!

ECKHARDT: Would you like to see more?

CHRIS: Oh, please!

(*He takes a rope from his pocket. Tugs and shows its wholeness to them.*)

ECKHARDT: We take a rope. We take one end of the rope. So! We take the other end. So! We take the middle of the rope. So! We take a scissor which by coincidence I have. We cut. We make knot. Now, we wind round hand. (*To* MAT) Blow, please.

(MAT *blows.* ECKHARDT *lets rope uncoil. Intact.*)

Voilà!

CHRIS: (*Thrilled*) A magician!

ECKHARDT: Perhaps you call them conjurors here?

(*At which he takes an egg from* CHRIS'S *ear.*)

MAT: If this goes on I shall *never* get to work.

(ECKHARDT *performs a third simple trick.*)

CHRIS: I thought you had to prepare for such things. Can you do them just anywhere, any time?

ECKHARDT: No, of course not, but I thought I would prepare a few simple things up my sleeve to soften the atmosphere which I supposed might not be too – er –

MAT: I know what she'll say, she'll cry out: 'At last! Your father's produced something magical in his life!'

CHRIS: More likely: 'The devil gives birth!'

MAT: No, no. She'll come in, pause while he takes an egg out of her mouth, or wherever, and say –

ECKHARDT: 'Welcome and are you hungry and would you like something to drink and . . .'

(*Again prompted they go with apologies to fetch him things to eat and drink from the fridge.* MAT *looks;* CHRIS *lays out.*)

MAT: Ham!

CHRIS: (*To* ECKHARDT) Ham?

ECKHARDT: Ham, thank you.

MAT: Cheese!

CHRIS: Cheese?

ECKHARDT: Cheese, thank you.

MAT: Tomato!

CHRIS: Tomato?

ECKHARDT: Tomato, thank you.

MAT: Milk!

CHRIS: Milk?

ECKHARDT: Milk, thank you.

(*He is presented with a full plate and glass.*)

PHASE TWENTY-ONE

Sound of a door opening. NITA *appears.*

NITA: And which waif are we feeding today?

CHRIS: Mother, I want you to meet Eckhardt from Germany.

NITA: Pleased to meet you. Did you travel back on the plane from Israel? Chris was always like that, ever since she was a child, she'd go off on a holiday, or out to the museum for the day and sure as hell she'd come back with a stranger, who'd have to be fed and stay the night and be made welcome like a sister.

MAT: Or a brother.

NITA: Right! Or a brother. Depending upon which sex she was. He was. (*Senses something is in the air.*) They feeding you well, Eckhardt?

ECKHARDT: (*Holding up plate and glass*) Thank you, I'm not *so* hungry, though.

NITA, CHRIS *and* MAT: (*Together*) You don't have to be hungry to eat.

(*Joyous sounds of Jane Oliver singing.* NITA *sits. She gives up and waits.*)

CHRIS: Now, Mother, sit down.

NITA: I *am* sitting.

CHRIS: Then don't stand up.

NITA: Ever?

CHRIS: This is Eckhardt. From Germany.

NITA: Pleased to meet you. Did you travel back on the plane from Israel? Chris was always like that, ever since she was a child, she'd go off on holiday, or out to the museum for the day and sure as hell . . .

CHRIS: Mother, Eckhardt is my half-brother, the son of Jason.

(NITA, *shocked, rises sharply, pauses, sits weakly. All three youngsters strain forward eagerly, to hear what she'll say. We all do. It's a long pause. Her eyes seem to travel back in time, mixed of bitterness and sad resignation.*)

NITA: I always wanted a son [*in addition to a daughter, not instead of*].

(*Blackout. Brief interval in half house-lights. Singing of Jane Oliver up.*)

Scene II

PHASE TWENTY-TWO

The first five minutes or so of this scene are taken up with ECKHARDT *showing his new family a collection of quite spectacular tricks. He's performing for them, and of course for the audience, a bonus show! He's using* CHRIS, *dressed in a cloak, as his assistant. Lights are (presumably) dim.*

Note: On no account must the performer be a second-rate magician. This part of the play must be stunning. And through it all the actors must remain in character, which, depending upon the tricks and ECKHARDT'*s patter, may involve the actors in extemporized dialogue which must be delivered as boldly as normal text.*

The last trick is the levitation one. CHRIS *is the subject. It is while she's suspended in mid-air that the doorbell rings.*

NITA: That's Jason.

ECKHARDT: Shall I bring her down?

NITA: No, leave her there. See what he says.

(MAT *goes to let in* JASON *who is accompanied by* MONICA. NITA

47

is momentarily chagrined at the sight of a beautiful young woman.
JASON, *confused by what confronts him, chooses to ignore it.*)

JASON: Monica, this is Nita. Nita – er – Monica.

NITA: A lecturer in philology?

MONICA: It's history, I'm afraid.

NITA: You're supposed to be old and dowdy.

MONICA: And you're supposed to be dull and without surprises.

NITA: Oh lordee, are we going to like each other?

MONICA: Not if we work at it.

JASON: (*To* MAT) Who are you?

MAT: Mat the printer.

JASON: (*Pointing to suspended* CHRIS) She your girlfriend?

NITA: No, she's mine. I mean, I'm hers. No! I mean, I'm his.

JASON: You're his? Well, who's hers? (*Meaning* CHRIS. *Then, pointing to* ECKHARDT) Him?

NITA: No, she's ours but he's yours.

JASON: She's our what, but he's my what?

NITA: She's our daughter but he's your son.

JASON: Christine? Christine, this is taking lethargy too far. *He's my what?*

(*All make way for* ECKHARDT.)

ECKHARDT: I'm very pleased to meet you, father.

JASON: Oh my God! Eckhardt! My lecture on 'Evariste Galois and the Birth of Modern Algebra', Hamburg University, 1953.

ECKHARDT: We moved from Hamburg when I was seven. My mother took up a post in Berlin. You see, Berlin was offering financial concessions to attract people to live and work there. You see . . .

(*Silence. No one knows how to continue.*)

JASON: (*Referring to the still-suspended* CHRIS) Did she arrive from Israel like that?

(*He's about to sit down.*)

ECKHARDT: (*Reaching under* JASON *to pull out a rabbit or something*) Excuse me.

MONICA: Skeletons in your cupboard, rabbits up your ass. What other surprises have you got in store for us?

JASON: At this moment I need friends.

MAT: At this moment we all need drinks.

(*He goes off to prepare them.*)

NITA: At this moment I need honesty.

JASON: And I don't need cant at this moment. At this moment cant about honesty is the last thing I want to hear. An overrated virtue.

NITA: You've *never* been able to take honesty about yourself.

JASON: Who the hell wants it? 'Get in touch with yourself!' But supposing I don't like myself? Why the hell should I want to get in touch with myself? What would you have done twenty-five years ago if I'd told you I'd fathered a child on a lecture tour?

NITA: If you'd been honest I'd have left you earlier.

JASON: So you say now. But honesty about what you don't understand results in distortion, honesty before fools results in abuse, honesty before those who can't take it results in confusion, pain and misery. Christine! Come down from there and act your age!

ECKHARDT: If you'll permit me.

(*He takes a black shroud, throws it over the levitated* CHRIS, *pulls it away. She's disappeared.*)

JASON: Good! (*Pointing to* NITA) Now her! A drink! I need a drink!

(MAT *gives him one as* ECKHARDT *clears away his box of tricks.*)

PHASE TWENTY-THREE

JASON: I can't take it. Redundancy! Passion! Hash parties! Visitations! Levitations! The past! It's all too much. Lights! Give me lights! I need light!

(ECKHARDT *snaps his fingers. Lights!* CHRIS *appears. He receives her as he would an assistant. Pah-pom! She's excited.*)

. . . and somewhere quiet.

CHRIS: That's it!

JASON: That's what?

CHRIS: My vocation.

JASON: Disappearing?

CHRIS: Yes, yes! Disappearing! (*Embracing him*) Hello, Daddy! Disappearing, reappearing, coming, going, rabbits in hats, sawn in half, endless flags from nowhere –

JASON: – your intelligence separated from your head!

CHRIS: Magic! Illusion! Fantasy!

JASON: (*To* NITA) Talk to her. She's your daughter.

NITA: And he's your son. Talk to *him*. The pied piper!

49

CHRIS: The first time I've ever really felt drawn to a profession and it sets them quarrelling.

JASON: *What* profession? To assist a trickster?

CHRIS: Not a trickster, a magician.

JASON: There are no magicians, only illusions!

NITA: Do you want to give your life to illusions?

JASON: The day will come he'll plunge a sword in the box and you won't have moved away in time!

CHRIS: (*To* ECKHARDT) Do you need an assistant? Have you got one? Can you train me?

JASON: Your daughter's running away with the circus. Do something!

CHRIS: Don't take much feeding, am very bright, learn quickly, will do anything.

JASON: Why is she talking like a telegram?

CHRIS: Anything!

JASON: She'll fall in love with him. Incest!

NITA: She's spontaneous, what can I do?

JASON: Spontaneous idiocy! Like mother, like daughter.

NITA: There's one important difference between your daughter and me.

JASON: She's young, you're old.

NITA: Two important differences.

JASON: What *could* it be?

NITA: She has half of *you* in her blood and genes, I've only ever had you in my hair.

JASON: But both ends!

NITA: When you could find the energy!

JASON: And you the desire!

NITA: And you the imagination!

JASON: And you the sensuality!

NITA: And you the know-how!

JASON: And you the passion!

NITA: And you the bloody wherewithal!

(*They hold, poised at one another to see who says what next.*)

MONICA: (*To* ECKHARDT) In case you're not understanding what's going on this is a match between ex-besters.

MAT: A bester is one who has to get the best, and last word over the other.

NITA: (*To* JASON) You're holding your breath again!

JASON: So are you! Don't evade the problem.

CHRIS: I am *not* a problem! Stop talking about me as if I'm a bundle of wool to be unpicked. It's simple! Nothing turned me on. Not school, not travel, not people, not Nita, not you. Nothing! Till now.

JASON: And now?

CHRIS: Now I know what I want to do, and *you're* the problem. *You're* turned off. What is there in the world can possibly turn *you* back on at your age?

MONICA: Well now, let's *talk* about this . . .

JASON: I have been turned off, daughter, because I've reached the age where a nightmare has affixed itself to me.

MONICA: (*To* MAT) I do hope he's not referring to me.

JASON: One day, everything's ending! Blown up! Scientific discoveries, works of art, books – gone! All those moral codes, philosophical precepts, political rights – painfully fought for, scrupulously lived by – for nothing! When a vision like that takes hold and haunts you, it's spiritual cancer. Terminal! But you? Nothing like that should've blemished you yet. You should be making revolutions.

CHRIS: I don't believe in revolutions.

JASON: Oh really!

CHRIS: They produce distorted values and revengeful commissars who liquidate old friends.

JASON: You don't believe in anything, that's the trouble.

NITA: Nor do you.

JASON: I've earned the right not to because I once did! But there's no excuse for the young.

NITA: Nor the old! We could all say we've earned the right not to believe in anything, then where would we be?

JASON: Oh, I'm not competing with a woman who's asking Europe to give up a week's wage for the poor.

NITA: The Third World is not the poor, it's the abused.

JASON: And can you describe the society *you* believe in?

NITA: Yes –

JASON: Oh good God, what've I asked!

NITA: One where a person helps their neighbour.

JASON: Puerile! Read Nietzsche!

CHRIS: I believe in magic.

JASON: Whimsy! Read Voltaire!

CHRIS: In illusion.

NITA: Irresponsible! Read Balzac!

ECKHARDT: Whose side is who on?

CHRIS: I believe in finding there what didn't seem to be there.

JASON: Like blood in a stone? Read Spinoza!

CHRIS: (*Screaming the supreme insult at those unfortunate enough to be educated*) Name-droppers!

ECKHARDT: Excuse me, but can I say something, please? You are all very frightening people, it's not easy to peek in.

MONICA: Right! Do you realize, Jason, that you've made no fatherly gesture to your son?

MAT: Yes, how about: 'Welcome and are you hungry and would you like something to drink and –'

ECKHARDT: '– and won't you sit down, you must be tired and tell me about yourself . . .'

JASON: If you've been with the overfed feeder of the Third World till now then I assume you've been feasted and made welcome; *she's* given you a drink, you *are* sitting down and I don't *want* to know about yourself. You're a conjuror and you've conjured fevered fantasies in my daughter's mind. She will *not* be your assistant. That's final. I'm her father!

ECKHARDT: And mine.

(*Pause.* JASON *relents, opens his arms. They embrace.*)

PHASE TWENTY-FOUR

JASON: Forgive me.

ECKHARDT: I've come at the wrong time?

JASON: No, no. The right time but–

NITA: – but piping the wrong tune.

JASON: That petulant half-child there is in fact quite sensible. The imbecility is a façade. In reality she's a talented photographer of reality.

ECKHARDT: Ah! A photographer. Can I see some?

NITA: (*Emptying the cartridges again*) Yes, there!

JASON: Undeveloped, I presume, like their maker.

CHRIS: Good photographers are ten a penny. I don't care about it. Don't you understand that? I just don't care, care, care! I want to be a magician!

JASON: She's not satisfied just being a witch!

CHRIS: Enough! I'm not arguing any more or I'll be slaughtered in your crossfire. I've had to live my life between you two outbesting each other and now – *you* fight, I'm retreating.

(*She goes to her room.*)

JASON: Which means I can concentrate on *you*.

NITA: (*Retreating*) If she thinks I'm fighting the beastly king of besting she's mistaken. I've already sacrificed my youth to him.

JASON: What youth! You never had a youth. You were born straight into second childhood!

MONICA: Why don't we change the subject, calm ourselves, talk about what we came to talk about . . . ?

MAT: Hash-judgement day!

NITA: I'm also retreating!

(*She enters her room.*)

JASON: (*Yelling after her*) They could all have died of hash-poisoning! You're an irresponsible woman!

NITA: (*Yelling back at him*) At last!

(*She slams the door.*)

CHRIS: (*Opening her door*) Eckhardt! I need Eckhardt to discuss my future. But out of range of the battling besters.

(*She slams the door.*)

ECKHARDT: Really, a most frightening family I was born into. These are English?

MAT: But, happily, cross-fertilized by the world.

(ECKHARDT *enters Chris's room.*)

NITA: (*Opening her door; a* cri de cœur) Mat! I need your youth!

JASON: So does he!

MONICA: (*To* MAT) To your duty.

MAT: My duty? Opportunities to enjoy what's been missed? Find what's been lost? Second chances?

(*They smile, bow to each other. He enters Nita's room, closes the door gently.*)

MONICA: And then there were two.

JASON: Is that how you see yourself? A dutiful youth? Easing the middle into old age? Giving me a 'second chance'?

MONICA: I'm not giving it, you're taking it.

JASON: I was really caught with my trousers down.

MONICA: Pick them up, lover. You can't walk the streets of Paris with me with your trousers down.

NITA: (*Opening her door*) If you were anything of a father you'd be building up your daughter's future instead of destroying my equilibrium.

(*She slams the door.*)

MONICA: With your trousers down you can't ski in the Alps, attend ballet in Moscow, go shopping in Samarkand.

JASON: I'm tired. That's why I don't want to work any more. I'm simply tired. I want to go somewhere where the only pressure put upon you is to decide between orange and grapefruit juice.

CHRIS: (*Opening her door*) If you were anything of a father you'd grow old gracefully –

JASON: (*Yelling at* CHRIS) Somewhere where literacy is not sneered at!

CHRIS: – and leave me to build my future in peace.

(*She slams the door.*)

MONICA: Bless your daughter's career as a magician, welcome your son into the family, and give up a week's wages to your ex-wife. (*Beat.*) With your trousers down you can't dance with me in New York . . . ?

JASON: (*Rising*) I think I need to go where no one can go for me, the last bastion of peace.

(*He moves to the loo. Slams the door.*)

MONICA: And then there was one.

JASON: (*Opening the door, his trousers round his feet*) Since I think I'm suffering from cancer of the pancreas this may take a long time.

(*He slams the door.*)

MONICA: And then there was one.

JASON: (*Opening his door*) Don't come looking for me.

(*He slams the door.*)

MONICA: And then there was one.

JASON: (*Opening his door*) Unless I'm gone an hour, then call an ambulance.

(*He slams the door.*)

TWENTY-FIFTH, AND LAST, PHASE – THE DOOR-SLAMMING SEQUENCE

MONICA, *left alone, wanders around, puts on a record or tape which is of Jane Oliver singing 'One More Ride on the Merry-go-round', finds herself by the fridge, opens it, eyes brighten. She takes cake out.*

MONICA: A cake! (*Breaks off a piece. Eats.*) Jason, I've come to a conclusion. I have nothing very important to say about life but – I do rather enjoy it. So put away your little complaints – you and I *will* travel, broaden our backs and our horizons. (*Makes herself comfortable.*) Samarkand, Mississippi, São Paulo, Quezaltenango . . .

JASON: (*Opening his door*) You need health to travel, and stamina, and bravery . . .

MONICA: No more jokes about dying, lover. Tehuantepec, San Francisco, Tahiti, Sumatra . . .

CHRIS: (*Opening her door*) We're making progress, discovering very interesting family traits in common.

(*She slams the door.*)

MONICA: . . . Borneo, Venice, Cairo, Alexandria . . .

NITA: (*Opening her door*) And I've got one last thing to say: I believe in a society where you help your neighbour because you *love* him, and leave him alone because you respect him, and . . . and . . . and . . . Damn!

(*She slams the door.*)

MONICA: . . . Addis Ababa, Sierra Leone, Yokohama, New York . . .

CHRIS: (*Opening her door*) Yippee! He needs an assistant!

JASON: (*Opening his door*) Yippee! Can he pay you?

CHRIS: (*Disappearing*) I'll let you know.

MONICA: . . . Jerusalem, Peking, Bangkok, Tashkent . . .

NITA: (*Opening her door*) And I've got another last thing to say: I believe in a society where you help your neighbour because you love him, and leave him alone because you respect him,

and . . . and . . . and . . . (*But she still can't find that last phrase.*)
Damn!
    (*She slams the door.*)

CHRIS: (*Reappearing*) He's broke! To begin with, our father must carry the can.

JASON: Impossible! Your father's sitting on it!
    (*He slams the door.*)

CHRIS: (*Ignoring him*) Next problem: can a half-sister make magic with a half-brother *sans scandale*?
    (*She slams the door.*)

MONICA: . . . Turkistan, Paris, Sri Lanka, Famagusta . . .

CHRIS: (*Opening her door*) Hallelujah! He's gay! Oh Father, your son's gay, your daughter's happy, and you're fantastic – you gave birth to my employer!
    (*She slams the door.*)

NITA: (*Opening her door*) Eureka! I've found it! I believe in a society where you help your neighbour because you love him, leave him alone because you respect him, and know the right time to do which!
    (*She slams the door. The joyous singing of Jane Oliver is swelling.*)

JASON: (*Returning, dressed*) Confucius say – man with trousers down, trip! Man with trousers up, dance!
    (MONICA *joins him, dreamily. They dance.*)

MONICA: . . . Barcelona, Karyupolis, Chióggia, Guadalajara, Katmandu . . .
    (*Joyous music up. Lights down.*)

CARITAS

Dedicated
with love and hope
to my nephew
Jake

Caritas is about the pursuit of the ideal through dogmas which lead to the destruction of things human.

There are two stories. They are not narratively related but it is hoped that through their juxtaposition the play will make a poetic impact, as a parable does.

One story relates the simple stages of the abortive English peasant uprising of 1381. It records that injustice existed which the peasants fought against, and that in the process they became intoxicated with blood-letting, and perpetrated other injustices.

The parallel story tells of a young girl's pursuit of an ideal state of mind through dogmas which lead to another kind of injustice. She becomes imprisoned by her dogmas; her pursuit of the ideal has led her to a denial of the life she thought would be divinely liberated.

The play is not contrived to prove a theory. The incident happened. I have attempted to extract meaning from the experience.

All dogma is anti-human because it presumes the way life *must* be lived, which kills spontaneous creativity. The human spirit must be given room to grow, enjoy, to innovate. Anything that suppresses this spirit, whether it is a capitalist or socialist or religious dogma, is anti-human.

Injustice cannot be tolerated but that does not mean the ideal is ever attainable.

It is right not to tolerate injustice, but it is foolish to expect people ever to be perfect.

Caritas is about the anti-human quality of dogma which presumes to dictate the way life must be lived.

A.W.
24 October 1981

One cause of disillusionment among certain types of young people is the new materialism which is sweeping Chinese society in the wake of the post-Mao leadership's emphasis on raising living standards and incomes. A Peking author who published a story about a young girl still under the influence of Maoist ideas received the following letter from one of his readers, describing her own dead sister:

All year round she would only wear black, white, grey and blue. She berated me for getting a special hairdo. She only read the *People's Daily* and the *Red Flag* [the Party's theoretical journal]. She thought everything else was decadent or pornographic or reactionary, feudal, capitalist, or revisionist. After the Gang of Four was overthrown she still persisted in her attitude. She worked in a factory and came home angry, saying the other workers were all reactionary; the younger ones would talk only about clothes, while the older ones would only talk about housekeeping and shopping for food. Why didn't they want to talk about global and national affairs? When it was payday, she didn't want to take any, saying, 'What do I want with stinking money?' She was living off her father, but couldn't even grasp what that meant. When bonuses began to be paid, she called it revisionist restorationism. She said people were trying to corrupt her with money. She kept a diary, but it was just full of Mao quotes. She had a few friends she had met during the Red Guard period, and she wrote to them. Their letters were always the same: first a bit about the 'excellent situation prevailing', then something on the latest slogans in the press, like 'plant the country with green trees'; then she would criticize a few people who were backward, and not revolutionary, and say, 'We are the only revolutionaries, we have the friendship of comrades in struggle' – and end up with some revolutionary salute. She wanted to go to university, but wasn't good at her courses because she didn't think it important to study culture. But she wanted to be a teacher, feeling this was 'noble and lofty' – not thinking that teachers have to accept wages too. She was madly revising for the exam, when

Father offered her some watermelon and advised her to go to bed. She said, 'You want to corrupt me with melon, but I won't eat it.' Father said, 'You've lived this long, and you still don't understand a thing.' Then she ran into her room, took poison, and hanged herself.

from David Bonavia, *The Chinese*
(Penguin, revised edition, 1989)

AUTHOR'S NOTE

I would like to thank the touring theatres of Norway and Sweden and Det Danske Teater of Denmark for generously commissioning this play.

I should also like to thank Professor Paul Levitt of the English Department of the University of Colorado for urging me to look into the world of anchoresses and in particular the scant story of Christine Carpenter.

The historical Christine Carpenter lived in the Surrey village of Shere. She became an anchoress in 1329. Documents have recently come to light revealing that the original Christine was immured, broke out three years later and then seems to have been persuaded by the authorities to re-enter her cell.

Note for Translators

The dialect, as in *Roots* and *The Wedding Feast*, is from Norfolk. I have not rendered everything in dialect. Simply, 'ing' is *in*; 'and' is *an*; 'that' is *thaas*; and the rest is peppered with the occasional *hev* and *hed* for 'have' and 'had'; *bein't* for 'be not'; *on* for 'of'; *ent* for 'is not' and 'am not'.

Note for Directors

This is a relatively short play, but the first and second acts must run together.

The lighting for the first act dictates itself. For the second act, although I haven't indicated it, the 'parts' being in the main very short, they need to be divided by 'puffs' of light fading in and out with sufficient darkness in between to allow Christine to move into a new framed position.

CHARACTERS

CHRISTINE CARPENTER   a young anchoress, between sixteen and twenty-one years old

AGNES CARPENTER   her mother, aged around forty

WILLIAM CARPENTER   her father, a carpenter, aged around forty-two

ROBERT LONLE   Christine's ex-fiancé, apprentice to William, aged about twenty

MATILDE   an old woman, in her sixties

HENRY   Lord Bishop of Norwich, aged fifty

MATHEW DE REDEMAN   Rector of St James's Chapel, Pulham St Mary, aged about thirty

RICHARD LONLE   Robert's father

VILLAGER/TRAVELLING PRIEST/BAILIFF   *to be played by one actor*

BISHOP'S CLERK/TAX COLLECTOR   *to be played by one actor*

Time   July 1377 to July 1381

Settings

Act One   a composite set to include: the wall, alter and circular window of the chapel; part of the anchored cell wall and its grille window; a carpenter's workshop

Act Two   interior of anchoress's cell

Caritas was first performed by the National Theatre Company at the Cottesloe Theatre, London, on 7 October 1981. The cast was as follows:

CHRISTINE CARPENTER	Patti Love
AGNES CARPENTER	Sheila Reid
WILLIAM CARPENTER	Roger Lloyd Pack
ROBERT LONLE	Martyn Hesford
MATILDE	Elizabeth Bradley
HENRY	Frederick Treves
MATHEW DE REDEMAN	Patrick Drury
RICHARD LONLE	
VILLAGER/TRAVELLING PRIEST/	
BAILIFF	Paul Benthall
BISHOP'S CLERK/TAX COLLECTOR	James Taylor

Director	John Madden
Designer	Andrew Jackness
Lighting Designer	Rory Dempster

A pre-production version of the text was published by Jonathan Cape in 1981. Substantial changes were made during rehearsals; further changes were made after the author had worked on the libretto for the opera during the summer of 1988.

68

ACT ONE

Scene I

JULY 1377

The interior of the church of St James in the village of Pulham St Mary, Norfolk; a carpenter's workshop; the window and part of the wall of the anchoress's cell anchored to the church.

CHRISTINE, daughter of William the carpenter, is about to be immured in the cell.

Sound of 'Alleluia te martyrum'.

Light slowly touches the opening in the wall. This is the first thing we see. Huge stones alongside, waiting to be put in place.

Light then touches the solitary figure of CHRISTINE, who stands before the altar, her back to us.

Light next touches the carpenter's workshop where stand three rough but solid pieces of furniture: a small table, a chair, a hard wooden bed. They are for Christine's cell, made by her father. The bed is not complete. One side is down and needs to be dovetailed to complete the frame, after which the boards must be hammered into position.

Note: What follows is based upon the recorded ceremony for enclosing anchoresses. Poetic licence is taken. But scene I must be performed in full, as a real church service, so that an audience is saturated in an intense religious atmosphere and feels itself witness to the ceremony of immurement. All the words of the service have relevance to what's happening and should be delivered as text, not mumbled.

HENRY, Lord Bishop of Norwich, enters, followed by MATHEW DE REDEMAN, Rector of the church, and then Christine's parents, WILLIAM and AGNES, followed by Christine's ex-fiancé, ROBERT LONLE, followed by an old villager, MATILDE, and two others, a VILLAGER and the BISHOP'S CLERK. A strong smell of incense is in the air.

Bishop HENRY begins the service.

HENRY: (*Intoning*) Psalm 6, which is David's:

O Lord, rebuke me not in thine anger, neither chasten me in thy hot displeasure.

Have mercy upon me, O Lord; for I am weak: O Lord, heal me; for my bones are vexed.

My soul is also sore vexed: but thou, O Lord, how long?

Return, O Lord, deliver my soul: O save me for thy mercies' sake.

For in death there is no remembrance of thee: in the grave who shall give thee thanks?

I am weary with my groaning: all the night make I my bed to swim; I water my couch with my tears.

Mine eye is consumed because of grief; it waxeth old because of all mine enemies.

Depart from me, all ye workers of iniquity; for the Lord hath heard the voice of my weeping.

The Lord hath heard my supplication; the Lord will receive my prayer.

Let all mine enemies be ashamed and sore vexed: let them return and be ashamed suddenly.

(*During this beginning* AGNES *stands before her daughter and begins to unbutton her dress. She is so distressed that she cannot complete the task. Sobbing, she is taken aside by her husband,* WILLIAM. MATILDE, *the old villager, takes over and soon the girl is in a white chemise. Another* VILLAGER *stands by with Christine's habit in his arms. The service is continuing meanwhile. Everyone responds to the psalm.*)

ALL: (*Intoned*) Glory be to the Father, and to the Son, and to the Holy Ghost; as it was in the beginning, is now, and ever shall be, world without end. Amen.

(CHRISTINE *prostrates herself.* HENRY *and* MATHEW *stand before her.* HENRY *holds a cross in front of her.* MATHEW *sprinkles her three times with holy water, then three times with incense.* HENRY *raises her up. Two lighted tapers are placed in her hands.*)

MATHEW: This is the Gospel of the Lord.

HENRY: O God, who dost cleanse the wicked and willest not the death of a sinner, we humbly beseech thy majesty that in thy goodness thou wilt guard thy servant, Christine, who trusteth in thy heavenly aid, that she may 'ever serve' thee and no trials may part her from thee. Through our Lord Jesus Christ.

ALL: Amen.

(CHRISTINE *moves forward, places her candles before the altar, steps back, reads her profession from a document.*)

CHRISTINE: I, Sister Christine, offer an' present myself to the goodness of God to serve in the order of an anchoress, an' according to the rule of that order I promise to remain henceforward in the service of God through the grace of God and the guidance of the church an' to render canonical obedience to my spiritual fathers.

(*A pen is handed to her. She scratches the sign of the cross upon it. Returns to stand before the altar. She is helped on with the rough habit as* HENRY *intones:*)

HENRY: May God put off from thee the old woman with all her works, and may God clothe thee with the new woman, for you who yearn passionately for union with her God are created in righteousness and true holiness.

ALL: Amen.

(CHRISTINE *prostrates herself before the altar.* HENRY *and the congregation continue in subdued tones to chant the hymn of Pentecost in Latin,* Veni Creator.)

> Veni, Creator Spiritus,
> Mentes tuorum visita,
> Imple superna gratia
> Quae tu creasti pectora.
>
> Qui diceris Paraclitus,
> Altissimi donum Dei,
> Fons vivus, ignis, caritas
> Et spiritalis unctio.
>
> Tu septiformis munere,
> Digitus paternae dexterae,
> Tu rite promissum Patris,
> Sermone ditans guttura.
>
> Accende lumen sensibus,
> Infunde amorem cordibus,
> Infirma nostri corporis
> Virtute firmans perpeti.

Hostem repellas longius,
Pacemque dones protinus:
Ductore sic te praevio
Vitemus omne noxium.
    Per te sciamus da Patrem,
Noscamus atque Filium,
Teque utriusque Spiritum
Credamus omni tempore.
    Deo Patri sit gloria
Et Filio qui a mortuis
Surrexit, ac Paraclito
In saeculorum saecula.
    Amen.

(WILLIAM, AGNES *and* ROBERT *break away to the workshop; she to finish the last stitches on a tablecloth, they to finish making the bed.*)

ROBERT: I know her passions. They have more to do with her than heaven.

AGNES: Why, why, why? I ask her, she tell me, but I understand narthin'.

WILLIAM: An' it's just you who should!

AGNES: (*Ignoring that*) 'All right,' I say. 'You want to retreat? Retreat! But fastin'? Beatin'? Prayin'? Weave!' I tell her. 'Mend the Church's clothes, collect for the poor, minister the sick, comfort the grievin'! But this?' An' she tell me, she say – with a scorn she get from I don't know who but I guess (*looking at her husband*) – she say, 'Mother,' she say, 'there's weakness in good deeds.' So I yell at her –

WILLIAM: Tryin' to be the right mother at the wrong time!

AGNES: (*Ignoring that too*) I yell at her: 'But where be the virtue in sufferin'? The divine spark is offended by sufferin'. Offended by it!' 'Nay, Mother,' she say. '*Life* offend the divine spark, which can only be found in heaven, an' thaas what I prepare myself for.' 'Narthin'! Narthin'!' I yell at her. 'That reveal narthin'!' 'Heaven! Heaven!' she yell back. 'The truth is revealed in heaven.' 'Huh!' I say. 'Huh! Huh! If heaven is where all truth is revealed then it must be hell!'

ROBERT: It were me to blame, me! 'Wanna marry Christ,' she say. 'Not you. Christ! Not you!'

AGNES: (*Meaning* WILLIAM) It's him! He's to blame. Had her taught words and grammar.

WILLIAM: Which she nagged for.

AGNES: Which *you* encouraged.

WILLIAM: An' who made her grow strange? Who took her from the love of fairs an' runnin' an' dancin' which rightly belongs to young girls? Who talked her silly about angels an' heaven an' hell an' the suffering of the Lord Jesus Christ?

AGNES: Which mother does different?

WILLIAM: Which mother has a daughter lock herself up in small rooms for months on end? Too much piety in the house! More passion than a child should take.

AGNES: But I warned against books.

WILLIAM: Too late, woman, the child was called.

AGNES: By the devil, called.

WILLIAM: She'll miss them fairs.

AGNES: An' the tumblin' an' the jugglin' an' the wrestlin'. Blust! She loved all that.

WILLIAM: There! A table an' chair for I don't know what.

AGNES: (*Mumbling on and quoting her daughter*) 'Change, change! There must be change!'

WILLIAM: And a hard bed to prevent her sleepin' too well.

ROBERT: Suppose we must be thankful she didn't ask for a coffin to sleep in.

(*They place the chair and table on the bed and carry all to and through the hole in the wall. Soon they return as the intoning of the hymn comes to an end. The ceremony continues over the prostrate* CHRISTINE. MATHEW *goes to the altar, plucks up one of Christine's candles.*)

MATHEW: O God, who willest not the death of a sinner, but rather that she should repent and be cleansed, we humbly beseech thy mercy for this thy servant who has forsaken the life of the world, that thou wouldst pour upon her the help of thy great goodness that, enrolled among thy chaste ones, she may so run the course of this present life that she may receive at thy hand the reward of an eternal inheritance. Through Christ our Lord.

ALL: Amen.

(CHRISTINE *rises.* MATHEW *turns, hands the taper to her.* HENRY *takes her hand; the others form a procession behind. They move towards the hole. A litany, 'Invocation to Christ', is sung. The procession moves through the family. Against the singing,* AGNES, WILLIAM *and* ROBERT *talk as though from afar.*)

AGNES: How will she wash when she sweat and she bleed? She'll die of her own smells, mad gal.

WILLIAM: No more games for you, my gal. Your runnin', dancin' days is done, all your fleet, sweet days, sweet daughter.

ROBERT: (*Angry*) She've seen blue skies, she won't forget that. She've seen mares mate, she won't forget that. She've seen lambs skip, the calves suck, the settin' sun, the rivers run, and once she've seen me naked, touched me once, an' she won't forget that.

(CHRISTINE *stands before her cell.* HENRY *intones his prayer.*)

HENRY: Bless, O Lord, this house (*signs the cross*) and this place, that in it may dwell health, holiness, chastity, power, victory, devotion, humility, gentleness, meekness, fulfilment of the law and obedience to God, Father, Son, and the Holy Ghost. And let a full measure of thy blessing (*signs the cross*) rest upon this place and upon all who dwell therein in thee, that, dwelling in all sobriety in these temples made with hands, they may ever be temples of thy Spirit. Through our Lord Jesus Christ thy Son, who with thee liveth and reigneth in the unity of the Holy Spirit one God.

(HENRY *takes* CHRISTINE *into the cell.*)

The Kingdom of the world –

(CHRISTINE *enters.*)

ALL: – and all the glory of it have I despised for the love of my Lord Jesus Christ, whom I have seen, whom I have loved, on whom I have believed, whom I have chosen for myself.

HENRY: Go, my people, enter into thy chamber, shut thy doors upon thee, hide thyself a little, for a moment, until the indignation pass away. *In nomine patris, filii et spiritu sancti.*

(HENRY *leads the procession off to the Gregorian chant which began the ceremony: 'Alleluia te martyrum'. Two* VILLAGERS *now slowly block up the entrance. It is a chilling sight. The cell is walled up. Empty. Silence. Then – a song is heard.* CHRISTINE *is singing to herself, very sweetly, calmly.*)

CHRISTINE: I will forsake all that I see,

74

Father and friend, and follow thee,
Gold and goods, riches and rent,
Town and tower and tenement,
Playing and prosperity,
In poverty for to be one with thee.
(*Between many of the scenes, like punctuations of comment, will be heard – loud or soft, vicious or sympathetic – the chanting of children. Like a street game. Now we hear it, tenderly.*)

CHILDREN'S VOICES: (*Off*) Christ–ine, Christ–ine, had a revelation yet? Had a vision, had a word, had a revelation yet? Christ–ine, Christ–ine, had a revelation yet? Had a vision, had a word, had a revelation yet?

Scene II

Loud scream from a man. RICHARD LONLE *is dragged into the centre space by a* BAILIFF. *His hands are tied behind his back. He kneels with his back to us. The* BAILIFF *carries a brazier of hot coals with an iron poking from it.*

HENRY *and* MATHEW *appear. It is some months later.*

HENRY: You know what's to happen, Richard Lonle?
RICHARD: Hypocrites! You preach labourers should be freed from all estates except your own!
HENRY: We think it's better it takes place here, before the Church, as warning to others.
RICHARD: The law says if I live in a town for a year an' a day I've earned my freedom.
HENRY: You were caught before then.
RICHARD: Three days! Three more days!
HENRY: And why *should* you have wanted to leave? The manor made you, fed you, rented you land, guarded you in sick times. Was I a bad lord? Was my bailiff here unfair? And in these times! When labour is desperately needed on the estate! You run away. *You* behaved unfair. And for why? To claim freedom! Freedom! No man's free! We're all bound by duties and responsibilities. So (*brandishing branding iron*) I want you to understand the justice of this punishment.
MATHEW: (*Reads from the manorial roll, his heart not in it*) Richard Lonle, bondsman to the Manor of Henry, Lord Bishop of Norwich, you did hold twenty-four acres of land for which rent of four pence an acre was due, also three hens at Christmas and fifteen eggs at Easter. Further, you were bound to perform two days' ploughing in the year, four half-days mowing grass, two half-days for hoeing, six days in autumn for reaping, and one day for your horse and cart to carry corn. You were charged with absconding from your local place of work and domicile, withdrawing your services, and dispersing your family, for which a right and proper jury found you guilty. By grace of his Lordship the Bishop Henry of Norwich, you have been granted the return of your house and land on condition of renewed service but that you be branded with hot iron upon the forehead as

sign to your neighbours and before God that you have broken your bond.

HENRY: Bailiff.

(MATHEW *holds the victim, and turns away in horror. The* BAILIFF *plucks the hot iron and brands* RICHARD *on the forehead. He screams, faints. The* BAILIFF *drags him away.* HENRY *and* MATHEW *move up into the church.*)

They wanted him hung but I wasn't having any blood-letting, besides we're short of labour. *You* think I shouldn't even have had him branded, don't you?

MATHEW: The times change and the Church should follow, my Lord Bishop.

HENRY: The Church will decide if times change.

MATHEW: With respect, the Church called not for plague to decimate the population, robbing labour from the land.

HENRY: God's plagues are God's affairs, God's Church is ours, to be obeyed, no matter what John Wyclif says. John Wyclif! Huh! An intellectual! (*Contemptuously*) 'Each man holding dominion from God!' The man doesn't know what he's talking about! Wants to do away with the power of the priests. Wants to do away with you, Rector, what d'you say to that? You! A Wyclif man! Individual conscience! Pah! Have every man acting according to his own dictates and you'll have chaos. First thing God did he made order out of chaos and then divinely fired Paul to build his Church that order be preserved. Order out of chaos! God's Church! To be obeyed! And I will see it is! Forgive me, Rector. Talk too loud. Unsettled times. I wasn't made for them. Not intellectual like you and old John Wyclif. I worked hard, learnt words, pursued my duty and – developed passions for the land. 'Divinely inspired are you not, Henry,' I said. 'Leave that to those imagining they are. Acknowledge your limitations and administer. Enough! You love the earth and its seasons like a mother her child and its tempers. Administer what you love. Enough!' And let me tell you something else. I don't approve of them! How is she?

MATHEW: She says her prayers, eats little, advises from her window, confesses through her quatrefoil. In the beginning her confessions were full of guilts for small sins. Now, she confesses to anger that the 'old life' still clings to her and she hasn't found the new one yet.

HENRY: After six months? Huh! Tantrums and fervours – not always easy to distinguish between them and the real thing. But you insisted. 'She's called, my Lord Bishop, it's her vocation, my Lord Bishop. She's in communication with the angels, my Lord Bishop.' Pah! (*Grumbling as he goes off*) I've always warned – some can't bear the touch of God so they scream loud hymns and prayers to drown him out. Fervours! Fervours! Tantrums and fervours!

Scene III

Light up on the cell and window. ROBERT *outside Christine's cell.*

ROBERT: It's not God's call you're serving, more a private devil.

CHRISTINE: There's things you say, young Lonle, I don't hear.

ROBERT: That's not what I say, that's what the Bible say. God didn't make you for that hole, he made you for the world which he made for you.

CHRISTINE: In here's the world. Out there is clutter.

ROBERT: There's cruelty, p'rhaps, unreason, killin'. But is that God callin' you or man a drivin' you?

CHRISTINE: Don't taunt me, Robert Lonle, pray for me. You love me? Pray for me!

ROBERT: You explain this, an' you explain that, black meanin' white an' white meanin' black! Your words is wind an' mist.

CHRISTINE: I don't have no other words.

ROBERT: Try village words, an' fairground words.

CHRISTINE: Them's for villages an' fairgrounds!

ROBERT: Then I'll keep askin'. Again an' again an' again.

CHRISTINE: Love, Robert, love! I can't say more than that. Love, Robert, love! I'm filled with love for him what took upon hisself great sufferin' an' torment an' death. To redeem us to God's grace. He suffered. For *us*. Can't you see the powerful pity thaas there? That make me weep. An' when I weep I know I got to share a tiny part on it.

ROBERT: In the silence an' the dark?

CHRISTINE: In a silence what is speakin' an' a dark what is light.

ROBERT: There you go! Wind an' mist an' black is white! You make no sense.

CHRISTINE: If I make no sense don't come no more. Don't taunt me! Don't taunt me! Don't! Don't taunt me!

ROBERT: Sorry, then. Sorry, sorry!

(*Long pause.*)

CHRISTINE: I hear tell a story, once. Mother and son. Lived at the foot of high mountains. And the son was drawn to them. He had to climb. The spirit of the mountains drew him. 'No!' his mother begged. She feared for him. 'No!' she begged. But come the day he knew his strength and he climbed. He climbed and he climbed. His mother watched and feared for him, and watched and feared. The long days passed. She suffered anguish but she marvelled and were proud. But oh the ache, the helpless ache. Until one day she made a resolution. She would trace his steps. For what was life without her son, without her lovely loving son? She needed to be with him, tread the road he travelled on, share the pain, the fate. Adored him, see? There were no other way.

(*Sounds of taunting children.*)

CHILDREN'S VOICES: (*Off*) Christ–ine, Christ–ine, had a revelation yet, had a vision, had a word, had a revelation yet?

ROBERT: Get off! Get away with you! Get off! Off!

(*But we hear them again, at a distance.*)

CHILDREN'S VOICES: (*Off*) Christ–ine, Christ–ine, had a revelation yet, had a vision, had a word, had a revelation yet?

Scene IV

Carpenter's workshop.

WILLIAM *and* ROBERT *are answering the questions of the* TAX COLLECTOR, *who's writing on sheets propped on a sawn tree trunk.*

TAX COLLECTOR: Name and age?

WILLIAM: William. Forty-two.

TAX COLLECTOR: (*Writing*) Willelmus. Wife?

WILLIAM: Agnes. Forty.

TAX COLLECTOR: Agneta. Children?

WILLIAM: One. Christine.

TAX COLLECTOR: Cristina. How old is she?

WILLIAM: The Crown will get no tax from her, she give her all to God.

TAX COLLECTOR: (*Sceptically*) Is that so?

WILLIAM: You've not been told of her? She've made these parts famous enough.

TAX COLLECTOR: Ah! The anchoress! A rebuke to rudeness and self-indulgence. Very chastening. But I confess, I am a mortal man of sins and shames. Some temptations I control; others have a power I'm not built to control. What's to be done? Nothing, I say, but guard against excesses and be what of a good man I can, and God can spit wrath and indignation as he will, I am what I am an' there's an end, for I can do no more.

WILLIAM: There speaks someone from the city.

TAX COLLECTOR: Right! The solitary life is not one I'd be fit or excited for, but I'm full of reverence and awe, full of it. You must be proud.

(*His tone is casual. The men are silent. The* TAX COLLECTOR *looks around, then at* WILLIAM *for confirmation.*)

WILLIAM: Aye, carpenter.

TAX COLLECTOR: Carpentarius.

ROBERT: He say one thing you write another.

TAX COLLECTOR: Latin, young man. They may preach sermons in English these days but tax returns must still be recorded in Latin. And who are you?

WILLIAM: My apprentice.

ROBERT: You'll know me from my father, Richard Lonle. You were there yesterday.

TAX COLLECTOR: (*Looking through sheets*) Lonle, Lonle. Ah. Ricardo, agricola, Alicia, Edmundo, Henrico, Johanna and Claricia. And you must be Roberto. (*Smiles.*) Latin! And you're all bondsmen to the Bishop's Manor.

ROBERT: Now. But next year us'll buy our liberty.

TAX COLLECTOR: Is that so? Now, possessions? And I want to hear everything. You know the penalty for hoarding. Although – arrangements can be made, eyes closed, this and that ignored.

(*He smiles.*)

WILLIAM: (*Coldly ignoring the invitation of a bribe*) Three saws, two axes, a spokeshave, two adzes, two hammers, four oxen, seven steers, two cows, two and a half quarters of winter wheat, five quarters of oats . . .

Scene V

William's voice dies away as CHRISTINE's *voice from the cell takes over.*

CHRISTINE: There was a oneness time. I search that. When I were
with my soul, an' my soul were with my body, an' my body were
with me, an' we was all one with God an' his lovely nature an' there
were oh such peace an' rightness an' a knowing of my place. That
really were a oneness time that were. An' I search that, Lord Jesus.
   (*Old* MATILDE, *the busybody and gossip, enters, places her stool
   beneath the window, cards her wool, and chatters.*)
MATILDE: You crossed your mouth?
   (CHRISTINE *grunts her replies.*)
Good! An' your eyes an' ears an' your breasts? Good! For as the
advice goes – an anchoress must love her window as little as
possible, especially a young'un. There's men in this village with
lewd eyes an' soft tongues, an' there's boys with taunts, an' old
women with useless prattlin'. Your mother bring you your food?
Good! Now here's a story about a Belgie saint called Yvetta, tell me
by a smithy who heard it from a nun who heard it on a pilgrimage to
Rome which is how I get all my stories being a collector of stories
'bout saints which you'll be one day if you work hard at it. Yes! Get
them from all over. Pilgrims. Vagabonds. Ole cooks at the fairs who
I growed up with but them's also old an' widows now. Full o' stories.
So, Yvetta. Sweet and pretty thing she were, an' happy, but, poor
gal, she had to marry. Howsomever, when her husband die she
renounce the world and go to serve in a leper colony where she so
much wanted to be a leper herself that she eat an' drink with them,
look, an' even wash in their bath water! Blust! You shouldn't catch
me doin' that! An' when she were enclosed she were visited by that
many temptations that she had to hev a haircloth on her an' an iron
chain with two heavy tablets hanging round her neck, an' added to
them she give her poor ole limbs a whole lot o' floggin', there! She
didn't eat too much, neither. Baked flour an' powdered ashes three
times a week! An' all her day an' nights were spent in prayers, tears,
genuflexions an' striking of the breast, an' when she sleep that were
on sharp pointed stones. An' she die exactly on the day she say she
were goin' to die. Hands outstretched an' eyes raised to heaven.

Seventy she was. An' they say that even though it were the middle of winter wi' a great storm of wind an' hail an' snow, yet the birds gathered round her cell an' sang as if it were a summer day. An' her face was all a brilliant glow, they say.

Scene VI

Inside the church.

    MATHEW *by the quatrefoil taking confession from* CHRISTINE.

CHRISTINE: . . . O all you blessed angels an' saints of God! Pray for me, a most miserable sinner, that I may now turn away from my evil ways, that my heart may henceforward be forever united with yours in eternal love, an' never more go astray. Amen. I've sinned, father.

MATHEW: What sins, daughter?

CHRISTINE: I find pleasure in my cell.

MATHEW: Who told you pleasure was a sin?

CHRISTINE: Time pass quickly. I look forward to each day.

MATHEW: That is a joy. God has rewarded you with joy.

CHRISTINE: I feel my suffering is false. I feel a fraudulence, deceit. I feel an emptiness.

MATHEW: Be patient, child –

CHRISTINE: I don't suffer.

MATHEW: Patience –

CHRISTINE: I do not suffer.

MATHEW: Patience, patience –

CHRISTINE: Not to suffer is a sin.

MATHEW: What are you saying, child!

CHRISTINE: My chains! My haircloth! I want my chains, I want my haircloth!

MATHEW: You will enfeeble your body.

CHRISTINE: My chains! My haircloth!

MATHEW: Enfeebled bodies cannot sing the praise of God.

CHRISTINE: Enfeebled bodies come from comfort, too much ease. You do not understand. My body needs the pain to help me concentrate on him.

MATHEW: No! No! Pain will intrude!

CHRISTINE: My chains! My haircloth!

MATHEW: What harmony can be known through torn flesh?

CHRISTINE: The torn flesh of our Lord brought harmony to the world. His suffering brought peace.

MATHEW: Suffering brings suffering.

CHRISTINE: I want my chains! I want my haircloth!

MATHEW: You *want*, you *want*! *Those* are the sins.

CHRISTINE: I'm dirtied! Unclean! Selfish! Wilful! I must destroy that selfish will.

MATHEW: To which end you apply the most extraordinary power of will.

(*He stops suddenly, realizing he's arguing against the entire concept of the solitary pursuit which the Church has sanctioned. He's caught in a moment of doubt which Christine senses. She's a powerful personality of which he is afraid.*)

CHRISTINE: Are you a priest or not? Do I have God or Satan here?

MATHEW: Beware, Christine. Into a life of solitude creep many evil beasts. The serpent of venomous envy, the bear of sloth, the fox of covetousness . . .

CHRISTINE: – the swine of gluttony, the scorpion with the tail of stinkin' lechery!

MATHEW: And the lion of pride, and the unicorn of wrath!

CHRISTINE: I know them!

MATHEW: I will come another time. You sound out of temper today.

(*He leaves. She calls after him.*)

CHRISTINE: Bring me my chains an' haircloth, father. Bring them!

CHILDREN'S VOICES: (*Off, taunting*) Christ–ine! Christ–ine! Had a revelation yet? Had a vision, had a word? Had a revelation yet? Christ–ine, Christ–ine. Had a revelation yet? Had a vision, had a word? Had a revelation yet?

Scene VII

Carpenter's workshop.

WILLIAM *and* ROBERT *at work on a wheel.* AGNES *and* MATHEW
alongside.

AGNES: Here's your bread an' some meat from the fair, an' some bean
and bacon soup which is good for you. (*Pause.*) And here's the
Bishop's priest. (*Meaning: who is not good for you. Pause.*) No! I
aren't leavin'!

 (*Awkward silence. The men don't know whether to eat or not.*
 AGNES *decides for them.*)

Eat up, look. That'll be cold presently.

WILLIAM: Worried about our daughter are you? Speak to (*pointing to*
AGNES) *her*, then.

MATHEW: I urged the Bishop, it's true. Even against his doubts. But I
believe she was called.

AGNES: You believe your church looks better with an anchoress to
boast of.

MATHEW: (*Attempting sternness*) My church is your church and you
remember I'm the Vatican's choice for this parish, granted me by
Pope Urban himself –

 (*But his feeble authority touches their stony defiance not one bit. He*
 relents. He's a good man really.)

(*Gentler*) She's asked for haircloth and chains.

AGNES: An' she'll get them. Somehow. An' go on to crueller things. I
know her.

MATHEW: There's such a powerful hold on her mind.

ROBERT: Ent that what you want?

MATHEW: The solitary life is a search for union with God, it should
bring freedom.

AGNES: Instead of imprisonment by stubborn love, you mean?

MATHEW: (*Dismissively*) Love's an intoxicant. It clouds the truth of
things. It makes you feel great good is done to you as hate can make
you feel great harm is done when neither is the case.

WILLIAM: (*Curious about him now*) An' *you* approved of her goin' in,
father?

 (MATHEW *is troubled. Every time he speaks he seems to surprise*

87

himself. Is he moving away from the faith? Is he a Wyclif man? He is fearful he will say too much to the wrong people.)

MATHEW: (*Leaving*) I promise I'll keep close to her.

ROBERT: Well, *he* didn't stay long!

AGNES: I should've offered him food.

(*Now moonlight falls on Christine's cell as she whispers desperately to herself.*)

CHRISTINE: A showing! A showing! Give me Jesu Lord my lovely Christ a showing! Touch me with your passion. That crucifix before me. Bleed! Weep! Smile! Whisper to me! I crave a showing, to stay with me every dark day of my dark life in this dark cell!

Scene VIII

Christine's cell.
  MATILDE *arrives, places her stool, cards her wool, and chatters.*

MATILDE: You crossed your mouth? Good! An' your eyes an' ears an' breasts? Good! Your mother brought your food? Good! Now here's a story. Saint Veridiana. Born two hundred years ago they tell me, place called Siena in Italy. This one fasted even as a child, an' wore a chain an' hairshirt. *Her* cell were ten feet long an' only three an' a half wide. No furniture, narthin', just a ledge in the wall an' two snakes for company. She tell her bishop they were sent in answer to a prayer that she be allowed to suffer similar to what St Anthony did, cos you know *he* were tormented by devils in the form of wild beasts. They say them snakes sometimes lashed her insensible with their tails. They killed one just before she died, the other never returned. In summer she slept on the ground, an' in winter on a plank with a piece of wood for a pillow, an' now she wore an iron girdle an' a hairshirt. Only one meal a day she had, sometimes bread and water, sometimes boiled beans, most times narthin' cos she give it away to the poor what used to come beggin' every night. Course she don't talk to no one but the poor an' afflicted, you know. An' she live like that for thirty-four years. Till she were sixty. Then she die. She also knew exactly *when* she were goin' to die cos she sent for her confessor, an' closed her windows. An' at the very moment she die all the church bells began ringin' by theirselves, look. An' when they pulled down the wall there she was, dead on her knees, with her psalter open at the Miserere! (*Pause.*) Is that another comin' to your window? (*Shouting*) Go off there! That ent the right time o' day to be callin'. (*To* CHRISTINE) My, they do come, don't they? All wonder an' excitement an' reverence. Think cos you cut yourself off from life you can explain life's mysteries. (*Shouting to* CHILDREN) Get away, I say! (*To* CHRISTINE) Your solitary life make folk uneasy. Your fastin' make them feel their greed. Your gentle ways make folk reflect upon their violence. The Church may be your anchor, gal, but ha!, she needs you, that she do. (*Calling*) You're persistent. What's your question then? (*Pause. She listens. Then, to* CHRISTINE) It's a young gal. No more'n about twelve. Says she wants to know how this life begin for you.

(*Long pause.*)

CHRISTINE: I hear rumours, little gal. My soul hear rumours. Rumours like whispers. Not in words but in feelin's, feelin's whispered that another place up there existed. I don't talk of heaven, not rumours of heaven but (*struggling*) rumours of another kind of knowin'. Oh, how shall I describe it for you? I couldn't make things fit together, rumour come and say it could. I couldn't walk beside myself, rumour come and say I could. I couldn't ever love myself but rumour come and whispered I was loved. Where did them whispered rumours come from? They must come from somewhere, little gal, I say, and so I listen hard, follow sound, hope for the truth. Sometimes I think I hear the truth. I get excited, eager but – thaas not the truth. Only an echo of the truth, an' so I rage an' weep an' have to start again. (*Beat.*) Rumours, rumours, little gal, beware the echoes but wait for the rumours.

MATILDE: (*Collecting herself, speaks to 'gal'*) There! You got that? Rumours! Rumours! Wait for the rumours. Beware the echoes, but wait for the rumours.

(MATILDE *leaves, shrugging, utterly lost.*)

Scene IX

Carpenter's workshop. February 1379.
  WILLIAM, AGNES, ROBERT *and the* TAX COLLECTOR.

TAX COLLECTOR: Be sensible! This new tax must be paid by everyone.

AGNES: The King had tax from us two years ago.

TAX COLLECTOR: Twelve pence from you but, look!, the rich have twenty shillings each to pay, the clergy six and eight. But you? Twelve pence!

  (*He's becoming increasingly fearful of their mood.*)

You know my policy: six in the family, I count five, we split twelve pence. (*Pause.*) Not to be sneezed at. (*Pause.*) If you don't work with me the King's men will send officers with greater powers and it'll be imprisonment for all of you.

  (*Silence. He tries authority.*)

Right! My good nature's at an end. This money's needed for the safety of the realm and to support the army in its wars abroad.

WILLIAM: The wars in France.

TAX COLLECTOR: Yes, them!

WILLIAM: Disastrous wars. Losin' wars. Costly, disastrous, losin' wars.

TAX COLLECTOR: They pay me to collect the tax not judge how it's spent.

WILLIAM: (*Threateningly*) We hear from Kent a tax collector raped a farmer's gal.

TAX COLLECTOR: (*Frightened*) Well, that's in Kent and that was him, and this is Norfolk, this is me.

ROBERT: The farmers hung him.

AGNES: Why! I do believe the tax collector's shit hisself!

Scene X

Interior of the church.
 MATHEW *at silent prayer. We hear* CHRISTINE *at her prayers.*

CHRISTINE: . . . We adore thee, O Christ, an' we bless thee, because of thy holy cross thou hast redeemed the world. We adore thy cross, O Lord. We commemorate thy glorious passion. Have mercy on us, thou who didst suffer for us. Hail, O holy cross, worthy tree, whose precious wood bore the ransom of the world. Hail O –
   (*She stops abruptly. Ecstatic joy enters her voice.*)
 Oh! Oh! A showing!
   (*She can hardly believe it.*)
 A showing! A showing! I have a showing! There before me!
   (MATHEW *raises his head.*)
 I see the world's shape. God shows me the world's shape. I see its joins, I see its links, I see what clasps and holds it together. There's the hole and there's the dowel, there's the dovetail, mortise, tenon. Oh! Oh! I hear the flower blossom, see the harvest grow, I know the colour of the wind, the dark in light. Oh! Oh! It joins and locks and fits and rhymes. That be no echo this time, Lord, I see the shape. There is no mystery for Christine now. Oh, blessed Jesus Christ, I begged and prayed and prayed. The cross! The tree! The precious wood! And you have give to me a showing, you have give to me a showing!

MATHEW: Beware, Christine, beware the vision. Awake, asleep, dreaming, beware the vision. They could be illusions. Satan's stratagems. Once he made a man believe he was an angel and his father was a devil, and he made him kill his father. Beware, Christine, beware the vision.
   (*Long pause.*)

CHRISTINE: The dark in the light? I said 'the dark in the light'. I *did* say 'the dark in the light', didn't I? (*Pause.*) That were no showing, then. (*Pause.*) Though it did make sense. Gone. An' I nearly named the parts. (*Pause.*) There's a foul stench in my cell. Arrgh! Who'll rid my cell of its foul stench?
   (*Long pause.*)

MATHEW: Christine? Christine? Are you all right, Christine? Shall I confess you?

CHRISTINE: (*Hissing*) Go away.

    (*Sad, taunting voices of the* CHILDREN.)

CHILDREN'S VOICES: (*Off*) Christ–ine! Christ–ine! Had a revelation yet? Had a vision, had a word, had a revelation yet? Christ–ine! Christ–ine! Had a revelation yet? Had a vision, had a word, had a revelation yet?

Scene XI

Carpenter's workshop. May 1381.
    WILLIAM, AGNES *and* ROBERT. *It's evening, dim. They sit over a pint of ale, animated by the events they discuss.*

AGNES: I hear plans an' plottin's in the villages around.

WILLIAM: Are you surprised? Our grazin' places gone, forbid to hunt an' fish which we have done for years, look!

ROBERT: A third tax comin'.

AGNES: Plans an' plottin's to set fire to the Manor documents.

WILLIAM: Burn them an' they won't have record of who's tied to who, for what, nor where.

ROBERT: Good rid on 'em, too.

AGNES: The documents an' rolls of Carrow Priory first. The Manor House at Methwold next.

WILLIAM: You know a lot.

AGNES: If I depended on your ear to know the world we'd all be lost.

ROBERT: Then tell us all you know, missus.

AGNES: I don't know, I just guess. There'll be killin's.

WILLIAM: What's the sense in that?

AGNES: You sit on people, you squash sense out, don't you?

ROBERT: A third tax! Want their heads examined!
    (MATHEW *enters.*)

WILLIAM: Come to share some ale, father?

AGNES: (*Fussing*) Sit you there, look. I'll see to him.
    (*She pours.*)

ROBERT: I know why he've come.

MATHEW: The Bishop has refused.

WILLIAM: Refused him what?

ROBERT: To study grammar.

WILLIAM: Even though his father's got the money?

ROBERT: No matters how much money my father've got, the Bishop ont take it. The yearly levy, thaas what he'll take. Ploughin' his lands, shearin' his sheep. maltin' his grain – thaas what he'll take. An' when we grind our corn in his mill an' must leave some, he'll take that! An' when we brew ale in his brewery an' must leave some, he'll take that! An' when we bake bread in his ovens an' must leave some he'll take that! Course he ont let me study grammar. Us study, us'll leave!

AGNES: An' be branded with hot irons on your forehead like your father.

ROBERT: That was then. Now my dad is saving hard to buy his freedom and he wants his son to read. He sees my talent for the word, my mother sees, my brothers, sisters see, and now they tell us English will replace the French in church and court and school and parliament I must command the word, and if Christine had not retreated to a hole then she'd've been my teacher of the word!

(*They all sit in silence for a while.*)

MATHEW: It's not in her to be solitary.

ROBERT: I could've told you that.

MATHEW: She sits demanding visions. Now! At once! After only three years! When there's some have waited sixty and not been graced.

AGNES: I know my daughter's ritual well. The dawn appears, she rises, genuflects and kneels upon that bed you made, and with bowed body prays and prays and prays some more. And prayin' still and mumblin' still she dresses into God knows what. Because you know I took her once a day a shift until she said 'each week' and now 'each month' and soon she'll live a year in one foul dress and, oh!, the filth, the smell, the misery and pain – for what? I ask myself for what? (*Weeps.*) My gal, my gal, my own poor gal.

MATHEW: To give up now she knows there's only excommunication, fire and hell.

WILLIAM: It's not in her to be solitary nor in you, it seems, to be a priest.

MATHEW: For this Church – no!

Scene XII

Christine's cell.

MATILDE *arrives, places her stool, cards her wool and chatters. But now a distressed and wild* CHRISTINE *mocks and mimics her familiar opening sentences.*

MATILDE: You crossed your mouth?

CHRISTINE: (*Mimicking*) 'You crossed your mouth?'

MATILDE: (*Surprised but impervious*) Good! An' your eyes – ?

CHRISTINE: 'An' your eyes?'

MATILDE: An' your ears?

CHRISTINE: 'An' your ears?'

MATILDE: An' your breasts?

CHRISTINE: 'An' your breasts?'

MATILDE: Good!

CHRISTINE *and* MATILDE: (*Together*) Your mother brought your food?

MATILDE: Good!

> (*But she does a double-take. Something is wrong. Waits. Will* CHRISTINE *continue to mock her?*)

Now here's a story.

> (*But she's uncertain what is wrong or what to do. She'll risk what she's always done, however.*)

My favourite. You'll like this one. St Christiana. Another Belgie, an' she weren't an anchoress or narthin', she were just – well, holy! A spirit! A real spirit who could climb trees an' church towers an' was so thin an' light from livin' in the wilderness that she could sit on the thinnest branches of trees, look, and sing psalms! There were three sisters, three on 'em, an' she were given the job o' lookin' after the cows. But did she mind? Course she didn't. She'd sit out there contemplatin', an' contemplatin' an' contemplatin' so much that she put herself into a trance. Yes, a trance! An' that were so deep they all thought she was dead so they took her to church to be buried. But halfway through Mass she got off her bier an' clamber up the walls to the roof, look!, an' she don't come down till her Mass is finished an' the priest promise to absolve her. An' when she *do* come down she tell 'em all how when she were dead she were

shown purgatory, hell an' then paradise, an' they give her the
choice o' remainin' in heaven or sufferin' on earth for the con-
version o' sinners. She come back! Cor, that congregation fled!
'Cept for her eldest sister who was too terrified to move. Glorious
life she led. In an' out o' the wilderness, livin' on herbs, prayin',
contemplatin', prophesyin', hevin' ecstasies. Like a sparrow she
was, very weird and wonderful.

(CHRISTINE *shrieks loudly. Three times.*)

Scene XIII

Inside the church. 17 June 1381.

A TRAVELLING PRIEST *is giving a 'sermon'. But* **not** *to the audience, rather from a pulpit to a congregation of our characters and 'extras'.*

TRAVELLING PRIEST: 'Blow ye the trumpet in Zion, and sound an alarm on my holy mountain.' Thus saith the prophet Joel. New sermons are being preached in our land, beloved. Here's one for you: to each man hath God given conscience! Dominion over himself! Therefore turn to your priests and tell them this: one vicar cannot be upon the earth, for each is vicar to himself.

'Beat your ploughshares into swords, and your pruning hooks into spears: let the weak say I am strong.' Thus saith the prophet Joel. One hundred thousand men are gathered under Wat Tyler, brothers. Canterbury opens her gates, the manor records burn and they have snatched the mad John Ball from gaol to sing his lovely sermons to us all. Have you ever heard John sing, beloved?

'Good people,' sings John Ball, 'good people, things will never go well in England as long as goods be not in common held. By what right', sings he, 'are they who are called lords greater folk than we? Clothed in velvet, warm in furs and ermines, while we are covered with rags! Tell me', sings John Ball, 'when Adam delved and Eve span, who was *then* the gentleman?' D'you like those songs, brothers and sisters? They sing them from the coast of Kent up to the Wash.

'And it shall come to pass afterwards that I will pour out my spirit on all your flesh; and your sons and your daughters shall prophesy, your old men shall dream dreams, your young men shall see visions.' Thus saith the prophet Joel. And –

(*Bishop* HENRY *storms in.*)

HENRY: In my church? Blasphemy and treason in my church?

(*Comic chase. The* TRAVELLING PRIEST *dodges here and there with confident fun, throwing out slogans and rhymes of the day.*)

TRAVELLING PRIEST: 'Help truth and truth shall help you!'

HENRY: Who gave him permission? Who let him in? (*Calling*) Bailiff! Rector! Who opens God's house to the wandering blasphemer?

TRAVELLING PRIEST: 'Now reigneth pride in price

And covertise is counted wise
And lechery withouten shame
And gluttony withouten blame.'
HENRY: I'll have you hung, drawn and quartered! You'll burn in hell!
TRAVELLING PRIEST: (*Fleeing*) 'God do bote,* for now is tyme!'
  (HENRY *strides after him.* CHRISTINE *screams again. Three times.*)
CHRISTINE: (*A voice of dread*) I do not have the vocation! Release
  me! I do not have it!

* God do bote = God claims.

Scene XIV

Inside the church. Lit away from the cell wall.
HENRY *and* MATHEW.

HENRY: Knew it! From the start! Wrong! I felt it, warned it! But you insisted. 'She's called, my Lord Bishop, it's her vocation, my Lord Bishop!' And now, on top of everything else, farmers and knights and Wyclif's mad Lollard priests on the rampage. They're burning records in the manor houses, d'you know that? How can we know who's bonded to who, now? And in the midst of all a mad girl raves to be absolved from that most sacred vow. You satisfied?

MATHEW: There must be a hearing, my lord.

HENRY: Who says so? I'll say what must and must not be.

MATHEW: We *must* be seen to be considering the pleas.

HENRY: I've considered them. She took the vows of poverty, chastity and obedience. A vow is a vow! It must be kept!

MATHEW: Perhaps she can be moved, share a life with another anchoress.

HENRY: She wanted unity with God? The perfect state? Upon her head the perfect state! A vow is a vow!

MATHEW: (*Persistent*) Her parents and the apprentice Robert Lonle are waiting to see you.

HENRY: Well, send them away! I trust not her, not him, not any of them. Their heads are full of discontent, confusion, and their tempers are insolent.

MATHEW: But what shall I tell them?

HENRY: Tell them! Tell them! Tell them they neglected to plough and harrow my lands in the spring. Tell them God's granted my corn to grow and they owe it to God and me and the land to reap and make hay and grind. Tell them that! A struggle, why is everything a struggle?

MATHEW: I'll call them in, my lord.

    (MATHEW *leaves.* HENRY *glares in the direction of Christine's cell.*
    MATHEW *returns with* AGNES, WILLIAM *and* ROBERT.)

HENRY: And was she an aggravation for you, too? Did she have tantrums as a child which you thought were visions? Thought you had a special little girl, so you indulged her? Fanned her fervours, inflamed her imagination?

WILLIAM: It were her mother made her pious.

AGNES: It was her father had her taught the word.

HENRY: (*Exploding*) The word? The word? She learned to read? And did you ask permission? Was the levy paid? And *you* (*to* ROBERT) want my permission to learn the word! (*Pointing to the cell*) See where reading leads? To notions that take power of minds too weak to contradict them. Notions have a life their own to chain you, grab you, bind you, hold you! (*Pauses to collect his temper.*) What have you come to ask of me?

AGNES: She's our only child, Bishop, sir. No sons to help our work, look after our old age, and bring us heirs. Thaas a hard life on earth, an' the promise o' heaven then an' a family now – them's the only relief in it. She give our Lord three precious years. She've tried to please God an' the Church. Let them be pleased enough, Lord Bishop, sir, your reverend. Let her go.

WILLIAM: What's to be gained from a reluctant solitary, my lord? You want your folk to take strength an' example from your anchoresses, don't you, sir? To give courage, light, set a standard? What standard can my poor daughter set? She've gone in there to fill her head an' heart but look!, she've emptied them instead. No light, no standard, lord, no use to God or Church, or Bishop Henry. Let her go.

ROBERT: She were betrothed to me for love of me, an' I to her for love of her. There ent a week passed in these three years I've not sat with her, an' she talk an' talk an' talk an' talk, and I know she love me still. Let her go, sir. Let her go an' we'll be married. You'll hear narthin' of us more if you relent and let her go.

(*Pause.*)

HENRY: We will think on it.

(HENRY *and* MATHEW *leave, followed by the other three. Now a red glow slowly grows, like a house burning, as we hear the children's voices.*)

CHILDREN'S VOICES: (*Off*) Christ–ine, Christ–ine, had a revelation yet, had a vision, had a word, had a revelation yet? Christ–ine, Christ–ine, had a revelation yet, had a vision, had a word, had a revelation yet? Christ–ine, Christ–ine . . .

CHRISTINE: Not fit! Not fit! Christine not fit! You have hell anchored to your church, Bishop Henry. Break down its walls, break them, break them. In the name of God, BREAK THEM DOWN!

(*Sound of drums and marching feet. They grow louder and louder, topped by the cry of a man being slaughtered. The red glow lingers. Light shifts from church to carpenter's workshop.*)

Scene XV

Carpenter's workshop.
  AGNES: *seems anxiously to be waiting for someone.*
  The TRAVELLING PRIEST *enters carrying the dead* ROBERT *in his arms. Lays him gently in wood shavings. The* PRIEST *is himself in tatters and blood.*

  AGNES *gasps, bends to wipe away the blood, her low moaning continues throughout.*

TRAVELLING PRIEST: London, the Friday after the feast of Corpus
  Christi, the boy King meets Wat Tyler at Mile End, agrees to his
  demands. I watch it happen. Watch the King bow to his people,
  listen to the roar, the cheer go up. Shivers down my spine.
  Exhilarating.

  Then the mood changes. People become intoxicated with their
  gains and powers. A people's court behead Sudbury and Hales and
  at the Tower the King's physician, which intoxicates their passions
  more. Then the crude and rough ones surface. Scum arising to the
  top to pay off ancient scores and murder aliens.

  I shout and warn but there are quick and easy tongues to call me
  traitor. Oh, those quick and easy tongues! We come to Smithfield
  where we give the King a second paper of demands. 'Come talk to
  us,' he says. Again I warn but oh the tongues were quick and easy.
  Wat the Tyler goaded by the quick and easy mob steps to the other
  side where – swish! The Mayor of London kills him quick and easy.
  That was that!

  The Freedom Charters are withdrawn. John Ball sings his last
  sermon and is hung, drawn and quartered at St Albans, and the rest
  come home. (*Looking at* ROBERT) One way or another.

  (CHRISTINE *is heard singing her song, but sadly now.*)
CHRISTINE: I will forsake all that I see,
  Father and friend, and follow thee,
  Gold and goods, riches and rent,
  Town and tower and tenement,
  Playing and prosperity,
  In poverty for to be one with thee.
    (*Light transfers to inside the church.*)

Scene XVI

Inside the church. Lit away from the cell wall.

HENRY *and* MATHEW *confront* WILLIAM *who is on his knees before them awaiting the verdict.*

HENRY: We cannot. It is not in our power to sanction the breaking of a vow, nor can we bless an adulteress to Christ. She cannot leave the cell.

(*The cell wall revolves slowly. We see the inside of the cell. Backed against the wall is* CHRISTINE. *The sight of her is shocking. She is dirty, unkempt and terrified as her eyes take in what she now realizes is to be her cell for ever.*)

CHILDREN'S VOICES: (*Distant*) Christ–ine, Christ–ine! Had a revelation yet? Had a vision, had a word, had a revelation yet? Christ–ine, Christ–ine! Had a revelation yet? Had a vision, had a word, had a revelation yet?

(*And on the chanting the lights slowly fade.*)

ACT TWO

One continuous scene – in eleven parts. The interior of Christine's cell.

Part 1

CHRISTINE *in the corner of her cell, terrified.*

CHRISTINE: I ent narthin', I hev narthin', I desire narthin', save the love of Jesus only. I ent narthin', I hev narthin', I desire narthin' save the love of Jesus only. I ent narthin', I hev narthin', I desire narthin' save the love of Jesus only. I ent narthin' . . .

Part 2

CHRISTINE *on her knees before her crucifix.*

CHRISTINE: O Jesus Christ whose flesh were torn and into which you bid us creep for comfort – comfort me. Comfort me, deliver me an' show me mercy, Lord. Have mercy an' deliver me from here. I ent no saint nor martyr but a little thing afeared wi' timid soul an' helpless heart an' no strong body like I thought. I tried, my Lord, wi' all I got. I give, my Lord, wi' what I had. But what I had and what I got was not what you and me imagined, Lord. I thought I heard you speak to me, sign me a path, but that were Satan, Lord, the devil givin' me ideas my feeble head weren't made to take. Your father made me, Jesus Lord. He know me what I am an' fit for. Speak to him, Lord. Tell him make a sign to Henry. Tell him what you see, Lord Jesus. Look at me and tell him how this little gal ent made for solitary life. I ent, Lord, I ent, Lord, I ent, Lord, I ent, I ent, I ent, I ent . . .

Part 3

CHRISTINE *in the corner of her cell.*

CHRISTINE: I ent narthin', I hev narthin', I desire narthin' save
the love of Jesus only. I ent narthin', I hev narthin', I desire
narthin' save the love of Jesus only. I ent narthin', I hev
narthin', I desire narthin' save the love of Jesus only. I ent
narthin' . . .
(*Sounds of taunting children outside the grille window of the cell. Their
hands come through, hoping to touch her. She ignores them, sits on in
her corner. Their chanting takes over from hers.*)
CHILDREN'S VOICES: Christ–ine, Christ–ine, had a revelation yet?
Had a vision, had a word, had a revelation yet? Christ–ine,
Christ–ine, had a revelation yet? Had a vision, had a word, had a
revelation yet, Christ–ine, Christ–ine . . .

Part 4

CHRISTINE *by the quatrefoil.*

CHRISTINE: I know, father, yes, I know, I begged to be a solitary, yes,
I did. But now I must return to people. Live among the living, see?
Thaas like this here. Alone, in the silence, in the dark, I see the
truth – thaas noisy, truth. 'Tis! People pullin', pushin' different
ways – 'I'm this, I'm that, here's right, there's right, I want this, I
want that, do that, do this!' Screamin', screamin'! I can't stop 'em,
I can't blot 'em, rub 'em out. But, thinks I, put me *among* 'em, *with*
'em, look, I'll only see a few, hear a few, believe me. Stands to
reason, father. Honest. Anchoresses hear the truth an' it's more'n
they can bear. You show me anyone who's born to carry *all* the
truth? So help me, father, please, or I'll go mad with the noise.
What good'll Christine be to God, then, poor little mad gal? Eh,
father? God don't want no poor little mad gals, do 'ee? So help me,
father, help deliver me from here. Please, father, help me, help me,
help me, help me . . .

106

Part 5

CHRISTINE in the corner of her cell.

CHRISTINE: I ent narthin', I hev narthin', I desire narthin' save the love of Jesus only. I ent narthin', I hev narthin', I desire narthin' save the love of Jesus only. I ent narthin', I hev narthin', I desire narthin' save the love of Jesus only. I ent narthin' . . .

Part 6

CHRISTINE *is lying flat on her back on her bed. After many, many seconds she sits bolt upright, swivels round, her face alight with a new thought.*

CHRISTINE: There ent one God, there's two! Why would one God make livin' difficult by putting good *and* evil in the world? There *must* be two! Both made the world! One shovelled earth from out a hole the other shovelled earth back again. One shovelled out, one shovelled in! One shovelled out, one shovelled in.

(*She's incredulous at the thought, then panics.*)

O Lord! O Lord! To which one do I pray? To which? To which one do I pray?

(*She moves to the crucifix, then away from it, then to it, then away, uncertain which end of the cell to go to. Finally she chooses the one she knows, and desperately kneels before crucifix.*)

Hail Mary, full of grace! The Lord is with thee, blessed art thou amongst women, an' blessed is the fruit of thy womb, Jesus. Hail Mary, full of grace! The Lord is with thee, blessed art thou amongst women, an' blessed is the fruit of thy womb, Jesus. Hail Mary, full of grace! The Lord is with thee, blessed art thou amongst women, an' blessed is the fruit of thy womb, Jesus. Hail Mary . . . (*Stops suddenly.*) Thaas a blasphemous thought, Christine Carpenter. Two Gods! Where'd a thought like that come from?

(*She returns to lying flat on her bed. Long silence. Then –*)

Two Gods, two Gods. One shovelled out, one shovelled in. Two Gods, two Gods. One shovelled out, one shovelled in . . .

Part 7

CHRISTINE *paces up and down her cell.* HENRY *and* MATHEW *are talking with her through the quatrefoil. They can't be seen by the audience.*

CHRISTINE: Two Gods, two Gods! One shovelled out, one shovelled in! Two Gods, two Gods! One shovelled out, one shovelled in.

HENRY: Be still, child. Sit. Take hold. You are a bride of Christ. Trust him. Now, are you sitting on your stool? The one your father made specially for you with his loving hands? You're loved, Christine. Loved and admired.

CHRISTINE: (*Sitting on the stool*) Not fit, not fit!

MATHEW: The villagers look up to you.

CHRISTINE: Not fit, not fit!

MATHEW: They're proud of you, their anchoress, their very own.

CHRISTINE: Not fit, not fit!

HENRY: Control yourself, be calm. I have some questions for you. Answer carefully. Have you told people of your vision?

CHRISTINE: Yes.

MATHEW: 'Yes, my lord.'

CHRISTINE: 'Yes, my lord.'

HENRY: And it's your own vision, no one put it to you?

CHRISTINE: No, my lord.

HENRY: Have you had fevers recently, sickness?

CHRISTINE: No, my lord.

HENRY: You don't have to *keep* saying 'my lord'. Only the first time.

CHRISTINE: The vision's mine! All burnin' bright and fresh and mine alone! *For* me! For the *world*! There be two Gods!

HENRY: That's heresy!

CHRISTINE: (*Hardly restraining her glee*) Not fit, not fit! Let Christine go, she is not fit!

HENRY: Do you still love Christ?

CHRISTINE: Yes! Yes!

HENRY: Still long for union with God?

CHRISTINE: Not fit, not fit!

HENRY: And it was not a temptation of the devil?

CHRISTINE: No, no! The Lord tell me. There's a God of love an' a God of hate. The good one shovelled out, he say, the evil shovelled in. I am the good God's son, he say, the evil God had Satan. All what you see an' all what's been, an' all that ever will be seen, the two on 'em created, look! An' thaas the truth, he say.

HENRY: That cannot be!

CHRISTINE: It is! It is! It is! It is!

MATHEW: Christine. Listen to me. It's Mathew talking to you. Calm yourself and listen. How can you be so certain it was Christ you saw?

CHRISTINE: Because, because, because –

MATHEW: Because?

CHRISTINE: (*Inspired*) Because beside him stood the other son.

MATHEW: The two together?

CHRISTINE: To prove, to prove, to prove.

MATHEW: Saying?

(*Long pause. She cannot answer.*)

HENRY: Convenience thoughts! She's seen two Gods? Possible, but conveniently for her, unprovable. It's as good a way of describing the workings of this damned life as any.

MATHEW: Just like the teaching of our Church?

HENRY: Except that it *is* our Church and the one in power with responsibility, and I want that Church obeyed, respected and strong. Order is order, duty is duty, a vow is a vow! And I think you'd do well to find another parish.

MATHEW: Or another Church!

(CHRISTINE *realizes her stratagem has failed. Desperation turns to fury. The doubter emerges at last.*)

CHRISTINE: (*Viciously*) There are no Gods, there are no sons. For, look you, would a God of *love* put *evil* in your heart, would he? Would he? Do you believe a God so careless? Answer me. A careless God?

You have hell anchored to your Church, father. Break down its walls, break them, break them, break them. In the name of God BREAK THEM DOWN!

Part 8

CHRISTINE *is by the window grille.*

CHRISTINE: Thaas no good comin' to me for advice, little gal. What advice can a miserable sinner like me give anybody? Go to the Bishop Henry, or the Rector, or my mother an' father. They'll give you good advice. (*Pause.*) Oh no, because I live here don't mean –

(*She thinks. Then changes her mind and decides to offer advice.*)

Hear me then. When you die your soul go to the terrors you've been afeared of all your life. You had no terrors then your soul's left in peace. You hev them – they go with you! So you live that you should have no terrors, little gal, you live like that, look.

(*Pause. The taunting voices of* CHILDREN *return. Their hands poking through the grille, close to her face. She stands, wild-eyed, listening to the words, transfixed by the waving hands, her teeth clenched tight.*)

CHILDREN'S VOICES: Christ–ine, Christ–ine, had a revelation yet? Had a vision, had a word, had a revelation yet? Christ–ine, Christ–ine, had a revelation yet, had a vision, had a word, had a revelation yet? Christ–ine, Christ–ine . . .

(*They give up. She relaxes a little. Struggles to collect herself.*)

CHRISTINE: Well, thaas an improvement. I give advice to somebody. Didn't know what I was talkin' about but I spoke, leastways. So there, now. (*Pause.*) So there, now. (*Pause. Looks left and right.*) So there, now.

(*She must establish a routine. She runs to kneel before the crucifix and begins fast praying.*)

Hail O cross, dedicated to the body of Christ, and adorned with his limbs as with pearls, save the sound an' heal the sick. (*Striking her breast hard*) Let what cannot be done by human power be done in thy name. (*Crossing herself each time*) We adore thee. We adore thee. We adore thee. (*With her thumb she makes the sign of the cross on the ground and kisses it.*) Hail Mary, full of grace! The Lord is with thee; blessed art thou amongst women, an' blessed is the fruit of thy womb, Jesus. Hail Mary, full of grace! The Lord is with thee; blessed art thou amongst women, an' blessed is the fruit of thy womb, Jesus. Hail Mary, full of grace! The Lord is with thee, blessed art thou amongst women, an' blessed is the fruit of thy womb, Jesus. Amen. (*Pause.*) What next?

(*She rises quickly and sits on her stool. Pause.*)

What next?

(*She rises. With the end of her dress she dusts the table, then the stool, then the bed, then the stool again. Pause.*)

What next?

(*She places the stool in a different position. Then another position. Then in another position. Pause.*)

What next?

(*There is a hairbrush in her cell, under her bed. She reaches for that and begins furiously to bring order to her unkempt hair.*)

It's because you don't look after yourself, gal. Thaas why they don't trust you. They look through them holes an' they see dirt an' filth an' there's smells an' goodness knows what, and they think they see a mad woman. So comb your hair and bring back the runnin' gal, the dancin' gal, the gal-at-the-fair gal what made the village proud. They didn't mind you then, your prayers for them an' preachin' them an' lockin'-yourself-up-to-suffer-for-them. So comb your hair and pull your old self together, there's folk at your window for words of advice. (*Moves to the window.*) Yes, little gal, I'll answer your questions. (*To herself*) You crossed your mouth? (*Crosses her mouth.*) Good! You crossed your eyes, your ears and your breasts? (*Crosses them.*) Good! (*To the window*) Now, ask away. (*Pauses. Listens. Laughs.*) Ha, ha! Ho, ho! 'The meanin' of life'? Thaas big! You're bold! (*Gaily*) There *ent* no meanin', little girl. None! But – ha, ha! There's purpose! To do good. In a word, a deed, a chair made, a tree planted, the poor fed, a wrong forgiven, in love . . . in love . . . in love . . . For, as 'tis written: 'An' God said, "Let there be light", an' there *was* light. An' God saw the light, that it was good . . . an' God saw everything that he made, an' behold, it was very good.' Love, little gal, the purpose is to love. Cos the Lord Jesus Christ loved you so much, look, that he suffer an' die for you. Love, little gal. There ent narthin' more powerful than that!

(*She is jubilant. Continues brushing her hair.*)

There! That weren't bad! I did well then. You did very well, Christine. Narthin' mad about that. She'll go away and tell people that the gal Christine Carpenter give her good words of advice, an' people'll start coming again, and the word'll spread, an' get to the Bishop's ears, an' he'll write to the Pope, an' you'll see, gal, you'll see, you'll see, you'll see, and then . . . you'll see . . .

What next?

(*Pause. She runs to kneel before the crucifix and recites three Aves.*)

Hail Mary, full of grace! The Lord is with thee. Blessed art thou amongst women, an' blessed is the fruit of thy womb, Jesus. Hail Mary, full of grace! The Lord is with thee. Blessed art thou amongst women, an' blessed is the fruit of thy womb, Jesus. Hail Mary, full of grace! The Lord is with thee. Blessed art thou amongst women, an' blessed is the fruit of thy womb, Jesus. Amen.

What next?

(*Pause. She rises. Sits on stool. Intones.*)

The remedy for pride is humility. The remedy for envy is love. The remedy for anger is patience. The remedy for sloth is work. The remedy for covetousness is contempt for earthly things. The remedy for avarice is a generous heart. The remedy for lust is mortification of the flesh. (*Beats her breast, hard.*) The remedy for lust is mortification of the flesh. The remedy for lust is mortification of the flesh. The remedy for lust is mortification of the flesh. The remedy for lust is mortification of the fle–e–e–e–esh!

(*She shrieks the last word. Rises, bangs her head against the stone wall, calling out at the same time.*)

Flesh flesh flesh flesh help help help help mercy mercy mercy mercy O Mother! Tell them, Mother, tell them tell them, Mother, Mother, I have no vocation I am not fit I am not fit I AM NOT FIT! (*Stops abruptly.*)

What next?

(*Pause. She sits on her stool. Defeated. Intones.*)

The remedy for pride is humility. The remedy for envy is love. The remedy for anger is patience. The remedy for sloth is work. The remedy for covetousness is contempt for earthly things. The remedy for avarice is a generous heart. The remedy for lust is mortification of the flesh. (*Beats her breast.*) The remedy for lust is mortification of the flesh. The remedy for lust is mortification of the flesh.

What next?

(*Pause. She rises, moves to a corner of the cell, hoists her dress, urinates, all hope draining from her.*)

112

Part 9

CHRISTINE *in the corner of her cell. She cradles the heavy crucifix in her arms. Laments and rocks backwards and forwards.*

CHRISTINE: The poor wail, the orphan sighs, the widow is desolate, the pilgrim needs water, there's danger for the voyager, hardship for the soldier, cares for the bishop. Come to me, come to me, come, come, come, come.

(*Pause.*)

I've loved him from cradle-time. No smile like my baby's. See, they humiliate him now. *I* can't comfort him, though. I've loved him from his first falls. No cry like my baby's. See, there are thorns on his head. *I* can't comfort him though. Was anything so tender? The smell of oil on his skin, the trust in his eyes as I wrapped him warm. See, they've given his poor body a cross to bear. Why don't *my* bones crack instead? I can't comfort him though. And that first word he spoke! Such cleverness. How swift he learnt. See, they nail him now. My lovely boy, my own, my flesh, my blood. An' did I feed an' watch you grow an' guard you 'gainst the plagues for this? An' did we look at blue skies, the matin' mare, the suckin' lamb, the settin' sun, an' watch the rivers runnin' – for this? (*Cries out.*) Put nails through me! Through my hands, my feet. Me! Me! Oh, the ache, the ache, the helpless ache. I can't bear it! Can't bear it! Cannot. Oh, oh . . .

(*Pause.*)

The poor wail, the orphan sighs, the widow is desolate, the pilgrim needs water, there's danger for the voyager, hardship for the soldier, cares for the bishop. Come to me, come to me, come, come, come, come, come . . .

Part 10

CHRISTINE *in the corner of her cell. She is squeezing one bare breast, part a caress, part a maternal longing, intoning.*

CHRISTINE: The poor wail, the orphan sighs, the widow is desolate, the pilgrim needs water, there's danger for the voyager, hardship for the soldier, cares for the bishop. Come to me, come to me, come, come, come, come, come, come, come, come, come . . .

Part 11

CHRISTINE, *by the quatrefoil, her back to the wall.*

CHRISTINE: It's my thoughts, father, I can't put my thoughts on *him*. I see him on the cross, I see that sweet face sufferin', I see that poor body hangin' limp on its nails, an' I feel the pain here an' here an' here an' here an' here, an' I stand with my back to the wall, my arms outstretched (*her movements follow her words*) my eyes closed, an' I cry out, 'Lord Jesus, sweet lord, I'm with you, here I stand, I feel the pain, I'm with you.' An' then, an' then – Oh forgive me, father, forgive me! – but as I stand, my arms outstretched, my eyes closed – I think new thoughts which I can't deny. (*Her legs move apart now.*) Cos, oh, they're sweet, so sweet. I'm naked. My body open to the sky, my skin in the grass, sun on my breasts. I feel cool winds bring me the smell of hawthorn and the wild mint. An' I see the birds sweep high an' singin'. An', oh, those clouds, those glorious, rollin' shapes, that sweet scent, that soft air – thaas not the devil's forms, I say. Forgive me, father, but I say thaas never the devil's forms. An' I'm torn between shame and delirium. The spring, father, the spring! I am crucified upon the spring!

(*The taunting chants of* CHILDREN *are heard. Their hands wave through the grille.*)

CHILDREN'S VOICES: Christ–ine, Christ–ine, had a revelation yet, had a vision, had a word, had a revelation yet? Christ–ine, Christ–ine, had a revelation yet, had a vision, had a word, had a revelation yet? Christ–ine, Christ–ine . . .

(*She stands with her back to the wall, arms outstretched, listening, watching the waving hands. Slowly she moves towards them. Watches. Then – she grabs one and plunges her teeth into it. There is a terrible scream. She releases the hand. The voices, screaming, move and die away.*)

What next?

(*Long pause. She looks around her cell. She turns to a wall, places her hand on it, mumbles to herself, turning her head slowly around the cell.*)

CHRISTINE: This is a wall, an' this is a wall, an' this is a wall, an' this is a wall, an' this is a wall, an' this is . . .

(*On which poor, mad, imprisoned figure the lights slowly fade till only a faint light comes through her grille. Then – darkness.*)

When God Wanted a Son

For Nuria Espert
dear friend, great actress,
rising *metteuse-en-scène du monde*,
in whose house by the sea
I finished this play

CHARACTERS

MARTHA   aged fifty-two

JOSHUA   aged fifty-five, her estranged husband

CONNIE   aged twenty-seven, their daughter

Time   the present

When God Wanted a Son, completed in October 1986, received its first airing as a reading to raise funds for the Jackson's Lane Community Theatre on 19 February 1989. The actors were

MARTHA	Elizabeth Spriggs
JOSHUA	John Savident
CONNIE	Nichola McAuliffe

It was narrated and directed by the author.

A production has been scheduled at the Young Vic for Spring 1990.

ACT ONE

Scene I

A rough cabaret club.

CONNIE, *'apprentice' comedienne, stands before her audience fearing the worst. Her material seems to amuse only her. Prominently hanging round her neck is a gold chain from which hangs a Star of David. Her 'audience' is not us but a gathering slightly offstage.*

CONNIE: Poland, 1875. Moshe Ben Levy. The richest Jew in his village. Comes the Cossack pogroms, Moshe's store – no chance. Burned to the ground. Stock looted, son murdered, daughter abducted, wife dead from a broken heart. Poor Moshe Ben Levy. Down to his last crust of bread, his last pat of butter, the last leaves of tea, the sugar gone. You couldn't get lower than Moshe was in that year of 1875, in the heart of Poland, the heart of winter, heart-broken and cold. Surely this was the end.

He places the last of his logs on the fire, fills the kettle for the last leaves of tea, toasts his last crust of bread, butters it with the last pat of butter – then, as though God hasn't punished him enough for sins he can't even remember committing – the last of his calamities.

The water boils. He reaches for the kettle. He's shivering from the cold. He's clumsy. Brushes against the last piece of toast buttered with the last pat of butter – plop! To the floor! The filthy floor!

Now, everyone knows that toast falls butter side down. Always. Without fail. But not this day. This day – a miracle! Moshe's toast, which should have fallen butter side down, falls butter side up! Is this an omen? A sign that his luck is about to change? He rushes off to the Rabbi.

'Rabbi, Rabbi. You know me, Moshe Ben Levy, once rich now poor, my son murdered, my daughter abducted, my wife dead from

123

a broken heart. But, Rabbi, this morning, this morning I knocked my toast to the floor and it fell butter side up! A miracle! Everyone knows that toast falls butter side down, always, without fail. Tell me, is it an omen? Is my luck about to change?'

The Rabbi thinks and thinks and says: 'I have not wisdom enough to interpret this sign alone. I must confer with the other Rabbis. Return tomorrow morning. You will have our answer.'

Moshe falls asleep only for one hour before the sun rises. All night his imagination is on fire with visions of a new life. Without washing or changing his shirt, pausing only to gabble his morning prayers, Moshe Ben Levy hurries to the Rabbi's house. The Rabbi emerges tired from a room full of tired Rabbis, grey and numb with the meaning of life.

'Rabbi, Rabbi,' cries the eager, demented Moshe. 'Tell me, the miracle, what does it mean? My toast that fell butter side up – is it an omen? Is my luck about to change?'

His language is Yiddish, of course.

The Rabbi replies. Also in Yiddish of course. 'We have stayed awake all night. Seven of us. The wisest in the district. We have prayed, we have argued, we have referred to the holy books. One of us even dipped into the Cabbala to search for the meaning of your toast which fell butter side up. And we have concluded – (*despair and sadness*) – you must have buttered your toast on the wrong side.'

(CONNIE *cups her mouth and yells as though she were one of the audience.*)

(*Yelling to right*) Gerroff! Women shouldn't tell jokes! You've *never* told a good joke and you never *will* tell a good joke! (*No longer audience*) Thank you, thank you. I thought you'd like that one.

(*She smiles ingratiatingly, a smile of gratitude which turns into contempt.*)

Scene II

The 'office' of Martha.

A room in her house. She speculates in stocks and shares. On the wall are three huge sheets. On each sheet is a graph. They are graphs of the daily movements in value of the stocks of three different public companies. They are named: CENTRAL CEMENT PLC, VIENNESE RESTAURANTS PLC, NATIONAL GARDENS PLC.

MARTHA *is scanning the pages of the* Financial Times. *Round her neck, very prominently, hangs a gold chain with a heavy cross.*

MARTHA: (*Reading*) 'Argyl Construction . . . Bounty and Buildings . . . B, B, C, Carlyle Construction . . . ah! Central Cement: 575 to 577, up two points.

(*She marks the graph up two points. Returns to the paper.*)
Now, catering . . . A . . . B . . . C . . . S . . . T . . . U . . . V . . . Vacations International, Various Holidays . . . Viennese Restaurants: 353 to 350. *Down* three? Mmm. Is it the coffee they're not drinking or the cakes they're not eating?

(*She marks the graph down three points. Returns to the paper.*)
Now . . . National Gardens . . . Leisure, leisure, leisure . . . Ah! leisure . . .

Scene III

Cabaret club.

CONNIE: All right! All right! So I'm not funny. I'm funny but not *very* funny. You don't like my jokes so let's play a game instead. Let's divide the world.

I believe the world's divided into those who are clever and die, and those who are stupid and do the massacring. (*Pause.*) Come on now, you tell me how *you* think the world is divided. (*Beat.*) I believe the world's divided into those who are clever and die, and those who are stupid and do the massacring. How do *you* think it's divided?

(*Silence.*)

You want another example? Right. Here's another example. I believe the world's divided into those who applaud achievement and those who begrudge it – pah pom!

(*Silence.*)

Thank you, thank you. I thought you'd like that one.

Scene IV

A young girl's room.

Unchanged. The signs of toddlerhood through to young womanhood are there. It's Connie's room.

MARTHA opens the door to let in her daughter. CONNIE regards her past.

MARTHA: I didn't want to change it, then I did, then I didn't, then I did . . . Finally, well, you can see. I didn't.

CONNIE: Except for my montage.

MARTHA: I tried, but you glued it. (*Beat.*) Didn't you *ever* think it would have to come down?

(*No response.*)

'His' room I dismantled. Call me if you want anything.

CONNIE: Thanks, Mum.

MARTHA: And don't start crying as soon as my back is turned.

(*She leaves. CONNIE moves around her old room picking up this and that. On the walls are pinned scraps of paper, some of which are written upon, some typed.*)

CONNIE: (*Reading*) 'Don't you think men overrate the necessity of humouring everybody's nonsense till they get despised by the very fools they humour?' George Eliot.

That was when Dad thought I was going to be an MP.

(*Reading*) 'A man may take to drink because he feels himself to be a failure, and then fail all the more completely because he drinks. It is rather the same thing that is happening to the English language. It becomes ugly and inaccurate because our thoughts are foolish, but the slovenliness of our language makes it easier for us to have foolish thoughts.' George Orwell.

That was when Dad thought I was going to become a philologist. (*Beat.*) Or a dipsomaniac!

(*Reading*) 'Are you saying what you mean? Is what you mean worth saying? Are you saying it with poetry, imagination and style?'

And that was when he thought I was going to be a writer.

(*She finds her old toy telephone. Should she? Hesitant, sheepish, she dials.*)

Hello? God? Is that you? Wasn't sure you'd still be there. It's Connie. Didn't recognize the voice?

(*She hops, arms akimbo in the one-liner joke routine.*)

Once a con always a Connie! Pah pom! No? Well, perhaps my voice *is* changed. Got a moment? To talk?

(*Long pause.*)

Tell me, why *wasn't* I any of those things?

(*She weeps.*)

Scene V

Martha's office.
  MARTHA *alone.*

MARTHA: All money is worth twice its value. (*Thinks about that.*) I
  know that means something. (*Beat.*) But what? I have a hundred
  pounds. I spend twenty. Not only do I no longer have a hundred
  pounds but in addition I'm left with only eighty pounds. (*Thinks
  about that.*) Stupid! That's merely describing the same state in a
  different way. (*Beat.*) *And* you now possess twenty pounds' worth of
  goods. (*Pause.*) And yet – all money *is* worth twice its value. I *feel*
  it. You have both got it and haven't *not* got it. To be aware of *that* is
  the secret of wealth. I'm convinced of it.

  (*She picks up the* Financial Times. *Scans it. It's another day.*)
  Central Cement: 577 to 578. Up one point. Interesting . . .

  (*She marks the graph up one point.*)
  Viennese Restaurants . . .

Scene VI

Connie's room.

MARTHA *enters with a tray on which are a pot of tea, a jug of milk, a sugar bowl, ornate silver tongs, a plate with two kinds of thinly sliced triple-decker sandwiches – the crusts cut away, sliced into triangles.*

MARTHA: I thought when you came through the door: this girl needs looking after but I'm not going to spoil her. And here I am –

CONNIE: – spoiling me.

MARTHA: You don't know what it's like when your children leave home.

CONNIE: I know what it's like for the child!

MARTHA: It's not simply the empty house, or that your usefulness is over. It's not that their company is missed – though God knows it *is* missed. It's imagining them lonely. I cried for days when you left.

CONNIE: So did I!

MARTHA: And felt helpless.

CONNIE: So did I!

MARTHA: That's a special pain – to feel helpless about your child.

CONNIE: Cried, couldn't sleep, heard every noise, feared every movement.

MARTHA: Children don't leave, parents are abandoned.

CONNIE: (*Reading a note on the wall*) 'It grows dark, boys, you may go.'

MARTHA: Who said that?

CONNIE: The last words of the Great Master of the High School of Edinburgh.

MARTHA: Not sure I always approved of your far – (*beat*) 'his' little notes to you.

CONNIE: Yes, you were sure. You *never* approved.

MARTHA: I suspect advice offered through other people's words. Especially if it's pinned on walls.

CONNIE: Oh, you're so English about things.

MARTHA: I don't know any other way to be about things. (*Changing the subject*) You going to guess the fillings?

CONNIE: How many kinds?

MARTHA: Two.

(CONNIE *picks one triangle. Eats. Considers.*)

130

CONNIE: Sardines, for sure.

MARTHA: No mistaking that.

CONNIE: Not Spanish onions. Spring onions.

MARTHA: Clever.

CONNIE: Do I detect garlic vinegar rather than malt?

MARTHA: You do.

CONNIE: No salt, I'm glad to say, there's enough in the brine – but – you've peppered it.

MARTHA: Yes.

CONNIE: And there's something else, something – unusual. It's, it's – must have another bite. (*Bites.*) It's – good God! It's alcoholic. Sherry! You've soaked your onions in dry sherry. That's crazy!

MARTHA: But is it tasty?

CONNIE: Well – it's – a surprise.

MARTHA: Which is what I always wanted to be, surprising.

CONNIE: I've learned a new game. 'Dividing the world.' Example. I believe the world is divided into those who surprise you and those who don't. Your turn.

MARTHA: I need another example.

CONNIE: You can be humorous about it, too. I believe the world is divided into those who squeeze their toothpaste from the bottom up, and those who squeeze their toothpaste from the middle.

MARTHA: I don't see the point of that.

CONNIE: The point is to make the most important perception ever about the human condition. There are *only* those who squeeze their toothpaste from the bottom up, and those who squeeze their toothpaste from the middle. All other divisions between people are trivial, irrelevant. (*Pause.*) You can be serious about it if you like: I believe the world is divided into those who are sick and those who are healthy.

MARTHA: You haven't guessed the other filling.

CONNIE: You *never* liked the games I brought home.

MARTHA: They were too clever by half.

CONNIE: Only the English use 'clever' as an insult.

MARTHA: (*Edgy*) Why do you keep talking about 'the English' as though you were something else?

CONNIE: (*Herself curious*) Not sure.

MARTHA: My family also go back centuries, you know.

CONNIE: It's just that –

MARTHA: 'His' is not the only ancient tribe.

CONNIE: I didn't mean . . .

MARTHA: Centuries! (*Beat.*) And half of you is me, remember.

CONNIE: (*To change the subject*) I believe the world is divided into those who are grateful the bottle's half full and those who complain the bottle's half empty.

MARTHA: Monopoly and Scrabble, those are my games.

CONNIE: That's because you know how to spell and you *love* money.

MARTHA: (*Too violently*) I hate money.

CONNIE: Ha!

MARTHA: I loathe any talk about money.

CONNIE: Ha!

MARTHA: Loathe it!

CONNIE: (*Diverting her*) I believe the world is divided into those who are fat and those who are thin.

MARTHA: (*As a way of taking control of herself*) I believe the world is divided into those who are tall and those who are short.

CONNIE: Good! I believe the world is divided into those who listen and those who talk.

MARTHA: You haven't guessed the other filling.

CONNIE: (*Biting into second pile of sandwiches*) Oh well, easy – very crispy bacon.

MARTHA: Obviously.

CONNIE: And obviously cabbage in mayonnaise.

MARTHA: But what kind of mayonnaise?

CONNIE: You mean it's not from a bottle?

(MARTHA *is disdainful. Preens herself.*)

Ah! You *made* it.

(MARTHA *nods. Happy.*)

With egg yolk and oil and – er – (*amazed*) lemon juice?

(*Happy* MARTHA *nods.*)

Without curdling it?

(*Beaming* MARTHA *nods.*)

Clever old you. (*Beat.*) Red peppers and – er – chicken!

MARTHA: (*Triumphant*) Wrong! Turkey!

CONNIE: Shit!

MARTHA: I believe the world is divided into those who curse life and those who caress it.

CONNIE: Very good. But is it true?

MARTHA: It also has to be true?

CONNIE: Mother! Did you notice how you sang that line? (*Imitates her going up on 'true'.*) 'It also has to be *true*?' Like Dad would have sung it.

MARTHA: Nonsense. How else can you 'sing' it?

CONNIE: 'Does it *have* to be true?' 'Has it *got* to be true, too?'

MARTHA: What's the difference?

CONNIE: Think about it.

MARTHA: You and him! You and him and your theories!

CONNIE: Very interesting theories they are, too.

MARTHA: (*Viciously mocking*) 'You don't really mean what you're saying', he'd tell people. 'The sound you're making doesn't match your words.' To their face! Insult them! Thought he knew what they didn't about themselves.

CONNIE: The best people are uncomfortable to have around.

MARTHA: You and him! Insufferable pair!

CONNIE: How do you think Dad divided the world?

MARTHA: I try not to think anything about your far – about 'him'.

CONNIE: Not succeeding, are you?

MARTHA: If you're going to talk about . . .

CONNIE: *I* think about him all the time.

(MARTHA *rises to go.*)

No, stay. Oh, Mother, why am I making such a mess of my life?

MARTHA: (*Contempt for her chosen vocation*) Comedienne!

CONNIE: I always made them laugh at school.

MARTHA: What makes children laugh embarrasses adults.

CONNIE: Where I tell jokes they're not adults.

MARTHA: But they think they are.

CONNIE: (*Yelling*) Gerrout! Gerrup! Gerroff! (*Beat.*) It's my father's humour, that's the problem.

MARTHA: His humour, his values, his arrogance were always the problems.

CONNIE: For God's sake, name him. Father. He's my father.

MARTHA: Analysing, probing, taking me apart. He was good at taking things apart, but could he put them together again?

CONNIE: Ah! You believe the world is divided into those who destroy and those who build.

MARTHA: And he never mixed with my family. Had no patience for them. Too dull for him.

CONNIE: I believe the world is divided into those who surrender and those who survive.

MARTHA: I believe the world is divided into those who are Jer – into those who are 'them' and those who are 'us'.

(*She abruptly gathers the tea things and storms off.* CONNIE *picks up the toy phone. Dials.*)

CONNIE: Hello, God? We have a problem.

Scene VII

Connie's room.

Through the darkness comes a man's voice on a tape recorder. Lights up to reveal CONNIE *listening to a tape of her father,* JOSHUA, *speaking.* CONNIE's *lips move to* JOSHUA's *voice. She pretends she's him giving a lecture. She has played the tape to herself many, many times.*

MARTHA *in the background in shadow.*

VOICE OF JOSHUA: It seems to me we reveal our true meaning through the musicality of what we say rather than through the words we use.

Each word is carried on a note. The words add up to meaning. The notes add up to meaning.

Sometimes the meaning of a word coincides with the meaning of a note. Sometimes they're different. Sometimes they're at variance with each other.

Example: Take a simple fact which one person wants to communicate to another: one and one is two.

If you say: 'One and one is two' you are doing more than communicating a mathematical verity. You are also saying, 'You were wrong before.'

Listen: 'One and one *is* two.' The music is the same as: 'You *were* wrong.' 'You were *not* right.' There is even an element of scolding in the music.

Or, again, it may be that we are sensitive, and other people's slow wit embarrasses us. And so we sing 'apology' into our voice.

Listen: 'One and one *is* too–oo.' Meaning, 'I feel terrible telling you this but – one and one *is* too–oo.' The 'two' is delivered in two syllables: 'too–oo' and the second syllable goes up. 'One and one *is* too–oo.' The music of apology.

Now, take the 'two' down and what do we have? 'One and one is *two*.' The music of impatience. 'One and one is *two*.'

Emphasize the word 'two' in yet another way and you can make the melody say, 'You're a fool as well.' Listen: 'One and one is *two*.' Meaning, 'Not three, you fool.'

You can even add a further layer on to those five words. You not only think the person is a fool, but you also show contempt. Listen:

'One and one is *two*.' Meaning, 'Will this stupid person never get it right? One and one is *two*.' Sigh! The music of contempt.

I will now rephrase my first sentence. It seems to me we reveal not simply our true meaning through the musicality of what we say rather than through the words we use but also our true personality.

(CONNIE *switches off the tape.*)

Scene VIII

Connie's room.

She plays with her old teddy bear. It sits in a chair facing her, a bib round its neck.

A plate of the sandwiches has been left behind. She sits waiting for it to eat.

And sits.

Picks up and offers a sandwich. No response. She feels his forehead. Is concerned. Takes his pulse. More concern. Finds doctor's outfit. Applies stethoscope. An ailing teddy. She sighs sadly at the pain of it all.

MARTHA *in shadow in the background.*

Scene IX

Martha's office.

MARTHA: All money is worth twice its value.
  (*Turns it over and over, willing it to make sense.*)
 All money is worth twice its value.
  (*She marks her charts from the* Financial Times.)
 All money is worth twice its value.
  All money is . . .

Scene X

Connie's room.

Through the darkness comes JOSHUA's *voice repeating the end of the recording. Lights up on* CONNIE *who has been listening to it again.*

MARTHA *in shadow in the background.*

VOICE OF JOSHUA: . . . I will rephrase my first sentence. It seems to me we reveal not simply our true meaning through the musicality of what we say rather than through the words we use but also our true personality.

(CONNIE *switches off the tape.*)

CONNIE: Dogs sniff one another out. Humans listen to each other's musicality. (*Thinks about it.*) But what about those of us who are tone-deaf, Dad? Will we always fuck up our relationships? (*Beat.*) Unless we can interpret eyes. (*Beat.*) Or facial muscles. (*Beat.*) Or body movements. (*Thinks about it.*) Pity those deaf *and* blind.

(*She repeats the mathematical fact again and again, imbuing it with: anger, incredulity, delighted discovery, sadness, defiance, simple fact.*)

One and one is *two*!

One and one *is* two?

(*And so on . . .*)

Scene XI

Martha's office.

MARTHA: What I have I am also not without.

I am twice blessed: for possessing and for not having been dispossessed.

Every state is two states. I *know* I'm right. It is important to understand: all money is worth twice its value.

All money is . . .

Scene XII

Connie's room.

    She stands with a packet of old cigarette cards in her hand. She is spinning them down in a game where one card must rain down and cover another. She is an expert.

    MARTHA *in shadow in the background.*

    Abruptly CONNIE *stops her play.*

CONNIE: Give up your toys, Connie. Give them up.

Scene XIII

Connie's room.
CONNIE *on the toy phone.* MARTHA *in shadow in the background.*

CONNIE: You should have trusted me, Billy Boy. There was evidence enough. I'd hit days of chaos, that's all. Couldn't you tell? Every gal hits her days of chaos. Most have it every three years. The menstrual cycle of despair.

Let me tell you about the ages of women. Age the first: little girl. Little girl in awe of loud-mouthed male intimidation. Sometimes little girl in competition with loud-mouthed male intimidation. Sometimes little girl turns intimidator and leads squad of mocking girls to diminish male pride.

Age the second: breasts! Little girl with big breasts. A new confidence or a new intimidation? Should she be afraid to be stared at or should she use them to command attention? I used them to command attention. Breasts turned me into woman. Nothing turned boy into man. I was ahead.

But not for long. Age the third: young woman! and – pah pom! Male expectations! Which were either crude or unfathomable. He groped you or demanded you appear in a certain way. From which followed – chaos. And so the menstrual cycle of despair began, Billy Boy. One day I was busy trying to be what I thought you wanted me to be. Next day I was as unfeminine as possible. If he wants me he'll have to take me for *who* I am not what I *look* like.

Stupid woman! I hadn't understood that what I look like reveals who I am. As everything does. The way I walk, talk, gesticulate, think about the world. Stupid woman! Stupid theories! I bristled with them. You must have felt you were making love to a porcupine, Billy Boy. Bit of a pain in the arse, was I?

Here, I have a Norfolk joke for you. An old, old widow called on her parson with a problem. 'Parson,' she say, 'Parson, I see my dead husband today, sitting in his ole chair next to the fire. What do it mean d'yer think?' 'Could mean many things,' say the Parson. 'What do *you* think it means?' 'Well,' say the ole dear, 'they do say it could mean rain.'

Oh, Billy Boy, you should've persevered. I'm not arrogant. It's just that half of me is my father's child.

(*She puts down the phone. Drifts to another note on the wall.*)

(*Reading*) 'If you think education is expensive you should try ignorance!'

Scene XIV

Connie's room.
    MARTHA *and* CONNIE. *Evening. Drinks.*

MARTHA: My favourite game is inventing haikus.
CONNIE: What's a haiku?
MARTHA: A Japanese three-lined poem in which the first and third
    lines have five syllables and the middle one has seven.
CONNIE: Example?
MARTHA: Well, (*coyly*) one of my best was:
    I buy you flowers
    Letters return on the scent
    Where will it all end?
    (*She repeats it tapping out the syllables with her finger.*)
    I buy you flowers. Five.
    Letters return on the scent. Seven.
    Where will it all end? Five.
    That last line. Gave me a shiver when I first wrote it. 'Where will it
    all end?' Very mysterious. Could mean great happiness or great
    sadness.
CONNIE: That's not a game it's an – art form!
MARTHA: It's a game if you play it with someone else and see whose
    comes out best.
CONNIE: Who's to judge?
MARTHA: Well, honest couples usually agree on what's self-evident.
CONNIE: And were you and Dad an honest couple?
MARTHA: Who said anything about playing with your far– with 'him'?
CONNIE: Oh, Mother! You didn't compose haikus with your local
    priest.
MARTHA: It might have been a lover.
CONNIE: Before or during?
MARTHA: Either.
CONNIE: Some women are temperamentally suited to adultery, for
    others it's as inconceivable as a flying hippopotamus.
MARTHA: And you're saying I'm a hippopotamus that can't fly?
CONNIE: Well, *you* confessed: 'I always *wanted* to be unpredictable,'
    you said. Meaning you never were.

MARTHA: (*Harshly*) I said 'surprising'. 'Surprising' I said, not 'un-predictable'. I said, 'I always wanted to be surprising.' (*Beat.*) And who says I never were? Was.

CONNIE: Soaking spring onions in dry sherry?

MARTHA: (*Caught*) I was frightened of where it would all end.

(CONNIE *doesn't want to press her point. Struggles with a haiku instead.*)

CONNIE: Drink wine with me discuss art.

MARTHA: More than five syllables there.

CONNIE: Drink wine discuss art.

MARTHA: Five. Good.

CONNIE: Drink wine discuss art
Illuminate life for me
Where will it all end?

MARTHA: Bit heavy.

CONNIE: Heavy?

MARTHA: Discussing art and illuminating life. Heavy. Try again.

CONNIE: (*Struggling*) Er – 'Wine loosens up my limbs.' No. Six there.
Wine loosens my limbs.
A button falls from off my blouse.
No. Eight there.
A button falls from my blouse.
Better.
Where will it all end?
There! Lighter for you?
Wine loosens my limbs
A button falls from my blouse
Where will it all end?

MARTHA: Sex, sex! That's all the young think about is sex!

CONNIE: Can't talk about art, can't talk about sex!

MARTHA: You think it's so smart being frank and open about everything.

CONNIE: (*Repartee. To annoy*) Two old men, two old men on a park bench. Says one to the other, 'What do you like best, sex or Christmas?' 'Christmas,' says the other old man. 'Happens more often!'

MARTHA: Can we agree not to talk about sex, please?

CONNIE: Two old men, two old men on a park bench. Before them runs a young man chasing a young woman. Says one to the other: 'Can you remember the days when we used to do that?' 'Very well,' says the other old man. 'Only I can't remember why.'

MARTHA: Please, please! I've asked you! If you want me to keep you company can we agree not to talk about sex?

CONNIE: (*Cod German, but not too heavy*) You vant about sex vee talk shouldn't. You vant about life and literature vee talk shouldn't. You vant about mine farter vee talk shouldn't. I sink vee somesing verrrrry significant here hef.

MARTHA: On second thoughts, 'Where will it all end?' is not a good last line. The last line of a haiku should be linked to the image created by the other two.

CONNIE: Example.

MARTHA: Oh, I don't know. I can't make them up that quickly.

CONNIE: I'll give you an image. The sea. Loneliness.

MARTHA: Ah. The sea, the sea! Er – swimming. The last swim. 'We took our last swim.'

CONNIE: (*Tapping and counting*) Five. Good.

MARTHA: Don't stand over me.

CONNIE: Come on! Don't stop to complain. You're inspired. 'We took our last swim.'

MARTHA: We took our last swim
    The sea was big enough –

CONNIE: Only six syllables in that middle line.

MARTHA: The ocean was big enough.

CONNIE: Better.

MARTHA: We took our last swim
    The ocean was big enough . . .
    The ocean was big enough . . .
  Er . . .
    We took our last swim
    The ocean was big enough –
    (*Long pause.*)
    But salt tastes linger.

CONNIE: (*That was sad.*) Oh, Mother.

MARTHA: Well they do, they do. (*Beat.*) Remember, half of you is me.

146

Scene XV

Connie's room.
Although in Connie's room, it is MARTHA's *scene. She's in light.*
CONNIE *in shadow. A listening figure.*

MARTHA: (*Talking over her shoulder*) Most women are married to men
who bore them. Have you noticed that? They sit around in pubs,
restaurants, social gatherings, with faces announcing to the world
that they deserve more from life.

Men confuse that bored look with female mystery. It challenges
them. Up they trot. 'I understand,' they say. But they don't.
Within five minutes of their conversation it's painfully obvious
they don't. They bore.

But 'he' understood. 'Women have the power to give or deny
happiness,' he once said, 'and through that power we are manipu-
lated.' He hated being at anybody's mercy.

I couldn't bear him.

And he was full of opinions. He *knew* who was a great writer, a
great painter, a great composer. He could actually say Bach was
boring. Passionately say it. It mattered to him. Me – I was
exhilarated by them all, Bach, Mozart, Mahler. Well, perhaps
not Mahler so much. Too solemn. Still, that's just *my* taste.
When you're *that* great, dismissive opinion seems irrelevant. Pre-
sumptious! Absurd! But he insisted: opinions made you a person.
'It's a guarantee of your freedom,' he'd yell at me. Always impatient. Him and his circle.

Frightening lot they were. Non-stop talkers. Opinions on this,
opinions on that. How can people have so many opinions about the
world? You'd think it was such a vast and complex place they'd be
confused most of the time. Not that lot. Solutions for and opinions
about everything and anything.

Not me. Nothing much changes about human beings I always
think. And the world we live in seems to be shaped by scientists and
inventors not by people with opinions. You take the opinion that
everyone should work. Work dignifies people! The work ethic!
Along comes the silicon chip and suddenly we have – the leisure

147

ethic! The opinion changes! Everyone's demanding more leisure for all.

What *was* it about him that I hated? What really was it? Even now as I think about him my teeth clench. He had an air. He had – an air.

Scene XVI

Cabaret club.
CONNIE *performing.* MARTHA *in shadows in the background.*

CONNIE: Two old men, two old men on a park bench. Says one old man to the other: 'A woman without a man is like a fish without a bicycle.'

(*Yelling back as though one of the audience*) 'Yeah! But who needs a stationary haddock?'

Or was it two old women talking about a man without a woman? Depends who's telling the joke, dinnit? (*Curious about the word*) 'Dinnit'?

Dinnit! Dunnit! Innit! Gissit! Wannit! Gotcha! Gerroff!

(*Yelling as though one of the audience*) Gerroff the stage, yer stupid wench. We're 'ere to be amused not edumicated.

Beautiful to be alive is it not?

Don't go away, ladies and gentlemen. Stay with it. Hang on to your pints because this evening is an evening packed and planned, picked and plotted, designed and divined especially for you with *the* most brilliant joke-churners, story-mourners and warning-brakers ever to weather this bar-pub's weather-beaten boards where they will suckle fools and chronicle small beer as Iago said. You all know who Iago was, don't you? He was de one who made a fool of de black man.

No, seriously, folks, let's not be intellectual about humour. Let's not be intellectual about anything if it comes to that. As the man says – we're here to be amused not edumicated.

I believe the world's divided into those who know and those who don't know, with those who *think* they know coming a close second and really fucking things up. So drink deep and pass out because here to open our show is –

Scene XVII

Connie's room.
  CONNIE *and* MARTHA.

MARTHA: If I said to you, 'All money is worth twice its value', what would you think I meant?

CONNIE: I thought you loathed talk of money.

MARTHA: Not as much as I loathe poverty.

CONNIE: You're not poor. All those stocks and shares.

MARTHA: What 'all those'? I wish they *were* 'all those'. I'm trying to *make* them 'all those'.

CONNIE: (*Turning it over*) 'All money is worth twice its value.'

MARTHA: Poverty says: FAILED!

CONNIE: (*Still turning it over*) 'All money is worth twice its value.'

MARTHA: A *constant* reminder. Poverty – failure.

CONNIE: It's meaningless.

MARTHA: It's meaningless because you don't understand its meaning.

CONNIE: Help me understand.

MARTHA: The condition of poverty is also the condition of not being rich. You're not only a failure, you're also *not* a success. Unhappiness is more than unhappiness, it's also not being happy. Each state is two states. Thus – the state of affairs in which you only have £10,000 in the bank earning you £1000 a year interest is *at the same time* the state of affairs in which you *don't* have £100,000 in the bank earning you £10,000 a year interest.

CONNIE: She has gone mad. Mother has gone mad. It is sad about Mother, she was once happy, she was once content, she –

MARTHA: The Big Bang has exploded. The system for dealing in stocks, shares and currencies has changed.

CONNIE: She does not even make sense any longer.

MARTHA: I mean to survive.

CONNIE: I am worried about her.

MARTHA: You don't want a lecture, do you?

CONNIE: Yes. Lecture me. I love lectures.

MARTHA: Lectures are oppressive.

CONNIE: The only lecture that's oppressive is an oppressive lecture.

When it's not oppressive it's informative, stimulating and full of other people's enthusiasms. I love other people's enthusiasms.

MARTHA: Oh, you're so confident. Nothing threatens you.

CONNIE: Everything threatens. I just try not to let it overwhelm. Lecture me.

MARTHA: The Big Bang – a mini-lecture by Martha Mankowitz.

CONNIE: Did you marry him because you thought Mankowitz sat prettily with Martha?

MARTHA: Are you serious or not?

CONNIE: The Big Bang – a mini-lecture by Martha Mankowitz.

(*But* MARTHA *is now hesitant. In the silence a thought occurs to* CONNIE. *She giggles. Tries to suppress the giggle. Silence.*)

MARTHA: Well?

CONNIE: To have a name like Mankowitz when you hate Jer–

MARTHA: (*Determinedly interrupting*) The Big Bang – a mini-lecture. In the money streets of London known as the City, the mode of buying and selling shares used to be as follows: there was a purchaser, a stockbroker, and a jobber. I asked my stockbroker to purchase shares for me. He sent his dealers running among the jobbers in the Stock Exchange looking for the cheapest price. The jobber quoted to the dealer, the dealer phoned the broker, the broker advised me. When the Big Bang came the stockbroker became the jobber as well, and carried his own selection of shares.

CONNIE: Bang!

MARTHA: Problem: whereas before my stockbroker could shop around for me he now becomes the shop. I have to buy the shares he's already bought at the price which will give him profit. If I want choice then *I* will have to do the shopping around. How will I judge?

(*Pause.* MARTHA *is obviously waiting for something.*)

CONNIE: (*Understanding*) How *will* you judge?

MARTHA: I'm training myself to be a Chartist.

(*Pause.* MARTHA *again waits.*)

CONNIE: (*Obliging*) What is a Chartist?

MARTHA: I'm glad you asked. Come with me.

(*They move to Martha's office and the charts.*)

To buy shares which will go up in value and provide me with a profit I have to be able to interpret a company's performance. There are –

roughly speaking, you understand – two ways to do this. I can study company reports, accounts and balance sheets, and try to know the personalities involved. That's the conventional approach and those who pursue it are called Fundamentalists.

CONNIE: Now Fundamentalists threaten me.

MARTHA: Or I can read charts – the graphs of the price movements of shares. The readers of charts are called Chartists.

CONNIE: Not too happy with people who make charts either.

MARTHA: See here? The charts of three new companies in which I'm interested: Central Cement, Viennese Restaurants, and National Gardens. The world is building and entering a period of increased leisure. Cement, food, gardens.

CONNIE: Shouldn't they be called 'opportunists'?

MARTHA: To read a chart you must understand four main rules – about patterns, trends, resistance and support levels. Is the trend up, down or sideways? Cement is generally up. Food and gardens are stable. They have support levels. That is to say their low points, bottom peaks, haven't broken down below a certain level. Someone has confidence enough to keep buying them to prevent them dropping too low. When they drop below a consistent level, you sell. Conversely, if a row of peaks at the same level is penetrated on the upside it means there are more buyers than sellers, the buyers have taken over and then you buy.

CONNIE: And did you?

MARTHA: I've watched these charts for a year and made imaginary purchases and sales. If they hadn't been imaginary I could have made . . . who knows what I could have made! But even to have read them right has been thrilling.

CONNIE: You amaze me.

MARTHA: (Intoxicated) The City is in upheaval. Mergers! Head-hunting! The poaching of expertise! Giants merging to become monoliths. Middle-sized firms merging to become giants. Small ones shiver and cross their fingers, hoping that somehow the world won't change –

CONNIE: – not too much anyhow.

MARTHA: But it will! The finger-crossers will go to the wall. Nothing will be the same again.

CONNIE: You astound me.

MARTHA: I can't wait.

CONNIE: You astonish me.

MARTHA: I mean to survive.

CONNIE: I am thunder-clapped.

MARTHA: And the key to survival is understanding the nature of money.

CONNIE: Which is worth twice its value.

MARTHA: Just so.

CONNIE: It is sad about mother, she was once happy, she was once content, a simple soul –

MARTHA: That's it! Simple! You both thought me simple. You and him. Well, let me remind you, Jesus Christ was a simple soul.

CONNIE: (*Incredulous*) But Jesus Christ wanted us to give our money away, not bank it at 10 per cent.

MARTHA: You will never, never, never understand!

Scene XVIII

Connie's room.
   CONNIE *facing her toys.*

CONNIE: She's right. I *will* never understand.
   No. Not true. I understand. I just – don't know what to do.
   Give up your toys, Connie, give them up.

Scene XIX

Connie's room.
    CONNIE *and* MARTHA *shelling peas.*

CONNIE: What would you do if he walked in here right now?

MARTHA: He couldn't. I made him give up the key.

CONNIE: If he knocked, rang the bell?

MARTHA: I wouldn't hear it.

CONNIE: If he banged, thumped, begged?

MARTHA: He wouldn't come near me.

CONNIE: Suppose.

MARTHA: Why should he? He despised me. What would he expect?

CONNIE: Never mind him. You. What would *you* do, feel, say?

MARTHA: I'd say nothing, feel nothing, do nothing.

CONNIE: That's not true.

MARTHA: Why ask if you're not going to believe me?

CONNIE: It can't be true. You may say or do nothing but you'd *feel* something.
    (*Pause.*)

MARTHA: Rage. I'd feel rage.
    (*Pause.*)

CONNIE: (*About to ask for something*) Mother?

MARTHA: Worried about the tone of that.

CONNIE: I need to borrow some money.

MARTHA: See! Money! I heard money in that tone of voice.

CONNIE: Perceptive.

MARTHA: 'He' never thought so.

CONNIE: (*Returning to original request*) About a hundred and fifty pounds.

MARTHA: Don't be absurd. You know perfectly well I don't have that kind of money. I can manage twenty-five.

CONNIE: I always pay you back.

MARTHA: I wish you wouldn't ask.

CONNIE: Make it a hundred and twenty-five then.

MARTHA: You know how I hate discussion about money.

CONNIE: You could have fooled me.

MARTHA: I can go up to fifty.

CONNIE: I've got two important dates coming up.

MARTHA: I know your dates.

CONNIE: A hundred?

MARTHA: Cancelled at the last minute on a whim. Sixty is all I can manage.

CONNIE: These are dead certs. What about eighty-five?

MARTHA: Dead certs! Ha! (*Beat.*) Seventy!

CONNIE: Eighty?

MARTHA: Seventy-five and that's my final.

CONNIE: You're my saviour.

MARTHA: Where will you find the other seventy-five?

CONNIE: (*All innocence*) What other seventy-five?

MARTHA: (*Slowly understands.*) You're a real scheming little Jer–
    (*She holds back in time.*)

CONNIE: Little what?

MARTHA: You're like your far– like 'him'.

CONNIE: Like my father was what?

MARTHA: He would never come out with what he wanted.

CONNIE: Was *he* a real scheming little Jer–?

MARTHA: Never direct. Always circuitous.

CONNIE: (*Feeding her*) Devious?

MARTHA: Devious!

CONNIE: Dissembling?

MARTHA: Dissembling!

CONNIE: Sly, treacherous, blood-sucking?

MARTHA: Nothing threatened *him* either. He had an air –

CONNIE: Ridiculous, depraved, greedy?

MARTHA: – an air. He had – an air . . .

CONNIE: Presumptuous, audacious, arrogant?

MARTHA: Yes! Yes yes yes! Arrogant! Audacious! Presumptuous! All that! And more . . . an air, an air . . .
    (*She can't define it.*)

CONNIE: I believe the world is divided into those who think and those who hate thinkers.

MARTHA: The world is divided into them and us and that's the *only* division that counts. The only damn and bloodying division that counts.
    (*Long pause.*)

CONNIE: Mother, talk to me about when I was a little girl.

(*Pause.* MARTHA *doesn't want to talk about anything.* CONNIE *feels contrite about goading her mother. Wants to make her feel more comfortable with her thoughts.*)

Artists are a bit like Jews. They not only *behave* as though they're in possession of the truth. they actually feel the need to impart it. (*Beat.*) And nobody much likes *them* either.

MARTHA: It's 'him' I hate, not the Jer—

CONNIE: (*Gently*) Say it. Say the word. You'll feel better.

(MARTHA *makes a huge effort to collect herself.*)

MARTHA: You were spoilt. You were adorable and he spoilt you. As soon as you were born you couldn't take your eyes off one another. No matter what you were doing – eating, crying, waking from sleep, as soon as you saw him you stopped, stared and smiled. It was uncanny. And he talked to you non-stop. *I* fed you, changed you, made sure you had pretty clothes but *he* talked to you like an adult. No baby noises or words for *his* daughter. Real words and long sentences. And stories you couldn't possibly have understood. He wouldn't ever allow you to be a little girl. He made you stand before your time and walk before you could crawl. You could say 'claustrophobic' before you could say 'sweetie'. 'Sceptical' before 'Mummy'. It was all wrong. We have our stages. Growing up must go through stages. 'Allow her to be childish,' I warned him. 'Let her play with dolls.' He wouldn't. No fantasy. He deprived you of fantasy and fear.

CONNIE: That's not true. I developed a strong sense of fantasy . . .

Scene XX

Connie's room.
     CONNIE *in light.* MARTHA *in the background, a shadow.*

CONNIE: . . . and *all* I have is fear.

Fear of time passing, of loss, of you dying, 'him' dying without me ever seeing him again. Of growing old, ending alone. I fear that no one will laugh, that no one *ever* laughed, that there's nothing to laugh at.

Do I have to start again, Mother? Could I? Look at my face. The skin is hardening. I see lines. I feel lumps. I see blotches. I feel terror. Oooo . . .

. . . hold me, comfort me. It goes. I feel it going. No anchor, me. No anchor. Anchor me, Mother.

I promised talent, once. Once I was a force. Anchor me. It goes. O God, who art in heaven and promised meaning, don't let me go. Don't let me splinter and shatter. Hold me. Comfort me. Anchor me anchor me oh how it goes.

(*Pause.*)

There were these two women on a beach listening to a concert on their transistor radio. One grey, the other greyer. Early morning. Hardly crowded. Quite hot. The sea dotted with sailing boats. Said the grey to the greyer: 'Yes, I think it's very much one of those modern concertos. Strindberg or someone.'

(*Pause.*)

Definition of Jewish genius: a boy with average intelligence and two parents.

(*Pause.*)

Georg Lichtenborg said: 'It's impossible to carry the torch of truth through a crowd without singeing someone's beard.'

(*Pause.*)

Who *was* Georg Lichtenborg?

Scene XXI

Connie's room.
  CONNIE *and* MARTHA. *Sounds off.*

CONNIE: What's that?

MARTHA: What's what?

CONNIE: Sounded like a key in the front door.

MARTHA: No one has a key to the front door.

CONNIE: Daddy?

MARTHA: I made him give it back to me.

CONNIE: That was distinctly a key in the front door.
  (*Knock on the door. The women are terrified.*)
  Who is it?
  (*The door is flung open.* JOSHUA *stands before them, a man of enormous spirit, intelligence, gaiety.*)

JOSHUA: The prodigal son returns! The war is over! Let us turn our swords into ploughshares. For remember: when God wanted a son he crawled up the skirts of a Jewish girl!
  (MARTHA *enters a hysterical outburst which begins, continues and ends at the same high, intense level as though she has become possessed.* JOSHUA *is incredulous.* CONNIE *is distressed. But it's an outpouring that cannot be stemmed and must run its course.*)

MARTHA: (*Screaming*) Ahhh! No! Tell him to go! Do you hear how he comes with offence? Look at him. He walks into everyone's room that way, as though he were born there, as though he can say anything anywhere anytime. We agreed. You promised. My home, my decisions, my privacy. Not everybody wants you around. Not everybody thinks God chose you to be their neighbour. Tell him to go. Tell him I can't bear anything about him – his arrogance, his opinions, his irreverence. No reverence for anything, only what *he* thinks, what *he* wants, what *he* believes. Him! Him! Him! Don't laugh at me. Do you hear his laughter? Do you hear his superior laughter? So superior, so confident, so happy, so eager, so interested, so talkative, so fucking full of his own fucking self. Listen to me. He makes me curse. He's made me decadent. He's never respected me. Destroyer of innocence, lecher, devil! Tell him to go. Tell him the world wasn't made for him. Tell him people want to be left alone. He disturbs everyone. Everyone feels unsafe, threatened. Look at him looking at me. His eyes mocking me. He always mocked me. Some of us have our own beliefs, some of us don't care what *you* believe. We care about our *own* little thoughts. Yes! Little to you, precious to us. Look at him! Full of contempt and derision. One day someone will gouge his cockiness from his eyes. Tell him that. Tell him to go. Before it's too late. Tell him he's an old man who's been in the world too long. Tell him he doesn't belong in this house. Tell him I can't breathe when he's in the room. I never know what I feel when he's in the room. I don't know what to do with my hands, where to look, what to say. Listen to me, my words are all jumbled. I'm screaming. He makes me scream. As soon as I see him I go into shock, I become unnatural, I hate myself. Tell him to go. Tell him to go. Tell him to go go go. I can't stop screaming. Tell him to go.

(*Blackout.*)

ACT TWO

Scene I

Connie's room.
   CONNIE *and* JOSHUA. MARTHA *in her office.*

CONNIE: She says she's not coming out till you leave.

JOSHUA: I'll cook her a meal.

CONNIE: 'And tell him I don't want one of his smelly-tasting meals,' she said.

JOSHUA: I bought her favourite wine.

CONNIE: 'And if he's bought my favourite wine tell him to drown in it,' she said.

JOSHUA: Irrational as always.

CONNIE: 'And tell him I'm not being irrational.'

JOSHUA: She'll come.

CONNIE: Irresistible, are you?

JOSHUA: She's a woman of second thoughts. Third, fourth and fifth thoughts to be precise, if one can be precise about your mother.

CONNIE: There was nothing imprecise about that outburst.

JOSHUA: Distressed you?

CONNIE: I've never heard her like that before.

JOSHUA: I've had it since the day we married.

CONNIE: Why did you stay?

JOSHUA: I have 'an air' about me, 'an air . . . an air . . .'

CONNIE: Which she can't name.

JOSHUA: Why do *you* keep coming back?

CONNIE: 'One half of you is me,' she keeps saying. 'Remember! One half of you is me.'
    (*Pause.*)

JOSHUA: My grandmother was the largest lady in her Polish village.

CONNIE: (*Music-hall*) The largest lady in her Polish village?

JOSHUA: The Jewish community had never produced such a large lady. She could lift a man in each hand by the scruff of the neck.

161

CONNIE: And frequently did.

JOSHUA: They say, the story came down to me, that she insisted upon two husbands.

CONNIE: And got them?

JOSHUA: And got them! And when the pogroms came every village in the district suffered except hers.

CONNIE: The Cossacks were terrified of being raped!

(*They are convulsed by laughter.*)

MARTHA: (*From her room*) Judas!

(*The laughter dies down.*)

JOSHUA: 'The first truth', says Buddha, 'is that all life is suffering.'

MARTHA: (*From her room*) Judas!

(*Pause.*)

CONNIE: I believe the world is divided into those who were born when God was around and the rest of us who were born when he was on holiday.

JOSHUA: I believe the world is divided into those who manage to get discounts on everything and the rest of us who have to pay the full price.

CONNIE: Dad, can you lend me a hundred and fifty pounds?

(*Special burst of laughter from* JOSHUA.)

A hundred then?

(*They both laugh.*)

Tell you what, I'll go easy on you. Make it seventy-five.

(JOSHUA *takes out his wallet and carefully lays out seven five-pound notes, two one-pound notes, some loose change.*)

JOSHUA: Thirty-seven pounds fifty-three pence. All the money I have in the world.

CONNIE: Ah!

JOSHUA: (*Trying to suppress laughter*) Sad, isn't it?

CONNIE: (*Trying to suppress laughter*) Yes.

JOSHUA: But it's even worse than that.

CONNIE: Worse?

JOSHUA: I've been forced to resign my post.

CONNIE: Forced to? I thought that couldn't happen unless you seduced a student.

JOSHUA: I did.

CONNIE: It's not true.

JOSHUA: She was brilliant. You know how I find brilliance irresistible. Nineteen years old. She knew everything. I had nothing to
teach her. Except one thing.

CONNIE: Dad, is this true?

JOSHUA: No. She seduced me.

(*They continue laughing.*)

CONNIE: Dad. We do not make jokes about seducing nineteen-year-
old girls when we're fifty-six.

JOSHUA: Fifty-five.

CONNIE: (*Warning*) Dad!

JOSHUA: Nothing happened. I couldn't make it. She tried everything. She sang to it, tickled it, honeyed it, oiled it, got down on
her knees and prayed to it. Nothing.

She played music to it, stripped, danced to it, whistled, even told
hair-raising stories. Nothing!

She whacked it, she shook it, she cursed it, she blew it, she
threatened, chanted mantras, salt-and-peppered it – wept.
Nothing!

(CONNIE *is convulsed.*)

Imagine! We were caught not doing it! In my rooms at college.
Among all that medieval oak panelling. The most uncomfortable
rooms in Cambridge.

(*Through his laughter*) Ah well, as the philosophers have
observed: we're all dying one way or another.

CONNIE: That's life, innit? (*Beat.*) Innit? Dinnit? Dunnit? Wannit!
Gissit! Gotcha! Gerroff!

(MARTHA *enters.*)

MARTHA: (*To* CONNIE) Judas! (*Referring to* JOSHUA) And him!
Why is he here?

CONNIE: Oh, Mother, stop this.

MARTHA: You don't know what it's costing to be in the same room
with him. Ask him. Why is he here?

CONNIE: Why are you here?

JOSHUA: (*To* MARTHA) I want you to invest in my project.

CONNIE: (*To* MARTHA) He wants you to invest in his project.

(MARTHA *can't believe such audacity.*)

MARTHA: He must be mad.

CONNIE: You must be mad.

Scene II

Martha's office.
  MARTHA *and* JOSHUA. CONNIE *in her room.*

MARTHA: He must be mad.
JOSHUA: Not mad, romantic.
MARTHA: He doesn't respect me, why is he asking me for help?
JOSHUA: We need each other.
MARTHA: Why should I need someone who doesn't respect me?
JOSHUA: Come, sit with me, be friends.
MARTHA: He's *pretended* to respect me. Only ever pretended.
  (JOSHUA *makes the effort he has always had to make to control his exasperation with her.*)
JOSHUA: What are these charts?
  (MARTHA, *despite herself, is pleased he's asked.*)
MARTHA: I'm studying the market.
JOSHUA: With charts?
MARTHA: Doesn't he know about them? Isn't he supposed to know everything?
JOSHUA: I thought one studied the stock market by looking at personalities and balance sheets.
MARTHA: There are other ways, you study the performance of the shares themselves.
JOSHUA: And then make predictions?
MARTHA: And then make predictions. What am I talking to him for?
JOSHUA: And you drew out all this?
  (*She nods.*)
  And you make a mark every day?
MARTHA: From the *Financial Times.*
JOSHUA: Have you done today's?
  (*She reaches for the pink sheets. Scans. Marks. Stops halfway.*)
MARTHA: It's me who's mad, talking to him again.
JOSHUA: Martha! I'm not a 'him'.
MARTHA: Showing him, explaining –
JOSHUA: I'm in the same room.
MARTHA: – tolerating his presence, his existence –
JOSHUA: Aren't you at least interested to know what my project is?

MARTHA: I don't care about his projects.

JOSHUA: We could make a fortune.

MARTHA: He's always had hare-brained projects for making a fortune.

JOSHUA: Martha, you *have* to acknowledge me.

MARTHA: I just want him to go. Please, God, make him go away.

(CONNIE *enters.*)

CONNIE: Two Jews, two Jews. About to be executed. The Nazi captain, a civilized man, sensitive, a lover of Wagner virtue heroes children dogs and the Alps, not being without pity, and mindful of tradition, asked the Jews if they had a last request before being shot. The first Jew asked for a cigarette and was given one. The second Jew thought a second and then – spat in the captain's face. At which the first Jew spluttered, choked on his cigarette, went pale and whispered, 'Hymie, Hymie, do me a favour, don't make trouble!'

JOSHUA: In my version the second Jew asked if he could learn to play the violin.

MARTHA: Jews! Jews! Always jokes about Jews.

CONNIE: (*In an Irish dialect*) Two Irishmen, two Irishmen. About to be executed. The British captain, a civilized gent, sensitive, a lover of brass bands horses Darjeeling tea Sunday mornings and his mother, not being without pity, and a stickler for tradition, asked the Irishmen if they had a last request before being shot. The first Irishman asked for a pint of Guinness. The second Irishman thought a moment and then – spat in the captain's face. At which the first Irishman coughed, spluttered, choked on his Guinness and went red in the face crying out, 'Jasus! Seamus! Do me a favour, don't make trouble!'

(*Pause. Silence. Nothing.*)

'Jasus! Seamus! Isn't it trouble enough we have?'

(*Still nothing.*)

'Jasus! Seamus! Haven't yers got me into enough trouble?'

(*Pause.*)

Not the same, is it?

MARTHA: And why is it, I wonder, that when a Jew tells a Jewish joke it's called Jewish humour but when anyone else tells it it's anti-Semitic?

JOSHUA: Because when a Jew tells a Jewish joke it's Jewish humour but when anyone else tells it it's anti-Semitic.

MARTHA: There! He looks for trouble.

JOSHUA: (*Ironically*) Can't get enough of it!

MARTHA: And because he looks for it he attracts it.

JOSHUA: That's really what you wanted, that I shouldn't ever make trouble.

MARTHA: I wanted respect.

JOSHUA: That I should be invisible.

MARTHA: His air, his air . . . he has an air . . .

JOSHUA: An air of what? What air? What, what, what, you foolish woman, what?

MARTHA: Fear! He has no fear!

JOSHUA: (*Incredulous*) Fear? Why should I have fear?

MARTHA: People without fear have no respect.

JOSHUA: Interesting.

MARTHA: He's mocking me again.

JOSHUA: People without fear have no respect. It's interesting.

MARTHA: He mocks me, and my thoughts jumble.

CONNIE: (*Warning*) Dad!

MARTHA: He always mocked me.

JOSHUA: *You* speak to your mother.

MARTHA: He was contemptuous –

JOSHUA: *I* don't understand the woman.

MARTHA: His voice was loud –

JOSHUA: And I *have* tried.

MARTHA: – he spent money before he earned it –

JOSHUA: How have I *not* tried!

MARTHA: He quarrelled with friends, wrote letters to the press, the Prime Minister –

JOSHUA: I called the fraudulent frauds, the faint-hearted cowards, the lickers of arses arse-lickers –

MARTHA: – and to the Pope.

CONNIE: The Pope?

MARTHA: Yes! The Pope, the Pope! He wrote to the Pope!

CONNIE: You actually wrote to the Pope?

MARTHA: At last Rome held an ecumenical council agreeing to forgive the Jews for the Crucifixion, and your father, your wise,

166

witty father wrote announcing the creation of a Jewish ecumenical council to decide whether to forgive the Christians.

JOSHUA: It's called irony.

MARTHA: It's called irreverence.

JOSHUA: I screamed at the pompous, the complacent, the tyrannical, the opportunistic – I screamed and I stirred and I made trouble because sometimes trouble had to be made.

MARTHA: Like seducing the innocent?

JOSHUA: I have my weaknesses.

MARTHA: Is it any wonder he's thrown out of everywhere?

JOSHUA: I think it's time to tell a funny story.

MARTHA: *I* have a background. *I* have a heritage. It must be respected. Tell him it must be respected.

JOSHUA: There were these thick Irishmen . . .

CONNIE: . . . Jonathan Swift . . .

JOSHUA: . . . Oliver Goldsmith . . .

CONNIE: . . . Oscar Wilde . . .

JOSHUA: . . . Yeats, Synge . . .

CONNIE: . . . Bernard Shaw, Sean O'Casey, Brendan Behan . . .
    (*Beat.*)

JOSHUA: Did anyone *ever* laugh at that joke?

CONNIE: Not in the clubs where I played, they didn't.

MARTHA: Neither of you. No respect. None at all.

Scene III

Connie's room.
  CONNIE *and* JOSHUA. MARTHA *in her office.*

JOSHUA: You at least will ask about my project.
CONNIE: A book on the difference between what people say and the way they say it?
JOSHUA: More than that. More, more than that. A book about the national characteristics revealed by language.
CONNIE: Frightening.
JOSHUA: (*Sarcasm*) Mock not the future.
CONNIE: What will you call it?
JOSHUA: Suggest a title.
CONNIE: *Hidden Meanings?*
JOSHUA: Excellent! Splendid! But my book's only the beginning. I want to construct a machine.
CONNIE: God help us. Science fiction?
JOSHUA: Let me explain. Just as there are only a handful of basic plots so there are only a handful of basic emotions. And each basic emotion has its own identifiable melody which the voice sings: love, hate, arrogance, modesty, false modesty, contempt, respect, sanctimony, demagogy, fear, and so on. And sometimes people utter *words* which are modest but in the *melody* of arrogance; or they utter words of love but in the melody of hate; or they offer words of respect but in the melody of contempt. And most people can't hear the *melody*, they're fooled and misled by the *words*.
CONNIE: So?
JOSHUA: So, my machine will be sensitive to the melodies and will show up as a colour on a screen. The melody of sanctimony – green. The melody of demagogy – red. The melody of arrogance – blue.
CONNIE: The melody of seduction – pink.
JOSHUA: The melody of mockery – yellow.
CONNIE: The melody of false modesty – brown.
JOSHUA: The melody of intimidation –
CONNIE: – grey, grey, grey!
JOSHUA: Everyone will have my machine attached to the TV set. No

politician, journalist, diplomat, actor, prize-winning novelist or born-again priest would be safe.

CONNIE: A lie detector!

JOSHUA: No! A 'distinguisher'! To make distinctions. Very important to make distinctions. A lie detector tries to detect what you *feel*. Feelings are not to be trusted. My machine will distinguish between what's honestly intended and what's dishonestly intended. Not by registering feelings but by identifying melodies. (*Beat.*) *You* ask your mother to invest.

CONNIE: Me?

JOSHUA: Appeal on my behalf.

CONNIE: When I can't appeal on my own behalf?

JOSHUA: One half of her is you, she said.

CONNIE: But the other half is *you*, dammit!

JOSHUA: She was left a great deal of money, your mother. Began after the steam engine was invented. The age of empire: philanthropy, long novels, a new sense of who belonged where in what place. I need her.

CONNIE: If you need her, be good to her.

JOSHUA: I trusted her, I advised her, I tried to love her but I am who I am what I am that I am. She couldn't suffer it.

CONNIE: And how am I expected to help her suffer who you are what you are that you are?

JOSHUA: It would help her feel benign.

CONNIE: I'm hearing a melody.

JOSHUA: It would help her set up the relationship she really believes is right and proper.

CONNIE: I'm hearing a melody louder than words.

JOSHUA: She believes the world is divided into those who need to be conferring favours and those who have no alternative but to beg them.

CONNIE: And the melody is of self-pity.

JOSHUA: Self-pity?

CONNIE: You thought you were identifying a fact about human behaviour. But the way you sang it revealed you were sorry for yourself. Powerless.

JOSHUA: Powerless? What are we talking about power for? The knowledge that my neighbour is a fool gives me power.

CONNIE: Wrong! It gives you superiority. There's a distinction.

JOSHUA: Your father's daughter.

CONNIE: Superiority is the *knowledge* you have over the fool. *Power* is when you can prevent the fool from *murdering* you.
  (*Pause.*)

JOSHUA: They planted a bomb outside a Jewish old people's home in Copenhagen.

CONNIE: How brave. (*Beat.*) Anybody killed?

JOSHUA: Injured merely. Nothing much. A leg here, an arm there. (*Beat.*) The Danish government protested, 'But we have been critics of Israel . . .'

CONNIE: And the Jewish community?

JOSHUA: Those who never attend synagogue want to fill it. Those who attend regularly say, 'Hush . . . be invisible.'
  (*Pause.*)

CONNIE: God's already invented a distinguisher. It's called 'woman'.

JOSHUA: Woman?

CONNIE: Men only listen to words, women listen to the melody of words. There's millions of us about.

JOSHUA: But flawed! Inaccurate! Unreliable! Like everything God invented.

CONNIE: Still, it *was* his first go.

JOSHUA: No excuse! You're not sure how to do something? Leave it to somebody else.

CONNIE: (*Sadly*) Who else was there, Josh?
  (*Pause.*)

JOSHUA: It *must* be possible to get at the truth of human intention.

CONNIE: Technology won't lead you to the truth.

JOSHUA: I need to try. I need her help. I need your help to get her help. Ask her.
  (*Pause.*)

CONNIE: I believe the world is divided into those who *know* the world is divided and those who *don't* know the world is divided.

JOSHUA: Or don't care, dammit, don't care!

170

Scene IV

Martha's office.
    MARTHA *and* CONNIE.

MARTHA: Tell him to ask me himself.

CONNIE: You just want him to beg.

MARTHA: I want him to face me.

CONNIE: His face angers you.

MARTHA: If he wants my help he must learn the art of normal social intercourse.

CONNIE: The art of social hypocrisy you mean.

MARTHA: We are talking about large sums of money.

CONNIE: The truth is expensive.

MARTHA: I have to hear from him the details of his plans.

CONNIE: You know he won't have detailed plans. A man like Dad has a record. His books, his honours, his standing in the world. The big foundations fund people not blueprints.

MARTHA: I am not a big foundation.

CONNIE: He's on to something important, Mother, possibly even lucrative.

MARTHA: I'm a small investor. I need facts and figures.

CONNIE: Think of the glory you'll reap.

MARTHA: I'm a pragmatist.

CONNIE: Think of your epitaph.

MARTHA: I'm Protestant and pragmatic.

CONNIE: 'Mammon helps Truth.'

MARTHA: 'Innocence exploited by Cunning' more like.

CONNIE: At least declare you're prepared to help in principle.

MARTHA: I will declare nothing. Tell him to ask me himself.

Scene V

Martha's office.
　　MARTHA *and* JOSHUA. *The middle of a conversation.* CONNIE *in her room.*

JOSHUA: Will you or will you not help me?

MARTHA: Nor did he ever like my father.

JOSHUA: I didn't ever like the image *you* had of your father. Otherwise I liked him. After my fashion.

MARTHA: I'll never forgive him the time he came for dinner and remained silent a whole evening. Deliberately. Rudely. Embarrassingly.

JOSHUA: Your father was a kind man, an intelligent man but he never talked *with* you, only *at* you. He *asserted* his ideas, didn't offer them. Disagreement was unthinkable. Even small contributions. You had to exist in his space, his world, at his speed, with his laws, his references, his choice of subject, his beginnings, his ends, for his was the kingdom, the power and the glory. It was not that he was *angry* if you introduced other values, other perspectives. He was bewildered. Hurt. One day I decided to stop hurting him.

MARTHA: He insulted him instead. With silence.

JOSHUA: You mean I should've said 'amen' now and then?

MARTHA: And he expects me to keep him while he writes his absurd book and assembles his absurd machine? This man without respect, with his sarcasm, his mockery . . . ?

JOSHUA: I do not mock. Mock is one thing I do not *ever* do. It's an English habit. I just have difficulty being reverential about some things.

MARTHA: *Some* things? *Everything!*

JOSHUA: No. *Some* things. You never listened to me carefully enough.

MARTHA: And did he ever love *me*?

JOSHUA: I'm at your mercy. Stronger than love.

MARTHA: Did he imagine I wanted him to crawl to me? That I married him for that?

JOSHUA: I think you married me to be your guest. I think you married me as one opens the front door to a visitor one wants to impress with one's interiors, one's culture, one's good manners, one's magnanimity. I think you married me that way. That's the way I think you married me.

MARTHA: And he expects me to keep him knowing he thinks *that* about me?

JOSHUA: You can afford it. It's your responsibility.

MARTHA: Afford or not afford, *I* will decide my responsibilities.

JOSHUA: You have an inheritance you don't know how to use.

MARTHA: My inheritance is my inheritance.

JOSHUA: One I contributed to.

MARTHA: Ha!

JOSHUA: But you were too grudging to acknowledge it.

MARTHA: He nags for attention.

JOSHUA: It embarrassed you.

MARTHA: He whines for praise.

JOSHUA: Talk about money was bad taste. Expressions of passion were bad taste.

MARTHA: Listen to his shrill self-serving.

JOSHUA: Enthusiasm, appetite, energy, ideas, touch, loud laughter, generosity, second helpings – all, all bad taste.

MARTHA: Guttural, strident, ostentatious.

JOSHUA: You mean, thin-lipped, tight-arsed, unimaginative, sanctimonious, hypocritical, gold-plated bitch, will you or will you not help me?

MARTHA: I will *not*. I *will* not. Oh, will I will I not!
(*Tense silence.*)

JOSHUA: One day I found myself peeing in the loo during the interval of a production of *King Lear*. And I looked up as is the wont of loitering urinists and read the following graffiti: 'God is love – as all bunglers are!'
(MARTHA *screams and screams and screams as though the intolerable incomprehensibility of this man is driving her mad.*)

Scene VI

Connie's room.

CONNIE, toy telephone in hand. MARTHA and JOSHUA in Martha's office.

CONNIE: You still there, God? I have this father and mother and one is and one isn't and one does and one doesn't so I don't know if I am or am not, do or do not. Know what I mean?

    (*She positions herself regally in order to play God. Looks around, slowly.*)

(*Booms out.*) Not only do I not know what *she* means, I never know what anybody means!

    (*She returns to the phone.*)

Sorry, God. I keep being blasphemous I know but – can't resist it. You understand, don't you? I'm my father's daughter and it's my profession to joke and my nature to be irreverent and – oh, I don't know.

    (*Something catches her attention.*)

Hold the line a minute, will you, please? Attend to the next caller, I'll be back.

    (*She moves to a jar tucked away in a corner. It's a jar of wonderfully rainbow-coloured marbles. She sparkles. Mesmerized. Takes one. Rolls it forward. Takes another. Rolls it to hit the first. Keeps rolling till five are on the floor. Collects them. Carries them and the jar to the phone.*)

Hello, God. You dealt with them? Got through for a change?

    (*She drops a marble into the jar with each word.*)

It – was – all – simple – once.

    (*Long, long pause.*)

Not true. It was never simple.

174

Scene VII

Connie's room.
   CONNIE *and* JOSHUA. MARTHA *in her office.*

JOSHUA: Do you think she finds me indigestible?

CONNIE: I think she finds you incomprehensible.

JOSHUA: I think she's like the second child who one day realizes her father was someone else's father first.

CONNIE: Pity the third child.

JOSHUA: Poor Jesus.

CONNIE: Poor Ishmael.
   (*Pause.*)

JOSHUA: And yet how often the third child is the most beloved.
   (*Pause.*)

CONNIE: I think you should have been a rabbi.

JOSHUA: My belief in God cannot be relied upon.

CONNIE: Rabbis don't believe in God, they just use him to control unmanageable Jews.

JOSHUA: What would you know! Only half of you is Jewish. And the wrong half at that.

CONNIE: Doesn't stop me feeling unmanageable. You're indigestible, I'm unmanageable.

JOSHUA: My father *wanted* me to be a rabbi. He said, 'Son,' he said, 'the world respects a scholar. You will never want for bread if you become a scholar.' The Enlightenment had passed him by so for him there was only one kind of scholar – a Talmudic one! I – wanted to study language. 'Language? Language is something you use, not study.' 'But, Daddy,' I said . . .

CONNIE: You called him 'Daddy'?

JOSHUA: I called *him* 'Daddy' and my mother 'Mummy' right up until they died. I was nearly fifty years old.

CONNIE: '"But, Daddy," I said . . .'

JOSHUA: 'But, Daddy,' I said, 'the history of nations is in their language and how it was formed and how it evolved.' He was amazed.
   (*Pause.*)

CONNIE: Josh, talk to me about when I was a little girl.

JOSHUA: There was the time you tried to milk a bull.

CONNIE: I never did!

JOSHUA: We used to go on holiday each year, for about four years running, to a little farm sublet by one of your mother's brothers from his 2000 acre estate – for a not inconsiderable rent, I might add. You were ten years old and you'd seen the farmer's wife sitting on a stool with a pail between her legs pulling at something hanging, so *you* got a stool and put a pail between your legs and you found something hanging and you pulled!

CONNIE: What happened?

JOSHUA: He kicked! What happened. You pull a bull's ding-dong he gets confused. He say – 'Who dat dere? Who dat dere pulling my ding-dong when I ain't ready to have my ding-dong pulled? Dat my ding-dong. *I* tell you when I ready to have my ding-dong pulled.'

(CONNIE *in fits of laughter.*)

Fortunately the pail was in the way.

(*Pause.*)

(*Quiet*) I remember we took you to concerts and theatre and on long journeys to foreign parts. You liked puddles, I remember.

(*Pause.*)

'The first truth', says Buddha, 'is that all life is suffering.'

(*Sad smiles.*)

Do we really accept that? Really, really accept that?

(*Pause. The question hangs in the air.*)

CONNIE: Daddy, I'm sorry I was none of the things you wanted me to be.

JOSHUA: *Wanted* you to be? *Wanted*? Only one thing I *wanted* you to be – free. Independent. Dependent upon no one. Not a husband for your keep, not a country for your identity, not a group for your cause, nor an ideology for your fulfilment. I wanted you to learn your way out of prisons. To be nobody's slave, nobody's guest. You make people laugh. I'm not complaining.

CONNIE: Only they don't laugh and I am.

JOSHUA: You want to know about laughter? Let me tell you about laughter. Laughter comes from the Jews. Why the Jews? Because we're a nervous people. When you invent God you make people uneasy. When you then say he's chosen you to bear witness to the beauty of his creation and to guard justice you make people feel

176

indignant. 'We have our own Gods, we have our own justice.' But does the Jew listen? He can't! When you've invented God no other authority can really be taken seriously. And so the Jew questions all authority. People don't like that. They burn you for it. Isn't that enough to make you nervous? Nervous people laugh. And that doesn't help either.

(*Looking up*) You there? I'm talking to you. We've got problems down here. You sure you put the parts together in the right order?

(*To* CONNIE) He even questions the authority he claimed was unquestionable. What can you do with such a people? And they write funny books about it all.

Look at the Bible, the largest collection of jokes in the world. The Book of Job. What could be funnier? To prove Satan wrong God lets him play dice with Job's fortunes. A man who had everything – beautiful wife, lovely children, wealth, a house in the country on the west bank, and then, all of a sudden, wham! He loses everything. His wife dies, his children all die, his car, his hi-fi, his washing machine – everything repossessed! And he's struck down with herpes. It's enough to make you nervous. So what does Job do? If he were a Christian, faith would be enough. But for a Jew nothing is enough. He has to go to the top.

(*Looking up*) You there? I'm talking to you. I've got problems down here. I'm an upright man, I take a little here give a little there. Is this just? Look at me. I'm a mess.

And what does God do? He laughs back. He shows Job a big fish, a leviathan he calls it. What could be funnier? 'Can you hook it?' God asks. 'It's a big fish,' says Job. 'How can I hook it?' 'Right!' says God. 'How much more difficult to hook me!' 'He's doing a Hamlet on me,' says Job. 'Very funny!'

The Jew can't help it, he questions authority with laughter. It's a nervous tick.

Take Einstein. Einstein questioned authority with laughter. You know how it is. You meet a Jew on the stairs and you ask him if he's going up or he's going down and he says, 'Well, it depends. Everything's relative!'

Take Freud. Freud questioned authority with laughter. 'Ernest,' he said to his biographer, Ernest Jones – another Jewish habit, talking to your biographer – 'Ernest, I'm half convinced by socialism.'

'How come, Herr Doktor?' Ernest knows the Herr Doktor is a thorough conservative. 'Well,' says Freud, 'I've been reading Trotsky on socialism' – Trotsky, another funny man who questioned authority – 'I've been reading Trotsky and he says that in the first phase of the transition to socialism there will be big problems: upheavals, misery, large-scale disaster. But in the second phase – the promised land for us all, paradise on earth, utopia! Well, Ernest, I am convinced about the first half.'

No, don't laugh. This Jewish humour, this laughing at authority, it causes such irritation. You're not supposed to laugh at the misery they bestow on you. It's unnatural. It causes a great deal of misunderstanding, better known as anti-Semitism, or anti-Zionism as the new jargon will have it. And what *is* anti-Semitism? It's hating Jews more than is necessary. It's enough to make you nervous. Especially when you're never certain whether you've got an audience out there or a lynch mob.

CONNIE: A lynch mob, a lynch mob! That's my problem, I'm telling jokes to a lynch mob.

Scene VIII

Between Cabaret club and Martha's office.
JOSHUA *in Connie's room. Fade in first on* CONNIE *in the Cabaret Club.*

CONNIE: Take Kafka. Kafka questioned authority with laughter. He was talking to his biographer, Max Brod – they all have biographers these funny men – and Kafka as usual was being gloomy and pessimistic. Dark, he was a dark, dark man. And Brod says, 'Frank,' he says, 'you're being more depressing than usual. The way you talk. Is there *no* hope?' And Kafka says, 'Who says there's no hope? Of course there's hope, Max. An infinite amount of hope . . . but not for us!'

(*As one of her audience*) Bloody hell!

All right then. There was an Englishman, Irishman, Scotsman and this Jew. No. There was a Norwegian, Dane, Swede and this Finn. No. There was a Russian, Hungarian, Czech and this Pole.

(*Yelling as one of the audience*) Make up yer mind, yer silly cow.

How about – there was this Finn, this Pole and this Jew?

(*Yelling*) They shouldn't 'ave bloody women telling bloody jokes. Women never was funny.

(*Fade in on* MARTHA.)

MARTHA: I don't mean to be what I am, say what I say. He drives me to it. Draws it from me. And when it comes I don't know where it comes from.

CONNIE: So God finally found this bloke called Moses on top of a mountain tearing his hair out cos his family down below were dancing naked round a golden calf and doing all sorts of rude and wicked things and he said to Moses, 'I'm *giving* them away' and Moses said, 'Good! I'll have ten!' (*Beat.*) Pity! Thought you'd like that one.

MARTHA: (*Getting to her knees*) Dear Lord Jesus, pray for me. Send me a sign. Teach me what to think, how to behave. Explain it to me. We suffered too, didn't we?

CONNIE: I had a Jewish grandmother – yes, you heard! We've all got our crosses to bear. And this Jewish grandmother used to say to me, 'You can live a long time, learn a lot and still die a fool.'

179

MARTHA: Why does he want to destroy me? I didn't *want* to hate him. Hate is not my nature.

CONNIE: There's a certain kind of English mentality which turns very nasty if you don't take its flippancy seriously. Know what I mean?

MARTHA: I wanted to love him.

CONNIE: The kind of people who buy fast two-seater cars so they can't give friends lifts home.

MARTHA: But I loathe him. With a passion.

CONNIE: So, she nudges her neighbour across the wall and says, 'My old man, my old man, 'ee's the only man I know 'oo's risen to the depths!'

MARTHA: No one to talk with.

CONNIE: (*Yelling as though one of the audience*) Gerroff! You've never told a good joke and never will tell a good joke.

MARTHA: If there's no one to talk with, you talk to yourself.

CONNIE: Gerrout! Gerrup! Gerroff!

MARTHA: Cigarette. Need a cigarette. Tried to give up. Can't.
(*She finds one. Lights it. The pleasure of inhaling is immense.*)

CONNIE: All right then, all right. Repeat after me: I believe the world's divided into those who drive on the outside lane and those who drive in *and* out. No? How about this then? I believe the world's divided into those who transfer their diminished chopped liver to a smaller bowl, and those who leave large half-empty bowls to take up space in the fridge when I need it for all the other bloody things I've got to stock up with, you klutz!

MARTHA: Focus, focus! I can't focus while he's around.

CONNIE: (*Yelling*) What's chopped liver?

MARTHA: What I feel is not what I *want* to feel, know what I mean, angel?

CONNIE: All right then, try this.

MARTHA: Who is angel?
(*A sound grows. Of protesting jeering voices.*)

CONNIE: I believe the world's divided into the conscious and the unconscious.

MARTHA: I'm angel.

CONNIE: The givers and the takers.

MARTHA: My father called me 'angel'.

CONNIE: The winners and the losers.

180

MARTHA: 'Angel,' he said, 'beware of everything beyond these shores.'

CONNIE: The submissive and the domineering.

MARTHA: 'Beyond these shores nothing is predictable.'

CONNIE: The sick and the healthy.

MARTHA: 'There has to be predictability.'

CONNIE: Those who need God and those who don't.

MARTHA: My father knew. My father warned – 'he will be unpredictable.'

   (*Crescendo of voices ends abruptly.*)

CONNIE: 'I must remember', said Florence Nightingale, 'that God is not my secretary!' (*Beat.*) *She* couldn't have been Jewish then!

   (*Fade out on* CONNIE. MARTHA *reaches for her phone.*)

MARTHA: Connie? Connie? Please come back. If I shout a bit it's because I hurt a bit, I'm confused a bit. You've nothing to be afraid of from me. Remember – half of you *is* me. (*Puts down phone. Pauses. Dials again.*) Hello, God? Is it true that you're – that you're – that you're Jer–Jer–Jer–

   (*The word sticks in her throat. She gags on it.*)

181

Scene IX

Connie's room.
  CONNIE *and* JOSHUA.

JOSHUA: Years ago I did a lecture tour of Canada. One of my hosts, a professor and his wife, had a dog. We got on well, this dog and me. I fed him bits from the table, talked to him, stroked him. We were comfortable together. On the second evening we went out for a meal. The dog had to be left. My host said something about the house not really being safe with the dog, who'd as soon wag his tail and lick a complete stranger as snap at him. At which I looked down at the dog and addressed it with what I thought was a friendly teasing tone. 'You too sweet to protect your lord and master?' I asked. 'Too soft and soppy to be much use to anyone?' Some such words. And do you know – he growled and snapped at me! The tease came through stronger than the friendliness. There was something unpleasant to him in my melody. (*Growls.*) I was very hurt.

CONNIE: That when the idea first came to you for the book?

JOSHUA: Could be. Could well have been. (*Growls.*) Quite upset by it.

CONNIE: Even dogs.

JOSHUA: Even dogs. Mad Marthas and mad dogs. (*Beat.*) Did you speak to her again?

CONNIE: I did.

JOSHUA: And?

CONNIE: She doesn't like being called a gold-plated bitch.

JOSHUA: Did I call her that?

CONNIE: 'Mean, thin-lipped, tight-arsed, unimaginative, sanctimonious, hypocritical, gold-plated bitch.'

JOSHUA: I couldn't have said all that.

CONNIE: In one breath. She wrote it down.

JOSHUA: No hope then.

CONNIE: But she *is* a woman of second thoughts.

JOSHUA: There *is* hope then?

CONNIE: Do you know what it's like having the two of you knock around inside me?

JOSHUA: Take what's best, my darling, the rest reject. What makes you think she may have second thoughts?

CONNIE: I'm talking about me!

JOSHUA: Talk.

CONNIE: I'm a mess.

JOSHUA: So was Job.

CONNIE: I tell Jewish jokes for a living.

JOSHUA: But God adored him and I adore you.

CONNIE: And like your Canadian dog they can hear other melodies – bitter, ironic.

JOSHUA: And we all need adoring.

CONNIE: Adoring me doesn't help.

(*Knock on the door.* CONNIE *opens it.* MARTHA *enters with a birthday cake and six lighted candles in one hand, a bottle of champagne and three glasses in the other.* CONNIE *and* JOSHUA *are astounded.*)

MARTHA: Cakes and champagne for the family.

JOSHUA: I exist for her!

MARTHA: (*To* JOSHUA) Couldn't let your birthday go by without a little celebration.

JOSHUA: But it's not my birthday.

MARTHA: It *was* on at least one day this year.

JOSHUA: And I'm not six years old.

MARTHA: Six is for sixty, silly.

JOSHUA: I'm not sixty, either. I'm fifty-five.

MARTHA: We're all ancient members of an ancient race. We're celebrating that, then.

JOSHUA: It's poisoned!

MARTHA: If you stop to think about any day you'll always find a reason to celebrate it. The day you met your husband. The day you moved into the house. The Lord's Day. The first rose is out. Midsummer's Eve. Your monthlies are finished. A hostage is released. The Lord's Day – oh! I've already said that, haven't I? Anyway, it could be cakes and champagne every day. If one could afford it.

JOSHUA: All lunacy has logic.

MARTHA: Of course I can't really afford it.

CONNIE: I'm glad we're a family, mother.

MARTHA: I know your father has these fantasies of my vast wealth

183

hidden in banks around the world but for all the wealth *I* know about they might as *well* be hidden in banks. Now Joshua, blow.

JOSHUA: It'll explode. As I blow it'll explode and she'll have solved all her problems. In one blow!

MARTHA: Come. I want you both to taste the cake and tell me what it's made of.

JOSHUA: Martha, I'm not understanding.

MARTHA: Oh well, you can't expect to understand everything in this life.

JOSHUA: You're showing one face and hiding another. Martha –

MARTHA: That's the trouble with you people –

JOSHUA: 'You people'?

MARTHA: Your lot. The educated ones. Don't be so sensitive. You always want to understand everything, explain everything. You're all scientists, linguists, professors – of psychology or biochemistry or genetics. Genetics! There! You'll end up filling the world with monsters. Leave it alone. Mystery. Let there be mystery –

JOSHUA: – and darkness. How about some medieval darkness around the place while we're about it?

MARTHA: (*Peeling free the champagne foil*) And opinions! You've always got to have opinions. Stop tampering with the world. Eat cakes and drink champagne. Celebrate the days. Blow!

(*He hesitates. Closes his eyes. Crosses himself. Clasps his hands in prayer. Mumbles a little, then blows. The cork pops.*)

(*Pouring*) Had no faith in your Adonai? (*To* CONNIE) Did you know I can recite the prayer for wine. In the days when we trusted and loved one another he taught me.

(*She raises her glass. Recites.*)
Baruch atah Adonai
Eloheinu melech haolam
Boreh pri hagofen.

(*They clink glasses. She drinks. The others follow, though* JOSHUA *waits for* CONNIE *to drink first.*)

Do you know why we clink our glasses? All over the world people clink their glasses before they drink – why?

(*Pause.*)

Don't we know? My clever darlings don't know? Or do we think it's

184

useless information? Ah, well, it's been Martha's role in life to be a fund of useless information.

The ancients had for years loved wine. Every sense was gratified but one. No one talked about it. It became a taboo subject – like not mentioning that one's beautiful, intelligent, happy child had an arm missing. Until one day glass was invented and like the silicon chip it changed all living thereafter.

It was the court jester during the reign of Rameses III – no! That can't be so. The Egyptians hadn't learned that laughter at oneself could heal. Or had they?

JOSHUA: (*Admiringly*) Keep going, Martha, keep going.

MARTHA: Do you think every civilization had jesters to help them through life? I digress. Wherever, whenever, whoever, said: 'How good it is that we have wine to gratify so many senses. We can look at it, we can smell it, we can taste it, and to make it we must touch it. But how sad that we cannot *hear* it.' At which the court jester, inspired as only court jesters can be, clinked the glass of the pharaoh or the emperor or the duke, and said (*clinks* JOSHUA'S *glass.*), 'Health to all your senses, Lord!'

(*She drinks.*)

CONNIE: That was a very beautiful story, Mother.

MARTHA: Martha not so useless after all? Good. Now. (*Cuts the cake.*) It's a new recipe and I shall be very disappointed if you guess all the main ingredients.

(*She hands each a slice. Neither eats.*)

I suppose I should be used to your humour by now.

CONNIE: (*Eating*) Well, half of me is her. I'm safe.

JOSHUA: Don't bank on it.

(CONNIE *chokes. Staggers around. Falls.*)

MARTHA: Come now, dear. The death of children is not game for ridicule.

CONNIE: (*From her prone position*) Butter, eggs, flour, for sure. Then – er – honey?

MARTHA: Couldn't miss that.

(MARTHA *drinks quickly. She will become drunk soon.*)

CONNIE: Now *there's* an interesting question. What's not game for ridicule?

MARTHA: You haven't finished guessing the ingredients of my cake.

CONNIE: Who, if anyone, or what, if anything, is too sacred to be ridiculed?

MARTHA: Joshua?

JOSHUA: Oh – er – walnuts. I taste walnuts. (*To* CONNIE) Everything must be game for ridicule.

MARTHA: Connie, he says walnuts. What do you say?

(*A subtle conflict ensues.* JOSHUA *becomes excited by the topic.* MARTHA *fights for* CONNIE'*s attention.*)

CONNIE: Oh – er – almonds. Honey and almonds. (*To* JOSHUA) Everything?

MARTHA: What else?

CONNIE: Is the martyr game for ridicule?

MARTHA: I mean, there is one very special spice which sets it off.

CONNIE: The freedom fighter? The missionary? The educator? Those in pain?

MARTHA: I did take the trouble to bake a cake . . .

CONNIE: (*Biting*) Cinnamon.

MARTHA: (*Giggling*) Nothing so ordinary.

JOSHUA: Yes! All of them are game for ridicule *if* they can be seen to be in love with or intoxicated by: the martyr her sacrifice, the freedom fighter his anger, the missionary his zeal, the educator her cleverness, and those in pain their suffering.

MARTHA: I'll give you a clue. It comes from –

JOSHUA: I'm a puritan. I believe everything has to be earned, and all those who engage in altruism and agony should do so with reluctance. Anyone caught enjoying it should be punished with ridicule.

MARTHA: I really am surprised you didn't get it at once, Connie.

(CONNIE *walks to a note on her wall.*)

CONNIE: (*Reading*) 'Wherefore I perceive that there is nothing better than that a man should rejoice in his own works; for who shall bring him to see what shall be after him?' Ecclesiastes, chapter 3, verse 22.

MARTHA: It's a spice often referred to in the Bible.

JOSHUA: In my opinion all opinions are provisional! Even Eccles—

(MARTHA *snaps.*)

MARTHA: Opinions! He has to have opinions about everything! Puritan? Huh! I'd say he was. Not an ounce of fun in him. Takes himself so bloody seriously. Too clever by half! He'll have a fall one day which will break his bloody neck, and serves him right –

CONNIE: Mother!

MARTHA: Serves them all right. I'm sick of being nice and tolerant and baking cakes.

CONNIE: Mother!

MARTHA: It's happening again. He didn't go and it's happening again.

CONNIE: Please, Mother.

MARTHA: His air . . .

JOSHUA: I feared it wouldn't last long.

MARTHA: . . . he has this air . . .

JOSHUA: I'm having an intelligent conversation with my daughter.

MARTHA: *His* daughter, *his* conversation, *his* intelligence. It suffocates me.

JOSHUA: *What* suffocates you?

MARTHA: (*Struggling to name it*) His air . . .

JOSHUA: Air! Air! What air, you foolish woman, you? What air?

MARTHA: (*At last*) He has no fear of God.

JOSHUA: Fear of God? Why should I fear God? I invented him!

MARTHA: There! That! That's it! Did you hear him?

CONNIE: Mother, I am going mad with all of this. Mother –

(MARTHA *once more goes out of control into hysteria.*)

MARTHA: Mother! Mother! Don't 'mother' me. I'm not your mother. *He's* your father, though. And can't you tell it! The way you stick together. You. You and him. All of you. Keeping to yourselves. Cosy. Exclusive. Private. Private jokes, private conversations, private plots for this and that. You'd like to take over this house, wouldn't you? Find some way of getting me out of the place I was born in, grew up in, welcomed him into. Eh? I bet that's what you're plotting to do. Take over. I bet you arranged – Oh, my God! Why didn't I see it before? Of course! Fool! Trusting bloody fool. You arranged to come together, didn't you, at the same time? You've been scheming behind my back. Why? Why?

CONNIE: Cardamom. You've put cardamom in the cake. What a clever idea.

MARTHA: It's happening again. He didn't go and it's happening again. I can't breathe, I don't know where to put myself, I don't

187

know what to do with my hands, I don't know what to say, I'm not making sense, I'm screaming again, I'm screaming, I can't stop screaming.

(MARTHA *is drunkenly weeping. Inconsolable. She lays her head in* CONNIE's *lap.*)

Why didn't he go? I've never understood. He's got his own little flat now, hasn't he? I've never understood any of it, any of it, never understood . . .

(*They watch her simmer down. She moans softly, as though trying to comfort herself. It is a long pause.*)

JOSHUA: (*Realizing it, as though for the first time.*) She will never have any peace.

(*Slow fade.*)

LADY OTHELLO
A love story

Give all to love:
Obey thy heart;
Friends, kindred, days,
Estate, good fame,
Plans, credit, and the Muse –
Nothing refuse.

Ralph Waldo Emerson

CHARACTERS

STANTON MYERS   aged forty-four, professor of American
literature, British, Jewish

ROSIE SWANSON   aged thirty, about to become a student, New
York, Catholic, black

STELLA-BELLA   aged thirty to thirty-five, waitress, drop-out, New
York, Jewish

FRANCESCA   aged forty, restaurant owner

DELI SHOP ASSISTANT

MAN   Stella-Bella's fella for the night

WOMAN   'Miss Minelli', outside Sardi's, a customer

And VOICES

This is a play for three actors. The actress playing STELLA-BELLA can
also play FRANCESCA, DELI SHOP ASSISTANT, and WOMAN, thus
commanding the talent of a first-rate actress. Stella-Bella's fella makes
a brief, fifteen-second appearance and can be played by a stage
manager. All the voices off except one can be played by stage
managers or can be recorded. One voice off is a central role and must
be recorded by, preferably, a well-known actress's voice. This is the
voice of STANTON's wife – JUDITH.

Time   New York. Late seventies.

Lady Othello was completed in the autumn of 1987. At the time of going to press no production has been scheduled.

ACT ONE

House-lights fade. Sound of a Boeing jumbo jet in flight fades up and retreats.
   In the darkness – VOICES.

JUDITH'S VOICE: By the way, did your father tell you he was going to New York to give a lecture?

DAUGHTER'S VOICE: (*Cheerfully*) No, he's not. He's going to see his girlfriend. Stop him.

JUDITH'S VOICE: Will you not suggest crazy things like that. They upset me.

DAUGHTER'S VOICE: How long's he going for?

JUDITH'S VOICE: Twelve days.

DAUGHTER'S VOICE: Twelve days to give a lecture? Mother!

Scene I

Aeroplane toilet.
  STANTON *finishing shaving with old-fashioned cut-throat. Dangerous! Probably belonged to his father. He's a professor of American literature; handsome, wry, gentle, confident by nature. When finished he puts on a black rollneck sweater. Till then –*

STANTON: Repeat after me: this relationship can't possibly work because, one: when I'm sixty she will be forty-six. Two: New Yorkers, bless them, are *afflicted* by democracy and feel it a duty to have opinions about everything! Three: she *has* to be right. Four: seems unable to distinguish between disagreement and hostility, rational exchange difficult therefore. Five: she doesn't converse, she lectures. Six: speaks too ardently too often, too loudly and in public places. Seven: she's never on time, imagines punctuality is a sign of servility. Eight: she has a therapist. Nine: she's combative, competitive, possessive and contrary. And ten: I love my family. (*Pause.*) I must be mad! (*Pause.*) Then why, professor Stanton Myers, are you travelling three thousand miles to tell a woman you've decided it can't work? (*Pause. Beaming*) Because, one: she's perceptive, supportive, positive and loyal. Two: her New York humour is irresistible, outrageous and infectious. Three: her personality is sunny. Four: she's breathtakingly beautiful. And five: she appears to be powered by an apparently endless and delightfully unashamed lust and I have come to put myself at risk!

Scene II

STANTON *asleep in aeroplane seat.*
  Gentle voice of his wife, JUDITH. *It is the letter she's written to him before leaving.*

JUDITH'S VOICE: 'My darling. All my instincts are to fight tooth and nail to keep you as part of our family. Sometimes I manage with dignity, other times not. And then I feel angry with myself. The situation calls for civilized behaviour, doesn't it? Forgive my outbursts, they'll get less and less as I feel more in control of my situation. I do so want you to carry a graceful image of me. You *must* go to New York, I understand that. I'd hate you to grow into a tormented man, and *if* you come back we'll be here, waiting for your old self to return. The days will get tense from now on with *your* excitement at going and *my* sadness at seeing you go. Be strong, and go knowing that mine is a long-standing love. I'm afraid you'll have to arrange your own luggage, forgive me for not driving you to the airport . . .'

Scene III

Kennedy Airport, arrivals.

* STANTON in well-cut brown tweed suit, a black, military-style raincoat over his arm. He's jetlagged. He's besotted.*

* ROSIE, made up, stunning, radiant, expectant, eager. It is autumn. She wears an old 1930s astrakhan coat with fur collar; beneath it a blue denim skirt and black rollneck sweater. She's a little plump, she's offbeat, she's a beautiful Jamaican-black New Yorker – a kind of Barbra Streisand.*

* They stand a long moment taking each other in. They're strangely shy. She offers him a cheek to kiss, and three roses.*

ROSIE: Tired, huh?

STANTON: Deliciously.

ROSIE: Flight wasn't late as you feared.

STANTON: I had to alert you though.

ROSIE: All you had to do was move heaven and earth to get here. (*Beat.*) I'll provide hell!

STANTON: Don't make jokes. (*Beat.*) Yes, make jokes.

ROSIE: Honey? You sound tired and in need of love and comfort.

STANTON: I don't need love and comfort. I need *you*!

ROSIE: Same thing!

STANTON: (*Playing the professor*) One may come from the other but they're not the same thing. Love and comfort I can get from lots of people. *You* I can get from no one.

ROSIE: Shithead!

Scene IV

Airport coach into New York.

   ROSIE *chatters at a ferocious rate, which she does well, fluently and
frequently.*

ROSIE: And then Stella-Bella my flatmate rings up from just downstairs by the porter's desk and says, 'Rosie, it's here, didn't you see
it?' And I say, 'What's here?' 'Your results, dumb-dumb,' she says.
'An envelope, here, with the university's name on it.' 'Stella-
Bella,' I say, 'you've forgotten what time it is. I haven't even
brushed my teeth yet' – because sometimes as a waitress she's on
early shift for breakfasts and gets back around ten, ten thirty and
maybe I've had a late night cos sometimes I do late shifts in the
same restaurant to subsidize the lousy alimony cheque I get from my
cautious anxious mean-as-arsehole ex-husband, and I say to her,
'Stella-Bella', I say, 'now you come straight up with that envelope
because I'm in no fit state to leave this flat and I don't care how late
you are this is life or death for me.' And she was kinda eager herself
to know, was I going to be allowed entry into the hallowed halls and
groves of academe for a second chance in life or not, so she rushes
up shrieking, 'I'm late! I'm late!' and I tell her, 'Stella-Bella, pray!
I'm opening the envelope, pray!' Which she did. Stood there like
a madonna – a Jewish madonna, you understand, because with
a name like Stella-Bella she couldn't come from Neapolitan
Catholic stock, you know what I mean? And she prayed. In
Hebrew! 'Stella-Bella,' I said, 'do you know what you're saying
because I don't want you mumbling the incomprehensible to the
Almighty . . .'

STANTON: Rosie, did they or did they not accept you?

ROSIE: They accepted me!

STANTON: Congratulations!

ROSIE: So now I'll study for a degree in political science by day and
   attend your lectures by night.

   (*It's her way of sounding out if he's staying or not. He avoids the
   hidden question.*)

STANTON: Why should you attend lectures on modern American
   literature – I only offer my enthusiasms for insular English

students. You have enough of your own enthusiasms
here.

(*She can't stop gazing at him.*)

ROSIE: Oh, those lips. I've made a list of all the landmarks where I
want those lips to kiss me.

STANTON: Every inch of you is a landmark.

ROSIE: New York landmarks, dumb-dumb. Jesus, don't look at me
that way or I'll have to drag you under the seat here and now.

STANTON: (*Sinking*) Drag me.

ROSIE: Sit up and behave. I want to be kissed on the Staten Island
ferry, in Times Square, on a buggy ride through Central Park, in a
box in the theatre, on top of the twin towers, in the middle of a
disco floor, in –

STANTON: How about in an airport bus?

(*She's been holding back for she knew not what or when but now no
longer can. Closes her eyes. It's their first kiss, and lasts a long time.
She wants to withdraw, he slaps her 'pushing hand' away, holds till
she's breathless.*)

ROSIE: That what you came all the way from London for, to choke me
to death? Get it over quickly?

STANTON: Why don't I just chew on your mouth for the rest of the
journey? It'll give me pleasure and your mouth a rest.

ROSIE: (*Quick-tempered*) Don't you get fresh with me.

(*He retreats. A dangerous moment. First-encounter nerves.*)

STANTON: Oh? Guard my English banter, must I? Here, (*reaching to a
pocket*) a present for you.

ROSIE: Wait! Let me give you mine first. As they're nothings it'll be
less embarrassing that way round.

STANTON: What makes you think mine is 'something'?

ROSIE: I expect you to have brought me the Crown Jewels. Here.

(*She rummages in her large, floppy bag and offers him one by one five
little packages, each neatly wrapped and bowed, evidence of time spent
on them.*)

STANTON: (*As he unpacks each one*) A miniature pack of cards! Of
movie stars! (*Reading title of second one*) Street Cries and Rhymes of
New York. (*Reading title of third present*) The Jewish Connection –
Amazing Jewish Achievements. (*Reading title of fourth present*) Ours is
a Strange and Wonderful Relationship – a book for friends, lovers and

other strange and wonderful people. (*The fifth is –*) Writing paper!

ROSIE: But you won't need that now cos you're gonna stay with me for ever, aren't you?

STANTON: (*Evading her question*) I love them all.

(*He withdraws his present – an old Victorian silver locket on a chain. She puts it round her neck, slips her arm through his, huddles up.*)
And I've discovered a new piece of music by Bach which I can't wait to play you. C.P.E. Bach, that is. The son, not the father. His *Magnificat.*

(*She is very happy.*)

Scene V

Rosie's apartment. (This will be the main setting.)

It has a hall, a lounge/dining room, a kitchen – only partly visible, a bathroom/toilet – only partly visible, two doors leading to bedrooms, not visible. One bedroom is rented to STELLA-BELLA. *The other belongs to Rosie's son.* ROSIE *sleeps on a divan in the lounge which opens out into a double bed.*

Her apartment is – well – not filthy, cluttered rather. She's indifferent to 'things' as evidenced by her records, which are mostly out of their sleeves scattered around. There's little furniture. The divan is in a recess. A round table with four chairs. A couch. An armchair. A chest of drawers. A wall of shelves filled mostly with books. Cushions on the floor.

ROSIE *is in the kitchen preparing a meal. The rest of the apartment is in shadow.* STANTON *is sprawled out asleep on the floor on the cushions. A record of* Jane Oliver's First Nights *plays softly in the background.*

The front door opens violently.

ROSIE: (*Whispering*) That you, Stella-Bella?
STELLA-BELLA: (*Too loudly*) That's me, Rosie.
ROSIE: Ssssh!

(STELLA-BELLA, *New York Jewish, bony, not beautiful but not plain. A dropped-out J A P.*)

You bought yourself Chinese takeaway to eat in your own room tonight?

STELLA-BELLA: (*Good-tempered patience*) I bought Chinese take-away like you said, Rosie, and I'll eat it in my own room like you ordered, Rosie, and you won't know I'm alive, like you want, Rosie.

ROSIE: Good girl. Now go and say hello to Stanton and don't maul him around too much cos I haven't unwrapped him yet.

(STELLA-BELLA, *arms full, moves to front room. She kneels to* STANTON *and showers him with loud kisses on his face, neck, chest, pausing in between to say:*)

STELLA-BELLA: Rosie said not to maul you around too much.

(*She continues kissing.*)

STANTON: Stella-Bellaaah! [Please.]

STELLA-BELLA: OK! OK! I'll continue in the morning.

(*She retires to her room.* ROSIE *tiptoes back and forth laying the table, setting up candles, arranging a cheese board. The phone rings. She rushes to grab it.*)

ROSIE: (*Whispering*) Oh hi, Merle. Yes. He's here. What d'you mean, how do I feel? I feel like a lump of jelly, that's how I feel. I feel like I'm back at college with a crush on my lecturer, which is what's happened of course, only now I'm a mother! No, we haven't talked yet. What chance have we had? This guy flew in a couple of hours ago, did Mark's homework for him then zonked out. And I'll tell you something else, buster, I'm not letting him talk tonight either. This lascivious woman has other plans and uses for the English gentleman's native tongue. Mark's staying with his friend, Stella-Bella's got Chinese takeaway and a Gary Cooper movie in her room and that leaves me the professor and a free lounge and I tell you neither *his* hang-ups nor *my* hang-ups nor his views on modern American literature are gonna be taking the floor tonight because I tell you I tell you he is more beautiful than I remembered and I'm more in love than I knew was possible so if you want news about how my future looks you better hang up now and don't call us, we'll call you. Do I make myself plain or do you want me to repeat all that? (*Long listening pause.*) Oh, Merle, that's awful. I didn't know your father had gone into hospital. Yeah – sure sixty is young these days. Keep me in touch. Byeee!

(*She lights candles. Pulls down blinds. Changes record to Johnny Mathis – 'The First Time Ever I Saw Your Face'. She kneels beside the sleeping* STANTON. *He is snoring ever so lightly.*)

Honey. You're snoring.

(*He opens his eyes. Smiles.*)

Don't you *ever* wake troubled?

STANTON: I feel loved, why should I wake troubled?

ROSIE: Me, I shoot up straight, usually out of a nightmare – zonk! Like that! My fists ready.

STANTON: You're lying to me again. I love your lies.

ROSIE: Oh, those lips.

(*She kisses him.*)

STANTON: You, candlelight, smell of food, Frank Sinatra, what more can a man want?

ROSIE: It's Johnny Mathis.

STANTON: Johnny Mathis, what more can a man want?

ROSIE: Come.

> (*She pulls him up, seats him by the table, tucks his napkin under his chin.*)

Don't you go anywhere, now.

> (*Alone, his face changes. Sombre. What an impossible situation! She returns, catches his expression. In one hand is the dish of kedgeree, in the other plates with a foilful of spare ribs on top. He rises quickly to take the plates with his napkin. He had thought they were hot. Feels one with the flat of his hand. They're not.*)

Something wrong?

STANTON: Reflex. My hand automatically feels to see the plate's hot.

ROSIE: (*Hint of pique*) Don't heat plates in *this* house, honey.

STANTON: Grounds for divorce.

ROSIE: (*Quick-tempered*) You want to ring now see if there's a flight out tonight?

STANTON: (*Slowly, calmly*) Rosie, can we agree on something? To give each other's humour space? I can take any amount of crude New York humour from you because I know what it's meant to be and I love it. Mine's English – wry, teasing, sardonic, even though I'm Jewish. The Jews take on the personality of the countries in which they find themselves. English Jews are frightfully English. French Jews are (*French accent*) terriblee French; German Jews, (*German accent*) zoes who are left, are zere, zere Deutsch. Only in New York has it gone the other way, all New Yorkers are very Jewish. You are more Jewish to me than most of my family in England. I love you, therefore my humour is not meant to hurt. You will know when it does.

> (*She's just gazing at him.*)

ROSIE: Would you mind saying all that again. You English! How come you speak the language so beautifully?

STANTON: Can I have my spare ribs, please?

> (*Holding his gaze she reaches for a spare rib, presents it to his mouth, he bites, she bites, offers it to him again, pulls it away, smears his lips with it then tongues the grease off his lips, melting into a kiss.*)

Let me play you the Bach *Magnificat*.

ROSIE: Wrong moment.

> (*She continues with the passionate kiss. Thus locked they rise from the*

*table, stagger to the cushions on the floor where he showers kisses on
her face, ears, neck, beneath which she writhes until –*)

Fuck the chicken kedgeree!

(*And she zips down the zipper of her skirt.*)

Scene VI

Rosie's apartment. Next morning.

She's on the phone. It's a phone you can talk to from a distance while doing other things. Dressed in an old dressing gown and wearing glasses she's putting her hair in curlers. It is as though she's daring STANTON to love her in any state. It's not difficult. Her sunny personality shines through.

ROSIE: Yes, Ma, of course he's here. The English are always on time, didn't you know? Frightened they'll lose out on something. (*Pause.*) Of course he's nearby. He's in the kitchen washing up. What else did I bring him over for? You know me. (*Pause.*) Yes, yes, you'll get to see him but I better warn you – he's heavy. Yeah, heavy, you know, Marx, Freud, Woody Allen – that crowd.

(STANTON *appears from kitchen with a handful of soap suds which he places inside her gown on her breast.*)

Ow! Don't do that! (*Pause.*) No, of course not you, Mother. It's this Englishman here, he's getting fresh. Still thinks we're a colony. (*Pause.*) I'll explain some other time. Ma, I must go. And listen, here's the bad news. You're gonna be seeing a lot of Mark over the next ten days. (*Pause.*) Yeah, I thought you'd hate that. Bye, Ma. Take care.

(*She looks at her watch. Too late to put in any more curlers. Bunches rest of her hair into an elastic band. Puts on a record of Stevie Wonder, sits on the floor and commences stretch exercises to the musical rhythm.* STANTON *appears. Watches her.*)

STANTON: Any other woman wearing curlers I'd walk out on.

ROSIE: (*Puffing*) Love me, love my curlers. Did you know I planned to meet you at the airport in curlers? Curlers and glasses. And then I planned to call your name loudly, kiss you loud and long, and unzip your hide-and-seek. What would you have done?

STANTON: Pretended it wasn't happening, that I didn't know you, or called for police.

ROSIE: Shithead!

STANTON: (*With mock eagerness*) Will you always call me that, please?

ROSIE: (*Pausing in her exercises*) Tell me, how did you leave London?

STANTON: Sadly.

ROSIE: I mean, who knows? Who said what?

> (*She flops to her back, exhausted and preparing herself for the worst.* STANTON *can't resist, and dives to her side.*)

Don't get too near, I smell all sweaty.

> (*Which seems not to worry him. Sniffs her like a dog.*)

STANTON: Mmm!

ROSIE: (*Tenderly*) Tell me.

> (STANTON *sits up, away from her.*)

STANTON: My sister said: 'It's because your mother died last year. You're an orphan!' Our friend Julie said: 'It's passion – passion lasts six months then it's over, done.' Another friend urged me to talk to another friend who's a psychiatrist who said: 'She's the personification of the American literature you love.' Well, they could all be right, but it struck me, I fall in love and immediately everyone thinks I'm unwell.

ROSIE: And Judith?

STANTON: Judith runs the house, guards the children, who guard her. They write witty encouraging notes to each other and leave them on the hall table. They are – waiting.

> (JUDITH'S VOICE *takes over.* STANTON's *finger traces the back of* ROSIE's *hand. But a distance is kept as all her female antennae are out.*)

JUDITH'S VOICE: (*Quietly, sadly*) Stanton. I'd like us to talk. Our friends tell me it happens to most men. Why is it, do you think, that wives can't be mistresses, or husbands be lovers? Is it bed? It can't *only* be that. A strong element, maybe, but not *only*. Am I keeping you awake? Do you want to sleep? I'm afraid I'm going to keep you awake for as long as I can every night until you go – talking, kissing, touching, remembering. You won't deny me that, will you, that I send you off as full of me as she sent you back full of her? I wish you hated me, I'd understand then, but I know you don't. How could you hate harmless, loving, wise, playful, faithful li'l ole me? So tell me. Why can't wives be mistresses?

ROSIE: And *did* you tell her?

STANTON: I don't want to talk about it.

ROSIE: Tell *me* then. Why can't wives be mistresses?

STANTON: Oh, I don't know. Wives can't be surprised. For a mistress everything's a surprise. You need to look in a woman's eyes and see that you're fresh, a delight for her, you need to catch her looking at you with expectation. Married couples make each other feel stale, predictable. In love – your nerve ends are charged.

ROSIE: Dammit, Stanton! I don't want to be your mistress. I want to be your wife!

(*The declaration disturbs him. He can't keep it out of his eyes. Nor does she miss it. She leaps up to the bathroom – an incredible female mess – and makes up.* STANTON *follows, leans against the door frame, watching, mesmerized. The ritual of contact lenses, spitting on make-up boxes, the order of creams, the different thicknesses of sticks of eye make-up, all fascinate him. She has a rhythm. It's compelling. After a while –*)

Stop watching. Makes me nervous.

STANTON: Let me. I love watching you.

(*She continues. But silence is not her territory.*)

ROSIE: My therapist says, 'Now, Rosie –'

STANTON: How can you afford a therapist? You've chickenfeed for alimony, you *sometimes* get social security, you *sometimes* get wages waitressing –

ROSIE: He's a nice guy. Likes me. He knows he'll get it sooner or later. So anyway he says, 'Now, Rosie,' he says, 'you do realize you're entering a classic situation, don't you?' 'Hell, Mr O'Conolly –' he's Irish –

STANTON: An *Irish* therapist? There are Irish therapists in New York?

ROSIE: Shut up and listen, will yer? 'Hell, Mr O'Conolly,' I say, 'not only am I entering into a classic situation I swore I'd never ever let myself get into, more! *I* was the one who was morally outraged when any of my friends got themselves involved with married men. "That's a disgusting thing to do," I'd tell them. Jesus! Look at me!'

STANTON: Can't take my eyes off you.

ROSIE: Not only is he married and got children but he's *happily* married. Or thinks he is, though I don't know how a man can be happily married and sleep around with a black woman.

STANTON: Are you black?

ROSIE: Well, it sure ain't Californian suntan.

(*He leans down to kiss her neck, lightly. She freezes with ecstasy. He*

*moves up, kiss by kiss, to her ear. When he moves to her cheek she
backs away.*)

You'll make me late for my swimming lesson, Stanton.

(*But he persists. They embrace.*)

God! But you're a creep, Stanton.

STANTON: Shithead, please.

ROSIE: Go understand an Englishman! Shithead!

Scene VII

A coffee shop.

ROSIE *is writing out cards fast, furiously, silently. They've quarrelled.*
STANTON *is appealing.*

STANTON: But the streets of New York are paved with gold and jet
and garnet and topaz and –

ROSIE: You don't look at other women when you're with me!

STANTON: (*Refusing to take it seriously*) Who can resist?

ROSIE: First you make me late for swimming, then you spend time
gawking at the other swimmers.

STANTON: (*Warningly*) Rosie –

ROSIE: Don't Rosie me.

STANTON: Rosie, I'm too old to be chastised.

ROSIE: You're too old to be philandering but you're philandering!

STANTON: (*Lecturer's sternness*) Don't play Lady Othello with me,
Rosie.

ROSIE: Push me and I'll play such a noble Lady Othello you won't
know what's strangling you.

STANTON: It's not just New York girls upsetting you, is it?

ROSIE: You know? Why ask! Now leave me be, I want to catch the
midday mail.

STANTON: Christmas cards! It's only the end of November. And so
many?

ROSIE: I like keeping in touch and I like receiving cards back.

STANTON: (*Trying to change the mood*) Don't let's play Othello,
Rosie. He was a fool. Shakespeare made a fool of the black man,
and a monster of the Jew. Play Kate and I'll be your Petruchio and
we'll roll in the hay and –

ROSIE: (*Dangerously*) '. . . if I stir, or do but lift this arm, the best of
you shall sink in my rebuke . . .' Take me seriously, Stanton. I
know *Othello* backwards. (*Offering him stamps*) Here. Lick these. Be
useful to me instead of an aggravation.

STANTON: (*Licking and sticking*) You may be able to quote the play but if
you think Othello was noble you don't *know* the play. It's Iago's play.

ROSIE: Not in my reading. Othello is a man who gives himself utterly.
Utterly to war, utterly to love, utterly to jealousy. Wouldn't catch
him cheating on Desdemona for a black chick.

STANTON: You want sober intellectual exchange or female back-stabbing?

ROSIE: You're right. Sorry. Ignore the second sentence. 'Othello was a man of passion.' Discuss.

STANTON: *What* passion? 'She lov'd me for the dangers I had pass'd, and I lov'd her that she did pity them.' He tells the sob story of his life as a slave who escapes to conquest and fortune, she sobs with pity, he's flattered by her pity, she sighs with admiration, he asks her for her hand, they marry. Where's the passion?

ROSIE: He braved the anger of her father and the Duke.

STANTON: He braved nothing! He sees her as something bought.

> '. . . come, my dear love,
> The purchase made, the fruits are to ensue,
> The profit's yet to come 'twixt me and you.'

'The *profit's* yet to come' not 'The *passion's* yet to come.'

ROSIE: That's a crude interpretation, Stanton. The passion is in his blood. His problem is he's got no language.

> 'Rude am I in my speech,
> And little blest with the set phrase of peace . . .'

He's a general, a man of action but he is endowed with a mighty magic, I tell you.

STANTON: And I tell you he's only endowed with a mighty prick. Iago has a halter round Othello's neck.

(He imitates Iago holding rope, and performs Iago and Othello, making Othello a 'stage' black.)

Iago   Here, boy, growl, be jealous!

Othello   I will chop her into messes .   .   . Cuckold me!

Iago   O, 'tis foul in her.

Othello   Wid mine officer!

Iago   That's fouler.

Othello   Get me some of de poison, Iago, dis night.

Iago   Do it not with poison, strangle her in her bed, even the bed she hath contaminated.

Othello   Good, good, de justice of it pleases; very good.

Iago snaps his fingers, Othello jumps.

ROSIE: That's sacrilegious! Sacrilegious and offensive!

STANTON: Sacrilegious, offensive, but very perceptive.

211

Scene VIII

Times Square. The 'same-day ticket-sales kiosk'.

ROSIE: Right! Here's the first landmark.

STANTON: Is this the best spot? I mean can enough people see us from here? How about out there? In the middle. We can be seen by the traffic going both ways then.

(ROSIE *grabs him. They kiss. Long and passionately to the hoots and honks of passing cars.*)

ROSIE: Thank you. Now, you wanna book for the theatre?

STANTON: Not really.

ROSIE: What the hell you mean, Stanton? Everyone goes to the theatre in New York.

STANTON: Except intelligent people.

ROSIE: I dare you to stand up on Broadway and say that.

STANTON: Here will do. (*Coughs.*) Er, good afternoon, ladies and gentlemen.

ROSIE: Oh no, Stanton, I wasn't serious.

STANTON: I'm a professor of American literature at London University and I've been asked to address you today on the demise of the Broadway theatre.

ROSIE: Christ almighty! These fucking Englishmen!

STANTON: I would put it to you, ladies and gentlemen of the New York theatre-going public, that when people enter the theatre they lower their intellectual and emotional expectations and accept a level of infantile relationships and utterances that no publisher of Bellow, Updike, Wharton, Roth, Ozick, Doctorow, Jong would contemplate for one moment offering a public. It is to the American novel that we must turn for any serious intellectual or emotional stimulation . . .

ROSIE: Stanton! Oh, Jesus Christ! Are you crazy? I've never felt so mortified. In my own city. How do you expect me to walk these streets again? You want to spend these next eleven days in gaol?

STANTON: I don't think I really mind where I have you as long as I have you.

ROSIE: Honey, we don't have mixed gaols here yet.

(STANTON *looks down the list of theatre tickets available.*)

STANTON: No Miller, no Williams, no O'Neill, no Albee, no Gelber, no Kopit – ha! *Othello*!

(*A mischievous grin spreads across his face. Then –*)

What? Twenty-five dollars each! *That's* half-price? Twenty-five bloody dollars each?

ROSIE: It's Broadway, honey.

STANTON: That's two days' pay. That's twenty breakfasts, half-a-dozen novels, fifteen films. No play can be worth that!

ROSIE: Buy!

Scene IX

Francesca's restaurant.
After the play. Waiting to be served.

STANTON: *Every*one in that play is a fool. 'A man he is of honesty and trust . . . honest Iago,' cries Othello. 'I never knew a Florentine more kind and honest,' cries Cassio. 'Good madam . . . I know it grieves my husband, as if the case were his,' cries Iago's wife. 'O, that's an honest fellow,' cries Desdemona. Iago has duped everybody! Villainy rings in every syllable of his speech and no one notices!

ROSIE: (*Gazing adoringly*) I could listen to you speaking English all day.

STANTON: And Othello, a general of men who cunningly sees through his opponents in war can't see through this transparent knave. Who can believe such a nincompoop capable of passion?

ROSIE: First of all there's no relationship between a power of perception and the possession of passion.

STANTON: (*Genuinely*) Oh, I like that. A very succinct formulation.

ROSIE: You want sober intellectual exchange or you want to trade put-downs?

STANTON: But I meant it! Kiss me!

ROSIE: Anyone ever tell you you were a shithead?

STANTON: No one's ever loved me enough!

ROSIE: (*Throwing screwed-up bread at him*) Shithead!

  (FRANCESCA, *the owner, approaches.*)

STANTON: Hello, Francesca. You probably don't remember me but about six months ago I was giving a series of lectures and I used to come here –

FRANCESCA: You don't have to remind me. You're the English professor of American literature. Right?

ROSIE: (*Impressed*) Right.

FRANCESCA: (*To* ROSIE) Who could forget a voice like that?

ROSIE: I keep telling him but he thinks it's just flattery.

STANTON: This is my friend, Rosie.

FRANCESCA: Nice to know you, Rosie. Welcome.

ROSIE: Lovely place you've got here.

214

FRANCESCA: We've got our friends, like this young man –

STANTON: Stanton, and no longer young, dammit!

FRANCESCA: Stanton-and-no-longer-young! He didn't forget us. And others don't.

STANTON: Can we think a little longer?

FRANCESCA: Sure. Take your time. The bouillabaisse is very good. And the veal in Mozzarella.

STANTON: But we *will* have some wine to be getting along with, please. (*To* ROSIE) White?

ROSIE: Depends what I eat.

STANTON: I see. It's going to be that kind of evening, is it?

FRANCESCA: The lady's right.

STANTON: Yes, but I was thinking of just a little starter – like a glass of cold Chablis.

ROSIE: (*Cantankerously*) Prefer red, myself.

STANTON: (*Alert to her changing mood*) I don't imagine that presents a problem. (*To* FRANCESCA) Do you sell wine by the glass?

FRANCESCA: No, but I've just opened a bottle of red for myself and I'd be happy to offer Daisy –

ROSIE: Rosie.

FRANCESCA: – Rosie, a glass of mine. And there's a nice half-bottle of Californian Pouilly Fuissé in the fridge.

STANTON: Splendid! I knew I'd come to the right restaurant.

    (FRANCESCA *leaves.*)

But have I brought the right guest?

ROSIE: What's that supposed to mean?

STANTON: You don't prefer red, you prefer white. I remember from last time.

ROSIE: Well, I've changed in six months, haven't I?

STANTON: No, you are as contrary as ever.

ROSIE: (*Sour, but glued to menu*) Zat so?

STANTON: (*Veering away*) You didn't finish telling me what *your* friends said.

ROSIE: (*Quick-tempered*) I'd like to concentrate on the menu, do you mind?

    (*He's hurt. Retreats.*)

I mean I'm a hungry girl, haven't eaten since before the show. You know me – I don't get to eat when I need I become neurotic. My therapist says it's rewards. I'm looking for rewards all the time. I tell him, 'Rewards for what? I spend most of my time feeling ashamed for doing nothing, why should I reward myself?' 'Precisely so, my dear child,' he says. 'The more you do nothing to earn rewards from society the more you feel the need to reward yourself!' Neat, huh? Now I can eat without guilts because I know *why* I eat. I feel guilty!

(STANTON *remains unamused. She becomes winningly tender.*)

Oh, honey, I'm sorry. But I'm getting vibes from you. You're ill at ease and that makes *me* ill at ease. We're gonna have to talk soon, cos I gotta know.

STANTON: No one has ever been so able to drain me of feeling one second and fill me the next.

ROSIE: Stella-Bella said to me when you left six months ago: 'Rosie, this is a one-off! They don't make repeats. This one *don't* let get away.'

(*They twist their hands round each other across the table. He opens her palm, kisses it, tongues it.*)

(*Rising*) Oh my God! Let's go!

STANTON: (*Bringing her down*) Each appetite in its place. Choose!

ROSIE: (*At him with deliberate ambiguity*) *I've* chosen.

Scene X

Rosie's apartment.

The lovers in bed. Passionate embraces. Candle flickering. Jane Oliver on the deck. Sound of a key in the front door.

STANTON: What's that?

ROSIE: My, you're jumpy. It's only Stella-Bella. Relax.

    (STELLA-BELLA *is trying to tiptoe quietly to her room.*)

STANTON: I'm not sure I can make love in the middle of a thorough-fare.

ROSIE: Stella-Bella? That you?

STELLA-BELLA: It's me, Rosie. It's me. Go back to sleep or however else you were passing the time away. Reading maybe.

STANTON: Not since my student days . . .

STELLA-BELLA: My student days were never like this. We had to be satisfied with backs of cars and the other girls moaning alongside.

ROSIE: Goodnight, Stella-Bella.

STELLA-BELLA: I didn't make it to a real bed till I was twenty-one.

ROSIE: Goodnight, Stella-Bella.

STELLA-BELLA: And I had to get married for that.

ROSIE: Goodnight, Stella-Bella.

    (STELLA-BELLA *kisses* STANTON *and leaves.*)

My first and last marriage. Divorced at twenty-two. I married a teenage mother-freak!

    (*The door slams.* ROSIE *returns her attention to* STANTON, *her hands exploring under the blankets.*)

STANTON: It's gone, I'm afraid. Took fright. Probably for ever.

    (ROSIE *makes a deep-throated, lascivious growl-cum-uhhh! and sinks under the bedclothes.*)

And I'll tell you something else. Othello's cruel. Ow! And a hypocrite. Ouch! And dishonest. Oweee!

    (ROSIE *emerges out from under the blankets.*)

ROSIE: Proof! Evidence!

STANTON: How about this, then. He doesn't kill his wife at once, no! He *announces* he's going to kill her, and then he lets her wait for thirty-three lines to be uttered before he moves in for the strangulation, at which point she begs to be allowed a prayer and he refuses!

First he lets her linger with the knowledge of her death and then he denies her soul its peace. Not cruel?

ROSIE: You're a pedant! You don't see the man's passion because you don't understand the nature of passion.

(*At which point she draws out a gun from under her pillow.*)

OK, buster, this is it.

(STANTON *is genuinely surprised.*)

STANTON: Rosie?

ROSIE: Stand!

STANTON: (*Braving it*) Me or him?

ROSIE: You know which one of you I'm talking to.

STANTON: Jesus, Rosie! At my age I'm only supposed to do it once in seven days, not seven times in one day.

ROSIE: Kiss me, then.

(*He does so.*)

That wasn't a kiss.

STANTON: Sorry.

(*She puts away the gun. Sits up in bed.*)

ROSIE: OK, let's talk. You've not been 100 per cent with me since you arrived. If you've made decisions I want to know what they are.

STANTON: Can I introduce you to the Bach *Magnificat* first?

ROSIE: No mood music. You're on your own.

(*Long pause.*)

STANTON: I've fretted and worried and lived through fantasies: me staying now, me coming back in a few months for good, you coming to London, both of us living partly here partly there, but – my feelings are not my priority. My children are. Them I adore above everyone.

ROSIE: Even more important than your whole future?

STANTON: Oh, infinitely. And from this, everything else flows.

ROSIE: (*Weeping*) I don't understand why you came back then?

STANTON: Selfishness?

(*She's not sure she can interpret that. He knows he mustn't console her. She struggles and succeeds to recover.*)

ROSIE: You're very gentle at least. I must tell you that. I don't feel kicked in the guts just – the fight's gone out of me. (*Pause.*) Your children won't respect you for your decision, you know. Thousands of case histories attest to it.

STANTON: And as many attest the reverse.

(*Pause.*)

ROSIE: (*Wearily*) So! Now I know what's been eating you. Good! I'd've hated you if you'd left it to the last day. This way I've got ten days to get over it while you're still here. (*Suddenly*) Damn you, Stanton! You've embarked me on an academic career which is probably out of my fuckin' reach and filled me full of discontent so I won't ever put up with second best now because now that I know what's possible you give me a choice of something or nothing and I'll choose nothing and you're gonna leave me!

(*They sit up side by side. She's deep in thought. He's watching her carefully to see which way she'll go.* JUDITH'S VOICE *creeps over them.*)

JUDITH'S VOICE: It'll be hard for you, Stanton, won't it? You listening or you asleep? It'll be hard. How will you be able to explain that we actually like and respect one another? She *will* think you odd. I mean *I* think you even love me. Poor Stanton, what a dilemma! You won't be able to say any of the traditional things like, 'My wife and I haven't slept together for three years.' Or, 'My wife doesn't understand me.' I mean, how will she be able to love a man who can't complain about his wife? And what about the family network and the friends you cherish and all our rituals of Sunday lunches, and Sunday teas, surprise birthday parties, and the musical Friday evenings? I mean, would she let a quintet of amateur musicians loose in her house playing obscure seventeenth-century music? Hard, Stanton, hard. I *wish* I could help.

ROSIE: Right! Ten days left? Boy! These are going to be ten days to remember. *I* shall remember them and *you* will never forget them! You will have pleasure and you will have pain, you will have heaven and you will have hell, and you will regret this decision for the rest of your fuckin' life.

STANTON: Rosie, that's not the most inviting tone for a ten-day love affair.

ROSIE: I didn't set it, you did. Now, on the last evening I want to have half-a-dozen of my best friends over for dinner to meet you. I promised them. (*Realizes.*) Oh Jesus! (*Despair*) What am I gonna tell them!

STANTON: (*Picking up*) And I'll cook.

ROSIE: You *cook*?

STANTON: Almost cordon bleu.

ROSIE: Oh holy mother of Christ! I'm losing him and he cooks as well! Would you believe my luck!

STANTON: We've got our landmarks to cover, and I want to play you one game of chess in Washington Square and eat one of our desserts at Serendipity, and go to just one concert –

ROSIE: – and I want us to go discoing and to a porno movie.

STANTON: A *porno* movie?

ROSIE: I've never been to one and I want to experience it with you. Now, be still and let me read some Emerson to you. (*Reaches for a book.*) I know just the one.

STANTON: I bet I know which one it'll be.

ROSIE: Which one, smart arse?

STANTON: 'Give all to love.'

ROSIE: You're too clever for me. Here (*gives him book*) you read it to me then.

STANTON: (*Reading*) Give all to love;

Obey thy heart;

Friends, kindred, days,

Estate, good-fame,

Plans, credit and the Muse –

Nothing refuse.

(ROSIE *begins kissing his body as he reads.*)

'Tis a brave master,

Let it have scope:

Follow it utterly,

Hope beyond hope:

High and more high . . .

(*Her embraces are too much. He snaps book shut, stretches, moans . . .*)

Scene XI

Rosie's apartment.
    STANTON *is making the meal, moving in and out of the kitchen.* ROSIE
is ironing. They're in the middle of a heated discussion.

STANTON: Let us formulate the question simply. Is *Othello* a play
    about Othello's jealousy or about Iago's villainy and Othello's poor
    powers of judgement?
ROSIE: Othello's jealousy.
STANTON: But they don't even have a love scene.
ROSIE: If it were now to die,
    'Twere now to be most happy, for I fear
    My soul hath her content so absolute,
    That not another comfort, like to this
    Succeeds in unknown fate . . .
                            . . . it is too much of joy.
    Did *you* ever say such things to me, creep?
STANTON: Shithead, please.
ROSIE: Shithead.
STANTON: A dozen lines of love and that's all.
ROSIE: Compose me *one* such line and I'm yours whatever you or your
    wife may say, shithead.
STANTON: Oh, that name!
                            If it were now to die,
    'Twere now to be most happy . . .
ROSIE: (*Throwing things at him*) Shithead! Shithead! Shithead!
    (ROSIE's *reactions are complex. Each time the pleasurable adrenalin
    from intellectual skirmishes flows in her she is reminded that one day
    soon they will end.* STANTON *will be gone. Which changes her mood.
    She becomes mean.*)
Well, I must say you disappoint me. I've seen your dilemma a
dozen times. Husband hangs on, wife despises him, kids fucked
up.
STANTON: Rosie, don't. You're being textbook again.
ROSIE: Stop putting me down. These are not textbook notions,
    they're *my* observations.
STANTON: They may be your *experiences* but they're not really

observations. To be an observer you must expose yourself to a *wide* range of experiences which –

ROSIE: Oh, you and your fuckin' distinctions.

STANTON: Very useful, distinctions. They prevent the successful from imagining they're eminent, and the eminent from imagining they're omnipotent.

ROSIE: You *don't* take me seriously.

STANTON: I do, Rosie, I do, believe me. But it hurts to hear you trotting out simplistic explanations of complex problems. In my house is love and warmth and comradeship and much joy. *That* is the problem. Grapple with that.

(*It is a problem. One she knows she can't overcome. She becomes cold. He approaches to touch and console her.*)

ROSIE: (*Viciously*) Get your hands off me, mister.

STANTON: Rosie.

ROSIE: I'm so angry. I'm so murderously angry to be at the end of your mistake.

STANTON: I could get a flight back tomorrow?

ROSIE: Please your fuckin' self.

(*He moves back to the kitchen. She weeps. Then –*)

Stanton! Where the hell are you? You come back here and stop leaving me everytime I scold you.

(*He returns. They embrace. She takes up ironing. He brings in a plate of goodies. Offers her a pickled pepper.*)

STANTON: Taste.

(*She bites. He bites. He offers her a small meatball.*)

Taste.

(*She bites. He bites. He offers her a forkful of cold creamed potatoes with onions.*)

Taste.

(*She sucks. He takes the remainder.*)

ROSIE: This the way you gonna feed me all evening?

STANTON: This evening I'm going to serve you and fuss over you like you've never been served and fussed over before.

ROSIE: To make sure I *really* suffer when you go.

STANTON: You've given *me* what to suffer for.

(*He offers her a pickled cucumber, she reaches for it but he pulls it away.*)

When will be the right time for the Bach *Magnificat*?

ROSIE: You'll know.

STANTON: Taste.

(*She bites. He bites. She returns to ironing. He returns to preparing the meal.*)

ROSIE: Food! My therapist is right. I'm a pig!

STANTON: Your therapist calls you a pig?

ROSIE: He says I've got an eating problem but he means 'pig'. I'll be all right when we're married. You *are* gonna marry me, aren't you? You're not? Why Mr Stanton Myers, I do declare, you're making the biggest mistake of your lifetime. You won't find anyone to wait for you, cook for you, care for you, suffer, forgive and adore you as I would. To say nothin' of the fuckin'!

STANTON: Rosie, we wouldn't last six months together.

ROSIE: Zat so, Mr Stanton, suh? Why I thought a thing of beauty was a joy fah iver.

STANTON: Things, perhaps. People not.

ROSIE: Mr Stanton! You're a cynic!

STANTON: Rosie, can we lay Scarlett O'Hara to rest? Tell me what your Ph.D. thesis will be?

ROSIE: Passion! Men are driven by passions. Makes them irrational. The conduct of political affairs is perverted by irrational men. That'll be my thesis. Surprises you, huh? Coming from a woman who's driven by passions which make her behave irrationally?

(*What follows is calculated to inflame him sexually and impress him intellectually. At the same time. That he may be fully aware of what he is surrendering. She undresses and then dresses in bra, panties, suspenders, stockings and a see-through dress. She does it all casually, far more interested in what she's saying. But in fact it is a stripshow. He is mesmerized.*)

You take protest. Nothing wrong with protest. Sign of a healthy society. What goes wrong? I'll tell you what goes wrong. People! They fuck it up. Start off wanting more democratic rights, end up wanting to overthrow democratic institutions.

You take commerce. People rage against capitalism. Nothing wrong with trading. Healthy instinct. What goes wrong? I'll tell you what goes wrong. People! They fuck it up. Get greedy. Produce cheap goods. Form totalitarian monopolies which become a law unto themselves.

You take politics. Nothing wrong with politics. It's the art of government. We have to be governed. Since Adam! So what goes wrong? I'll tell you what goes wrong. People! They become politicians, fuck up politics. Ambitious! Dishonest! Opportunist!

You take religion. Nothing wrong with wanting to believe in a God. Jesus! Buddha! Muhammad! They're all saying the same thing – be good, love one another, look after the kids! So what goes wrong? I'll tell you what goes wrong. People! They become fanatics. Scream at one another. 'I'm holier than thou and all must be as holy as me!'

You take the study of art. Nothing wrong with that. You can't make the insensitive sensitive but a little bit of analysis here or history there helps! So, what goes wrong? I'll tell you what goes wrong. People! They become critics, professors, journalists – get on ego-trips. Fuck it up! Suddenly everyone's discussing the merits of critics rather than the artist they're supposed to be criticizing. Crazy!

You take science. 'Science will blow up the world! Pollute the earth!' Bullshit! You wanna attack Newton, Galileo, Benjamin Franklin? Science gave me my contact lenses and saved Mark dying of diphtheria. So, what goes wrong? I'll tell you what goes wrong. People! Along come the crooked industrialists, the dishonest politicians and the righteous fanatics, and *they* fuck up science.

(*She's finished and beams her full power upon* STANTON *who is sagging.*)

Guess I tired you out, huh? And we haven't even started *tonight's* studies, honey.

(*She nibbles his ear. Tongues it.*)

STANTON: Rosie, I don't think I'm going to make it tonight, Rosie . . .

ROSIE: You're not *what*? Are you talking to *me*? Are you saying I can't rouse your banner high?

(*His neck.*)

Are you saying there's no arrow for my bull's-eye?

(*His chest.*)

Are you suggesting I can't make your fella meet my requirements?

Because I do have requirements, you know. I'm not just a house-wife or a brilliant intellect. You're sleeping with a creature. A ker—reecha!

(*She bites his nipple and slides her hand down to his crotch.*)

Uh-huh! And what have we here? You only use this thing for stirring yaw tea, honey? You don't think I can fall asleep with this piercing my back all night, do you? It has to be attended to and tamed and I'm just the kiddy to do it.

(*She pulls him down to the cushions.*)

I mean you take sex. There's nothing wrong with s—

(STANTON *claps his hand over her mouth and plants upon her lips a wild kiss. Poor, tormented* STANTON . . .)

Scene XII

Rosie's apartment.

Next morning. Still dark. Hint of dawn. They're in bed. ROSIE *is trying to sleep.* STANTON, *roused, is now going to prove insatiable.*

ROSIE: Oh no. It's awake. Stanton, how can I be beautiful for you if you don't let me get my beauty sleep? (*Pause.*) You're an animal, you know that? (*Pause.*) Is this a dagger which I feel behind me?

STANTON: Now could I do such things . . .

ROSIE: Stanton, can I tell you what time it is?

STANTON: What matter the hour, the day, the time, the place . . .

ROSIE: (*Curling up to sleep again*) Well, if you're just gonna be literary about it . . .

STANTON: (*Nibbling her between lines*) Pray do not mock me.

I am a very foolish fond old man,

Fourscore and upward, not an hour more or less;

And, to deal plainly,

I fear I am not in my perfect mind.

ROSIE: Stanton, could me and King Lear get another hour's sleep? We've a swimming lesson this morning. I'll drown.

(*Movement in bed.*)

Jesus! Stanton! You're an animal, you know that? I think you're a brute, an animal and a sex-fiend. (*Beat.*) And I want you to know I appreciate it. Yes. Oh my God, yes, yes, yes, yes! Oh my golly God, Stanton, what the hell are you doing to me? No one's ever – I mean how – I mean, yes, yes, yes! Jesus Christ, Stanton, it's eight thirty in the morning, I've just seen my kid off to school, I haven't read the papers yet, and I'm coming, I'm coming, I'm – aaaaaaaah!

(*Orgasm.*)

Scene XIII

Rosie's apartment.

Bright morning. ROSIE *in a dressing gown, glasses, reading a newspaper by the breakfast table.* STANTON *opposite her, also in a dressing gown. He has a strange look in his eyes. He's slowly slipping off his chair and under the table as though drugged. A low hung cloth hides him.* ROSIE *lowers her paper.*

ROSIE: Stanton, where are you going, Stanton?

（*She realizes where he's going.*）

Stanton, are you crazy? Stella-Bella could come through at any moment. Get up from there.

（*But he doesn't. Something is happening. She smiles. Is aghast. Shocked. Delighted.*）

Stanton, I think you're disgusting. I don't think you're English at all. Stanton, don't *do* that –

（*But she positions herself to make it easier.*）

– we've just had breakfast, Stanton, my milk will curdle. What's got into you this morning, you're possessed? I mean – Oh my God! Again! Stanton, you keep doing this and I'll turn grey. Oh, oh, oh, my Lord. Oh, I don't believe this is happening. I just don't believe this – yes, yes, yes! There! Oh yes, there, there! Oh lordee – here I come again, before I've had a chance to read the gossip column I'm comin', comin', comin' . . . aaaaaaaah!

（*Orgasm.* ROSIE *flops over the table. Stillness. Then – from somewhere beneath the table there reaches up to us the defiant – if unskilled – mating call of a Tarzan. Of sorts!*）

Scene XIV

Rosie's apartment.

Some minutes later. ROSIE *in the bathroom making up.* STANTON, *still in his dressing gown, still zombie-like, approaches. Takes her arm and pulls her to the wall against which he places her. She regards him as though he were a madman. Feigns terror.*

ROSIE: Ahhh! It's him! The sex-crazed Hebrew from outer space. Stanton, give a girl a break, will ya?

(*To no avail. She's wrenched up and clasped in his arms. The brute!*)

Stanton, I've just made up and make-up's expensive and – don't look at me that way. I mean – would you believe this? I mean is this happening?

(*He's covering her with kisses, slowly slithering down her body.*)

Stanton, you're beginning to worry me. I mean, one or other of us is gonna have a heart attack and as I've got fourteen years on you guess which one it's gonna be! And, Stanton, may I remind you your lecture's tomorrow and there's folk expecting serious thoughts on American literature from you.

(*His head is now inside and covered by her dressing gown, in the region below her belly.*)

Stanton, you're a psychotic! You know that? An Anglo-Saxon psychotic. I don't believe I'm in the same world as this occurrence, I just don't. Ah! Ah! Aaaaaaaah!

(*Over which moan we hear the glorious opening Magnificat section of the C. P. E. Bach Magnificat. And blackout.*)

ACT TWO

Scene I

C.P.E. *Bach Magnificat.*
  Scenes of New York. ROSIE *and* STANTON *kissing at each landmark.*
  Guggenheim Museum.
  Macy's.
  Twin Towers.
  And less familiar landmarks:
  Bridal Path Arch, Central Park.
  Flat Iron Building.
  167–169 West 23rd Street.
  Grace's Church in the Village.
  Finally –

Scene II

Francesca's restaurant.

ROSIE *and* STANTON *waiting for their meal. They seem unable to stop touching one another – face, hands, palms, in and out of each other's fingers. He is besotted.*

ROSIE: Promise me something?

STANTON: Anything.

ROSIE: Promise me you won't be too proud to come back if you change your mind.

STANTON: Promise.

ROSIE: Cross your heart.

STANTON: Who, me?

ROSIE: Well, he *was* Jewish, dammit.

STANTON: (*Loving her humour*) Ah, Rosie. I'm creating such needs in myself now.

(FRANCESCA *arrives with champagne and pours.*)

ROSIE: We didn't order champagne, Francesca.

STANTON: Yes, we did.

ROSIE: Stanton, Jesus, you're so extravagant. You won't have enough left to keep me in the style you're accustoming me to. I mean he doesn't think I'm breaking open my kid's money box for him, does he?

FRANCESCA: Lovers, lovers, lovers! I love lovers.

ROSIE: Christ! Another crazy romantic.

FRANCESCA: Some people hate them, you know. Nothing drives them madder than to see two people kissing. Love's an affront. You ever thought about that? Love's an emotion so charged and pure that it can attract a pure and charged hatred. That's why I don't think lovers should love in public. Some people have murder in their eyes when they see lovers but somewhere out there is a person so disappointed with their life, so full of self-contempt, they're going to be carrying murder in their pocket. A gun to blow away lips that were blowing kisses. (*Imitates a gun.*) Pyeach! Pyeach! 'Put that tongue back in your mouth, lover!' Pyeach! Pyeach! 'Put them arms down by your sides, lover!' Pyeach! Pyeach! 'Wipe that shine from your eyes, lover! Who gave you the right to be happy when I'm not?' Pyeach! Pyeach! So drink up, lovers. Here you can hold hands, gaze at each other, touch and blow kisses. You're safe. Drink!

(*But nowhere is safe from each other.*)

ROSIE: I'd break open my kid's money box for a man who was staying *by* me, but for a deserter? Yuk! Cheers!

STANTON: Cheers!

(*Her mood, imperceptibly, has changed.* FRANCESCA's *speech has reminded her what she's losing.* STANTON *doesn't see it for a while.*)

ROSIE: You buy your wife champagne like this?

STANTON: You really want to know?

ROSIE: Why not? What've I got to lose? Tell me. She beautiful? She educated? A raving beauty and a dazzling intellect? Does she like your friends? Are they your friends or her friends? Did you meet her in university?

STANTON: (*Now sensing the wind*) Which question first?

ROSIE: You got a *lot* of friends?

STANTON: No, a small circle of friends but a wide circle of acquaintances. It's an open, busy house; large, Jewish family; colleagues staying from abroad; kitchen full of the children's friends; phone ringing constantly; steady flow of invitations to lecture in foreign parts . . .

ROSIE: You're famous, huh?

STANTON: No, obliging.

ROSIE: So?

STANTON: So what?

ROSIE: Tell me. She beautiful?

STANTON: Rosie, don't.

ROSIE: I'd never run my household the way she runs yours – all that entertaining. Not so often and not so many. And no one, but *no* one except a special few would ever stay! Jesus! Cleaning up after house guests. Not this lady. *Your* lady may be a good little house-lady but not this little lady.

STANTON: Rosie, you're misjudging the mood.

ROSIE: (*Snapping*) I can take care of myself! (*Pause.*) Tell me. I got a right to know who I'm giving you up to.

STANTON: I'm not sure she'd see it quite like that.

ROSIE: Oh, fuck how she'd see it. This is my party.

(*He's beginning to be chilled by her crudeness over* JUDITH.)

STANTON: We're on dangerous ground, Rosie. (*Lowers his voice. 'Other guests' are sitting close by.*) Especially here.

ROSIE: (*Loud*) Oh, shucks, Stanton, I got a right.

STANTON: (*Firmly, in low tones, hoping to still her*) She is a very extraordinary person who grows luminous under threat. In our circle she's an anchor. People don't tell her she's beautiful, they tell her she's radiant. Once a friend said to her, 'Everyone leaves your house happier.' There. You asked. And you better know, Rosie, any tantrum you can manufacture I can match.

(FRANCESCA *comes with one bowl of chowder soup. As they spoon – the fun gone now from the idea of spooning together – we hear* JUDITH'S VOICE.)

JUDITH'S VOICE: Stanton, you won't talk to her about me, will you? She'll want to know, but don't. Not only because I don't want you to but because she'll hate you for it. It'll spoil your holiday. Oh, I'm sorry. It's not a holiday, is it? It's a business trip. To discover if you're in love. Don't pretend you're asleep by snoring, Stanton. You never snore. I warned you I'd keep you awake one way or another. If *I* can't sleep why should *you*? Don't tell her about our family, our friends, our children. She won't really understand such a set-up, or even want to know. It'll lead to such wretched moments, my darling . . . believe me . . .

(*By which time they've come to the end of the soup.*)

STANTON: Want the dregs?

ROSIE: They're yours.

STANTON: You can sip them out, like a cup?

(*She declines. He lifts the bowl to his lips.*)

ROSIE: Even on you that looks grotesque.

STANTON: You don't mean 'grotesque' you mean 'gross'.

ROSIE: (*Viciously*) *Don't* correct me!

STANTON: Reflex. It's my job to know about words.

ROSIE: Fucking professors.

STANTON: Words are my passion. I make distinctions for my children, and –

ROSIE: Well, I'm not one of your fuckin' children.

STANTON: (*Anxious about neighbours*) Rosie, hush.

ROSIE: And don't hush me, either! I'm not one of your fucking anything!

STANTON: Rosie, I may be young at heart but I'm too old for petulance and infantile scenes in public which I hate, just hate. My parents quarrelled in public and public quarrelling mortifies me.

ROSIE: Well, ain't that a shame now!

(*At which she rises, looking for the loo.*)

(*Gruffly*) Where is it?

(*He nods a direction. She leaves. Though he tries to maintain a cool, controlled stance the scene has unnerved him. Is this confirmation that their relationship could never work?* FRANCESCA *brings the main course. She registers his glum face.*)

FRANCESCA: I never promised you a rose garden.

(*No response.*)

Here, take our matches and write something nice on the flap so it's here when she gets back.

STANTON: Like what?

FRANCESCA: Oh, I don't know. How about 'I love you'?

(*No response.*)

Someone has to say it.

(*She leaves. He writes and places it on top of her chicken.* ROSIE *returns. Glares at the propped-up matchbook. Ungraciously flings it aside.*)

ROSIE: You stuck that thing right in my sauce, you idiot.

STANTON: (*With dignity*) Rosie, I don't enjoy *anyone* speaking to me rudely.

ROSIE: (*Ignoring that*) If you love me why are you such a fuck?

STANTON: OK. Let's call a halt, shall we?

(*She attacks her food but knows she's gone too far.*)

ROSIE: Do you realize you never apologize?

STANTON: Because it's always you who starts a quarrel.

ROSIE: That's just not possible, Stanton. It takes two to make a fight, it always takes two.

STANTON: No. It takes two to become *involved* in a fight, but only one is needed to *cause* it.

ROSIE: And what about the conflict between the German people and Hitler which led to the extermination of the Jews?

(STANTON *is shocked by this non sequitur. It's not the level on which he's used to conducting exchanges.*)

STANTON: Rosie, what on earth are you talking about? That doesn't make sense.

ROSIE: Don't say that!

STANTON: And how can you trivialize a monstrous event like the Holocaust by comparing it to our petty squabble?

ROSIE: (*Relentless, indifferent to his arguments*) Because everyone knows the German Jews deluded themselves that it couldn't happen to them.

STANTON: (*Wanting to end it*) OK. I accept that point. I too believed this quarrel couldn't happen to me, and for that reason I'm guilty and contributed to it.

(*He retrieves the matchbook to tear it up.* ROSIE *had actually planned to keep it.*)

ROSIE: (*Pleading*) Don't do that, don't tear it up, Stanton.

STANTON: (*Continuing*) That's my mistake, to have stood in line as victim.

(*He rips as* ROSIE *cries out, 'No! No!'*)

I should not have been there! Now, change the subject.

(*Neither can finish the meal.*)

ROSIE: You were so quick to tear that up.

STANTON: Not true. It was lying around for many minutes. My kind of apology. You rejected it.

(*Silence. She weeps.*)

ROSIE: (*Pathetically*) You have no respect for me, for my opinions, my education, nothing –

(*But do they both know that was their watershed?*)

Scene III

Rosie's apartment.

Later that evening. Jane Oliver on the turntable. They lie on cushions, ROSIE *in* STANTON'S *arms. She's been crying.*

ROSIE: I feel so mediocre. So washed up and mediocre. Huh! University! Me! That's quixotic for you. (*Pause.*) Shut up being silent, Stanton. It's a sign of superiority, it gets on my nerves, and it isn't helping.

(*He extends a hand.*)

Oh, I don't want your fuckin' hand, I want your fuckin' being. All or nothing, me.

(*At which she lifts up his arm and crawls into him.*)

I've blown it, haven't I?

(*He makes no response.*)

What am I gonna do? Jesus Christ, what am I gonna do?

(*She plies his chest with kisses, reaches his lips, urgently. He responds, till – Slam! The front door!* STELLA-BELLA *has entered, pushing a young, embarrassed, virginal and terrified* MAN *ahead of her.*)

STELLA-BELLA: OK. Easy now. You didn't hear me. My hands are full of groceries and I'm a little drunk on account of this fella who's kindly helped me up the lift. (*Whispering to him*) In there! In there! No, not that door, shmuck, I don't sleep in the bath! (*Back to them*) So if I've woken you up forgive me; if I've interrupted your conversation that's not, believe me, the end of the world; if I've fucked up your relationship deduct it from my rent. No! That didn't make sense. I pay *you* rent. (*To* MAN) Hey, shmuck! Jesus Christ, I wish I could remember his name. Hey, I'm in distress, close the door!

(*Her bedroom door slams.* ROSIE *and* STANTON *lie back. Tension eased.*)

STANTON: Which French philosopher was it, do you think, who said: 'Life is like a cucumber; one minute it's in your hand, the next it's up your arse!'?

(*She smiles, snuggles into him. They are happy just to be in each other's arms.*)

ROSIE: OK. Here's what we do. You want to shop for records for your kids? We'll do that in the morning. Lunch and kiss in a little Italian place I wanna show you. Whitney Art Gallery in the afternoon for postcards and more kisses, and then we'll think of some place extraordinary for dinner. Wadja think?

STANTON: Whatever you say, sweetheart.

ROSIE: He called me 'sweetheart'! Oh! I'll die! Call me that again, quick.

STANTON: Call you 'what' again, sweetheart? 'Sweetheart'? I prefer 'Rosie'. You can variate a name like Rosie. My Rose, my rose-bud, my rosy-lipped, my rosaline, my rosamunda, my rose of thorns, my rosanna. I can sing 'rosannas' to a Rosie.

ROSIE: (*Kissing him*) Oh, those lips. What am I gonna do, what am I gonna *do*?

STANTON: Continue plotting.

ROSIE: Right! Tomorrow night's the night!

STANTON: The night?

ROSIE: Porno-movie night! At last! Someone I can trust to go with. After which – discoing!

STANTON: (*Mock serious*) Are you absolutely certain you want to go through with this?

ROSIE: (*Gazing at him*) Your lips will be the death of me.

STANTON: I need a drink.

> (STANTON, *trying always to control the temperature, frees himself and goes to the kitchen. Light from fridge. Sound of pouring. Silence. Sound of running water.* ROSIE *can't understand what's happening. Gets up to investigate.*)

ROSIE: (*From the lounge*) What the hell you doing, Stanton?

STANTON: (*From the kitchen*) Cleaning the tiles in your kitchen. They were filthy. (*Returns to lounge.*) If I leave you nothing else I'll leave you a clean kitchen and a Hoovered flat. And your records! Didn't anyone ever teach you how to look after records? You hold the edges, don't touch the surface with your fingers and always always always put them back in their sleeves. You've unobtainable Morgana Kings lying around being scratched to pieces by Johnny Mathis. Those are artists and you're ruining their life's work! And –

> (ROSIE *flares up. Snatches record from him.*)

ROSIE: You don't like my flat you can clear out. And you leave my kitchen be. I'll clean it when I'm ready, when I don't have to have a flatmate, when I've got the time, when I've got the money and the peace of mind and someone to look at it – and – no! (*Returns the record.*) No! Take it back! Clean them! Everything! Touch everything of mine. I love you looking after me. I want your presence in every corner – oh –

(*She weeps. He takes her in his arms.*)

What am I going to do? What, what, what am I going to do?

STANTON: (*Taking control of her*) It's the dinner party in two days' time, so we have to do the shopping for it tomorrow. Mustn't leave things till the last moment.

(*He pulls her down to the cushions, gently plies her with kisses while he recites:*)

Organization! The secret of cooking is organization. Wash up immediately you've finished with a utensil. Lay all your ingredients out before you prepare. Boil water while you slice onions. Season and soak your meat while the onions fry. Mix your fillings in the morning. Prepare your pastry the day before. And remember, don't go shopping at six for a meal to which you've invited friends for seven thirty. Now, where shall we shop?

Scene IV

Zabar's deli. But unlit yet.
   ROSIE *is leading* STANTON *in with his eyes closed.*

ROSIE: OK. Now keep your eyes closed. Imagine you're blind. I'll lead you so you won't fall. You know you can trust me. I wouldn't let one tiny thing hurt that person of yours. Every limb, every tiny limb and drop of blood is precious to me. OK. Now! Open!

   (STANTON *opens his eyes as though he were in wonderland. Lights full up. Copper utensils hanging, salamis, jars, boxes, tins, a vast variety of breads, deli-dishes, cakes – a fantastic deli alive with shapes, colours, food – a riot of Jewish/Italian New York.*)

STANTON: Rosie! Oh, Rosie!

ROSIE: Like it, huh? Isn't this something? Now here I *have* to be careful. Here's where I get orgasms which my therapist says are more dangerous. Look at that bread. You seen a bread like that before? I mean, don't you just want to go berserk? First there's the goodies I want to eat here and now, on the spot. Then there's the goodies I want to take home with me. Then there's the goodies I want to buy for this one, and that one, and the other one. And before I know it I've blown my week's wages. Have you ever observed the relationship between food and sex? I mean you take food –

STANTON: Rosie! This is driving me mad. I've got to taste something – salami, cheese, a pickle, something!

   (ROSIE *is delighted with his delight, and draws him to the cheese counter behind which is an* ASSISTANT.)

ROSIE: Come. (*To* ASSISTANT) OK now, my friend from England here is made speechless by your shop. He can't talk until a morsel of your most exceptional cheese passes his lips. What's your suggestion?

   (*The grinning female* ASSISTANT *cuts with a huge knife.*)

ASSISTANT: He from England? I got a cousin lives in England. Here. Try this.

   (STANTON *takes, tastes.* ASSISTANT *gives a second piece to* ROSIE.)

A little-known cheese from southern Italy.

ROSIE: (*Savouring*) Oh, my God. That's bliss. Now *that* – is bliss. Stanton?

STANTON: I'm overwhelmed. Let's go. You attack the breads and cakes, the salamis and the cheese. I'll go for the cuts of meat, the deli-stuff and the fruit. Agreed?

(STANTON *rushes off.* ROSIE *can see the* ASSISTANT *is impressed.*)

ROSIE: Special, huh?

ASSISTANT: Special is not the word. He's not afraid of women! In New York that's more than special. It's unnatural. Where d'you find yourself such a present?

ROSIE: He likes American literature. What can I tell you!

ASSISTANT: You bewilder me. Explain.

ROSIE: Take too long.

(STANTON *reappears with a bottle of champagne and three glasses.*)
Jesus, Stanton, it's the middle of the day. This is decadence.

(*He pours for them.*)

ASSISTANT: You crazy? You want me to lose my job?

STANTON: We are given but one life to live. Take risks! Lechayim!

(*They drink.*)

ROSIE: I love you, cuckoo. You take my breath away and give me palpitations. And I swear to you, *no* one's ever done that. (*Raising glass*) May you always be unpredictable.

STANTON: And may you always be as loved.

ASSISTANT: And may I always have such dangerous customers.

(*They drink.* STANTON *wanders off, swigging from the bottle.*)
Funny people, the English. Noble but poor. Poor, you know what I mean? Not many cars and no baths in the houses. But they speak the language. You gotta give them that, they speak the language like they invented it.

Scene V

The porno-movie house.

Two seats facing us, ROSIE *and* STANTON *with popcorn. They're giggly and embarrassed like naughty kids. They're waiting for the show to begin.*

ROSIE: I think they've opened it just for us, honey.

STANTON: This is going to be very tatty and corny, you do realize?

ROSIE: Not for me. Not the first time. All first times are an experience.

STANTON: If only the movie houses weren't so seedy I wouldn't feel so guilty.

ROSIE: Watcha feeling guilty about? You're with your mummy. (*Pause.*) How's ma fella?

STANTON: (*Looking around*) Which one?

ROSIE: Creep! There's only one fella in my life.
(*She glances down.*)

STANTON: Rosie, can we make a deal? No touching in this film.

ROSIE: Not even holding hands?

STANTON: Not even –
(*Lights go down.* ROSIE *throws popcorn into her mouth with greater speed.*)

ROSIE: Sssh! Here we go.

STANTON: Look at that! Even in porno movies the makers are Jewish!

ROSIE: And we'll soon see if the actors are!
(*The film begins. To accompany the flickering comes the heaving and puffing of cheap passion, exaggerated, like the smell of cheap scent.* ROSIE *and* STANTON *freeze. They can't believe what they're seeing. Incredulity, gasps, bewilderment. Some scenes are so dark they even lean forward trying to understand what's taking place. Hilarious! Then –*)

Scene VI

– Disco music!

The disco. Dark. Mirrored walls. Cushioned areas. Constantly moving lights. The music is loud but the best of its kind. Impossible not to feel young to it.

STANTON *and* ROSIE *are on the floor. She moves beautifully of course. And he, surprisingly, moves imaginatively and energetically. That, in fact, is his fault. He's too energetic – not absurd but exaggerated. Both are high with pleasure. As a number is changing, she stops.*

ROSIE: Here!

STANTON: Of course here.

(*They embrace and sway. Till –*)

ROSIE: OK now, honey. You're a great mover, I mean it. You're Jewish and English, you've got everything against you but you're doing fine, just fine. Only a few tips. There's more than one beat in disco. You hear this one? It's fast, yes? You dance to that and they'll carry you out. But you hear the slow beat? (*Moves to it.*) It's subtler. Easy, easy. And move more from the hips. Keep the top straight. You bend and fly too much. On a full floor you could knock someone out the way you move.

(*He succeeds in following her subtler movements. He has a sense of rhythm. They move as one. He's thrilled, takes balletic risks, twists and swirls. She's just bursting with joy at his pleasure. The music changes now to a more dynamic beat and they really go! Neither can sustain the pace though. They collapse on to the huge cushions, exhausted, panting.*)

STANTON: My heart. Feel it. (*Takes her hand to it.*) Not worked like that in years. All that cholesterol – racing away.

ROSIE: Oh, honey. That's unbelievable. No heart should pump like that.

STANTON: Rosie, Rosie, Rosie! How can I go back to normal living after this?

ROSIE: Stay with me, then, Stanton, stay. I'd do such things for you. Such marvellous and wonderful things.

STANTON: Do you know what it's like moving your body the right

241

way for the first time? I soared, Rosie, soared! I haven't soared like that since I won a race at school.

ROSIE: Stay, Stanton, stay!

STANTON: The body! Jesus! Why haven't I used it more? Why haven't I swam and walked and danced more? Everyone should dance, Rosie. Taught at school, compulsory, properly, with imagination, grace, dynamic – Oh! My heart!

ROSIE: Stay, Stanton, stay with me.

STANTON: It won't stop. It races on.

ROSIE: Your heart's not pumping from the dancing, Stanton, it's pumping from love.

STANTON: I think I'm going to have an attack.

(*He crashes back.* ROSIE *drops to him, kissing him, kissing.*)

ROSIE: Stay, Stanton, stay. You'll never find anyone to adore you like I do. Every part of me is alive, all systems are go. Stay, Stanton, stay.

STANTON: Don't tempt me, Rosie. I'm in a weak state. Don't be cruel.

ROSIE: Stay! Stay!

STANTON: I have this overwhelming desire to become a different person, change my skin, to disappear from everyone I know, everything I am, everything I feel.

ROSIE: Stay! Stay!

STANTON: I'm tired of myself, Rosie, so tired of my thoughts, my habits, what's expected of me.

ROSIE: Stay, honey, stay!

STANTON: Every time I catch up with myself I'm not there anyway.

ROSIE: Stay! Marry me, and stay!

STANTON: Tonight I want to say 'yes'. But on the plane over I said to myself – when I'm sixty she'll be forty-six.

ROSIE: (*Frantic*) What do I care, what do I *care*! I want you, your children *and* your old age.

STANTON: Let's dance.

ROSIE: (*Rolling away*) Oh, what will I do, what will I *do*?

Scene VII

Outside Sardi's restaurant.

Next day. They've been shopping. They're tired. They've set down bags. Subdued, too.

STANTON: Here?

ROSIE: (*Unenthusiastically*) Yeah! Why not! Fill the entire fuckin' city with places I won't be able to visit again.

(*He tries in this embrace to console her. She's inconsolable and breaks away, frustrated rather than angry. A* WOMAN *is about to enter Sardi's.*)

STANTON: (*Stopping her*) Excuse me, Miss Minelli, can I have your autograph, please?

ROSIE: Jesus Christ! I've brought a nut into the country.

WOMAN: Minelli??!!!

ROSIE: (*To* WOMAN) He's not mine, lady.

(*The* WOMAN *enters.*)

STANTON: And I say it's a play about Iago's villainy and Othello's poor powers of judgement.

ROSIE: How so?

STANTON: Within seconds of Iago pouring the poison of doubt into his ear Othello misjudges Desdemona *and* Iago by believing him and not her. Within seconds!

ROSIE: Not seconds. Iago worked hard.

STANTON: Took him a mere page and a half.

ROSIE: Into which Shakespeare packs more incredible dynamite it would take a lesser playwright ten pages to pack.

STANTON: That was a very interestingly structured sentence.

ROSIE: Shithead!

(*He embraces her again. She remains inconsolable.*)

What the hell did we think we were doing anyway! Nothing was right, was it? You're English, I'm American; you're a Londoner, I'm a New Yorker; you're a professor, I'm a student; I'm Catholic, you're Jewish . . .

STANTON: . . . I'm male, you're female . . .

ROSIE: Don't make jokes! I'm serious! And to cap it all, as if we

243

wouldn't have had enough to cause fights, you're black and I'm white . . . I mean . . . I'm . . . Oh, fuck it!

STANTON: She's colour-blind! All this time she's imagined she's white . . .

ROSIE: I'll beat your fuckin' brains out!

STANTON: You're making a scene in public again.

ROSIE: Sorry.

STANTON: But say it again. You make vulgarity sound so human.

ROSIE: Stop mocking me! I'll tear you limb from fuckin' limb!

(*He kisses her again. She buries her head in his neck. Weeping.*)

Stay, Stanton, stay with me.

Scene VIII

Francesca's restaurant.

That evening. STANTON *and* ROSIE *holding hands dejected, resigned, waiting to be served.* FRANCESCA *arrives.*

FRANCESCA: You ready to order yet?

(*No response.*)

OK. Take your time. You're my only customers and you know what? It feels like you're my only customers for the night. Want some music?

(*No response.*)

OK. I'll play you some music. What would you like? Music to go with the mood or against the mood?

(*No response.*)

OK! With the mood. You want the classics? The pops? The classic classics? The pop classics? The pop pops? The classical pops?

(*No response.*)

OK. I'll aim it high – the Classical classics. You want early? You want Renaissance? You want Romantic? You want modern?

(*No response.*)

OK. I'll go for broke – something so early you won't know what hit you.

(*She disappears. Silence. Then – Guillaume de Machaut's* Messe de Nostre Dame.* *After some moments –* BLACKOUT! SCREAMS!)

No panic! No panic! It's only a power failure.

ROSIE: Is it here or everywhere?

STANTON: No street lights. Must be everywhere.

(FRANCESCA *appears with candles.*)

FRANCESCA: It's like 1965 all over again. Remember 1965? Biggest power failure ever.

(*Sounds of street voices and smashing glass.*)

Stay calm! Everything's under control. Don't panic.

ROSIE: (*Rising, grabbing coats*) Francesca, I'm gonna panic. And if you take my tip you'll panic too.

---

* Deller Consort with Collegium Aureum and Ensemble Ricercare de Zurich, Harmonia Mundi HM 917.

STANTON: Where we going? We're safe here.

ROSIE: Don't argue with me. I *do* remember 1965. Looting! Fires! Bodily assault. Come! I know my city. Sorry, Francesca.

(*Sounds of police cars. Sounds of fire engines. Headlights and blue lights flash across the stage.*)

Scene IX

Street of New York.
Sounds of running, shouting, screaming. It is a riot.

MAN'S VOICE: (*Off*) Beat it! Get the hell away from this store. Anyone touch this store they get this across their back. You hear me out there? You fuckin' hear?

FIRST BOY'S VOICE: OK, man, no sweat. We don't want no trouble, just loot, man, just easy loot.

SECOND BOY'S VOICE: Hey, man, can't see, man. Gotta see, man.
(*Whoosh of ignited paraffin. Flames.*)
Can see now, man. See plenty. In we go.

ROSIE'S VOICE: OK, brothers, where's the action?

FIRST BOY'S VOICE: All around you, sister, all around, the Lord be praised.

ROSIE'S VOICE: Hal – lelujah! Hal – lelujah!
(ROSIE *appears, pulling* STANTON *into doorway. They're breathless from running.*)

ROSIE: Know the right jargon, you survive!

STANTON: You don't sound sympathetic.

ROSIE: Sympathetic? For *what*? We'll be lucky to come out of this alive. Another gang comes I don't know *you*, *you* don't *me*. OK? Strangers!

STANTON: 'The cock shall not crow till thou hast denied me thrice.'

ROSIE: Don't be scripture-smart with me, mister. Quote me no Gospels. I know this area, I know these mentalities, I know these moods.

STANTON: Would you really deny me?

ROSIE: (*Tender*) Oh, honey, no. No, no! That was just my black humour. Mamma will protect you.
(*She stands protectively in front of him, surveying up and down the street. Sounds of frantic skirmishing, as in war. His hands creep from behind her to cup each breast.*)
You have exactly three hours to remove your hands.
(*He turns her around. They kiss. Sound of a huge crash. He wants to run. She holds him back.*)
Safer here.

(*Pause as they listen.*)

STANTON: High unemployment, slum conditions, neglect, indifference – it's understandable.

ROSIE: Understandable, huh?

STANTON: Turn out the lights and look what happens.

ROSIE: Oh? And what *do* you see happening?

STANTON: In a word?

ROSIE: Or two.

STANTON: In a word or two I see around me looting and arson as an expression of rage.

ROSIE: Do you, now?

STANTON: As an expression of rage from a minority youth who feel hopeless members of a hopeless community.

ROSIE: Rage? Seemed to me they were having the time of their lives, mister.

STANTON: (*Surprised with this unfashionable view*) You don't see them as victims of apathy? You don't see all this as revenge, desperation, pent-up torment?

ROSIE: Pent-up torment? Cant! They're positively intoxicated with their dumb, fuckin' luck. Desperation? Cant! I don't see all this happening in slums. Revenge? Cant! Revenge on who? Spicks and niggers with small shops? The poor, fuckin' long-suffering New Yorker whose city taxes have been spent plenty on social schemes? Don't tell me – I was once a social worker! Look!

(*They look offstage.* ROSIE *calls out.*)

Hey there, fellas. I'm a reporter from the *Star*. Why you stealin' from your own kind, man? Tell me.

FIRST YOUTH'S VOICE: I ain't stealin', sister. This is lootin', lootin'. Root toot de toot, tootin' lootin'.

ROSIE: That's stealing in my book, sonny.

SECOND YOUTH'S VOICE: It's the name of the game, lady.

FIRST YOUTH'S VOICE: Aw, Jesus, man, let's go now, we gotta go.

(*Sound of feet running off.*)

ROSIE: (*Ferocious mockery*) 'And we got permission, man, we got permission from all you white liberals cos you told us being black and poor is good enough reason for being lawless. Yes, sir, thank you, sir, we're specially greedy and specially insensitive and specially immoral on account of underprivilege, thank you, sir. We's anti-social cos we don't know no better, thank you, sir. We loot and burn cos we's inferior, yes, sir, thank you, sir! That's just the go-ahead we need. Thank you, thank you.'

(*She's almost in tears but controls herself to continue.*)

But did *you* loot and burn when you were poor and lived in the slums? Right! Nor did I. So what makes you think you're better? How come you had standards but you think they can't have? How come your mother gave you self-respect but you don't think their mothers could give it to them? What makes you think being black demands special exemptions from being honest? You know what you're saying? They're not fully enough human to be held morally responsible for their own behaviour, that's what you're saying. And you know what that makes you? That makes you a liberal racist! (*Tears almost.*) A fuckin', patronizing, liberal racist!

(STANTON *has been regarding her with growing, loving admiration.*)

STANTON: Do you think we could make love here, now, in this doorway?

ROSIE: It'll be our last fuck, ever. Now – run!

(*She grabs his hand and they run.*)

Scene X

Rosie's apartment.
   The dinner party. Table laid. Candles waiting to be lit. Soft music.
STANTON *appears in a suit, struggling with his tie. When it's tied he uncorks a bottle. Pours two glasses.* ROSIE *appears in a beautiful black dress. She's stunning but – dreamy in a resigned way.*

STANTON: Rosie, you're breathtaking.
   (*He gives her a glass.*)
ROSIE: Stay, Stanton, stay.
STANTON: Think we bought enough food?
ROSIE: Stay! I'll feed you honey, massage your neck every night –
STANTON: Will I like your friends?
ROSIE: – I'll be your researcher, I'll write your lectures –
STANTON: Think we can take the covers off the plates now?
ROSIE: – I won't scream in public and I'll be beautiful for you every
   day. Stay with me, Stanton.
STANTON: Dance?
   (*The move around the lounge kissing between times, passionately, unhappily, desperately, hopelessly. A slow ballet around the room. Over it, for the last time,* JUDITH'S VOICE, *sad and gentle.*)
JUDITH'S VOICE: Oh, you'll have such a lovely time. Eventful and
   sweetly sad. You can make every hour an event when it's only over
   twelve days. Rather more difficult, I find, over twenty years. How
   lucky she'll be. You ought not to stay longer than twelve days with
   her, Stanton. That way she'll have the illusion it would *all* have
   been like that. Are you listening? Wake up. It's the midnight
   reflective hour, dear listeners, and this is your radio midnight
   friend, Judy Myers, delivering it to you. Did you look forward in
   middle age to those holidays with your husband, exploring
   new lands and sights together? Did you look forward to a new
   release, a fresh start, becoming lovers again. Ah, dear listeners,
   ah . . .
ROSIE: Stay, Stanton, stay!
STANTON: The dying words of a famous British actress: 'We didn't
   rehearse it like this.'

ROSIE: She's had a fair share of you.

STANTON: Do you know what the last words of Lytton Strachey were? 'Well, if this is dying I don't think much of it.'

ROSIE: Do you know how difficult it is to find a man worth living even a bit of a life with? This entire fuckin' city is full of women without men.

STANTON: Overheard in a Chinese restaurant: 'It's not the eggroll, Henry, it's the last five years.'

ROSIE: Oh Christ, what am I gonna do?

STANTON: You'll do, Rosie, what we all do: that which belongs to our nature.

(STELLA-BELLA *bursts in from her room. She's dressed for the party – idiosyncratically!*)

STELLA-BELLA: If he's short and with glasses and wearing the wrong-coloured shirt, he's mine. You hear me, Rosie? But for Christ's sake don't let him in here. Just give him a large neat whiskey. I want him drunk before I see him.

(*She retreats.* STANTON *flicks through the records.*)

STANTON: You know you don't have to come with me to buy my kids' records tomorrow.

ROSIE: It's my last day. I'm not letting you out of my sight.

(*Music of Jane Oliver.*)

STANTON: What would you do if I came back in a year's time, or thereabouts?

ROSIE: Drop him, take you! You crazy? There *is* no one else for me. Can't you understand? I don't *want* anyone else crawling over my body.

STANTON: Christ! You make me go weak at the knees, Rosie.

ROSIE: But don't give me false hopes, creep!

STANTON: 'Shithead', please.

ROSIE: Shithead! I'd be looking out for you every day. There was a boy in college who said to me once, 'I'll call you one Friday for a dinner date.' And, do you know, I watched for him over eight weeks? For eight Fridays I made no dates.

(*Pause. Her mood changes.*)

But you'd never change your mind. To leave home would be taking risks. Only big people take risks, burst out of their tight, narrow life . . .

STANTON: That's an incredibly trite observation, to say nothing of inaccurate.

ROSIE: (*Mocking*) 'To say nothing'!

STANTON: I kiss all my close friends, male and female, on the lips – would you tolerate that? I keep open house – would you tolerate that? I make friends of failures – would you, *could* you, in view of how competitive and possessive you are, cope with that?

ROSIE: Creep!

STANTON: 'Shithead', please.

ROSIE: Shithead!

STANTON: And as final proof that it's Iago's play and not Othello's, Shakespeare gives Iago more lines.

ROSIE: Not true.

STANTON: Betcha ten dollars.

ROSIE: You're on, shithead.

STANTON: Othello has 825 lines, Iago has 1,077 and thirteen lines of song.

ROSIE: You made that up.

STANTON: Disprove me.

(*She reaches for a volume of the Bard's work. Lights fade down and up to denote the passing of minutes.* STANTON *holds out his hand.*)

Ten dollars!

ROSIE: It still doesn't prove it's Iago's play.

STANTON: Ten dollars or a quickie.

ROSIE: Oh, you're so smug with it!

STANTON: (*Tenderly*) I don't *care* about *Othello*, Rosie. Christ! What does it matter who's right or wrong. Why do you have to compete over everything?

(*The phone rings.* ROSIE *rises to answer it. She paces backwards and forwards.*)

ROSIE: Oh hi, Merle. Yeah! Sure I'm OK. You know me. Just nursing a broken heart. Yeah. I did! He's leaving me. The romance is over. Not only is he leaving me but on the last night he packed. Couldn't wait. His plane leaves at two thirty and he packed six thirty the evening before. No, no, it's too complicated. I'll explain next week. No, of course I'm not gonna shoot myself. For an English-man? A colonizer? You crazy?

(*Long pause.*)

Oh, Merle. I'm so sorry. Yeah – see ya!
(*Phone down.*)
His father's in hospital, dying, wouldn't you know! He said to me, 'Oh no! You didn't lose?' Lose! Didn't even know I was fuckin' competing. (*Pause.*) You make sure you tell everyone it was you rejected me, now. I don't want any misunderstandings.
(*She suddenly rushes out of the front door.*)

STANTON: Rosie! They'll be here any moment. Rosie!
(*But she's gone.* STELLA-BELLA *comes through.*)

STELLA-BELLA: That was Rosie going, wasn't it?
(STANTON *nods.*)
A mess, huh?
(STANTON *opens his arms in despair.*)
You sure you doing the right thing?
(STANTON *is silent.*)
I know! I know! Who knows what's right till after it's done? Why do I ask?

STANTON: She *will* come back, won't she?

STELLA-BELLA: How far you think she'll go in that dress?

STANTON: Like that dress, Stella-Bella?

STELLA-BELLA: Crazy about it. You wanna marry me instead?

STANTON: I bought it for her in the middle of the riots. This shop, run by a couple of terrified gays, and there, in the window, this remarkable dress. Very odd feeling dealing with a shopkeeper who takes your money with one hand and wields a hatchet with the other.

STELLA-BELLA: You know you've broken her heart, don't you? She's never, never, never ever been in such a state.

STANTON: Don't make me feel worse than I do.

STELLA-BELLA: I'm confused. Tell me. Why come back at all? To tell a woman it couldn't work you flew three thousand miles?

STANTON: I had to face her.

STELLA-BELLA: As simple as that?

STANTON: Nothing's as simple as that.

STELLA-BELLA: So?

STANTON: I came . . . I came . . . I came to be overwhelmed.

STELLA-BELLA: And you were *not*? By Rosie you were *not* overwhelmed?

STANTON: Oh, I was, that. Overwhelmed and whelmed over and tossed around and about and up and down and brought to the brink . . .

(*She waits for more.*)

STELLA-BELLA: . . . and brought to the brink . . . ?

STANTON: . . . and saw . . .

STELLA-BELLA: . . . and saw . . . ?

STANTON: . . . such sights!

(*On which ambiguous line the doorbell rings.*)

They're here.

STELLA-BELLA: It's her.

STANTON: How do you know it's her?

STELLA-BELLA: (*Going to her room*) It's *her*! Believe me!

(STANTON *opens the door. It is* ROSIE. *She's determinedly revived.*)

ROSIE: Hello, cuckoo. Miss me? Thought I'd run out on yer, huh? Where's the champagne? You *are* gonna say goodbye to me on champagne, you know. On your last night you're doing what *I* want.

(*She goes to the fridge. Returns with bottle for him to open.*)

STANTON: (*Incredulously*) I was missing you.

ROSIE: (*Tenderly*) Hurt to be apart, didn't it? Well, you better get used to it.

STANTON: Right now I would love a cigarette.

ROSIE: When did you give up?

STANTON: When I started to puff making love.

ROSIE: *I* used to drink a lot. Stopped when I began telling friends the truth.

STANTON: I dreamt about a friend last night. Now what were the details? Can't remember. But as I was coming out of the dream he was saying something to me about 'as sad as a field of mint'. And when I was awake I had this line going round and round in my head: 'They came down off the mountain into a field of melancholy mint.' (*Pause.*) Is mint melancholy?

ROSIE: (*Stroking his face*) We are going to make love all night. Non-stop.

STANTON: What, no breaks at all?

ROSIE: Only to feed you a steak now and then.

STANTON: And what will *you* eat to regain strength?

ROSIE: I'm twelve years younger, remember?

STANTON: Creep!

ROSIE: Know what I love about you? You're not competitive. The boy I had before you *he* was competitive. Even in bed. No peace. I've always gone after boys, men who were my inferior, so's I could mother them. They gave me nothing. Well, not any more. You made me realize I've never touched heights. From here on I'm not putting up with anyone I don't really care about.

(*Sound of doorbell. Sound of guests. Music changes to Sinatra.*)

Scene XI

Rosie's apartment.

After the party. After tempestuous love-making. In the subdued light of a solitary candle ROSIE *and* STANTON *naked on the cushions. Exhausted.* ROSIE *pinches herself.*

ROSIE: Fleshy, huh?

STANTON: Who thought I'd ever make love to pop music?

ROSIE: Stay, Stanton, stay!

STANTON: I'm dry. My back's broken, I've lost seven pounds, my heart's racing and I'm dry.

> (ROSIE *staggers to the kitchen. We hear and see fridge door open, clink of glass, pouring of liquid, bottle returned, fridge door slammed.* ROSIE *returns with one glass full.*)

ROSIE: Soda suit you?

STANTON: Nothing better.

> (*She kneels to him, glass to his lips – nurse to a soldier wounded in battle. Suddenly her eyes catch something.* STANTON *follows what she's looking at. It's his 'fella'. A used, limp, 'fella' is a very comic and pathetic sight, worn-out and zonked-looking.* ROSIE *picks it up by its loose skin between two fingers.*)

ROSIE: *What* – is this?

STANTON: Don't know. Wasn't there this morning.

ROSIE: Poor thing. Someone beat you up, little fella?

STANTON: Less of the little.

ROSIE: Don't be offended. Size isn't everything. (*Whistles, as to a dog.*) Up, Rover, up! Good boy! Ah – Rover too tired to jump for his bone? Rover been hunting all day?

> (*She again picks it up. Lets it drop. Again and again.*)

STANTON: Rosie, it is *not* a piece of meat on a butcher's slab! Will you please show a little more respect for the service he's done you?

> (ROSIE *moves to a surface cluttered with something from every room; rummages, extracts from the clutter a kid's tin flute, squats cross-legged beside the 'fella' and plays, trying to charm the 'snake' to raise its head. Which sends them both into fits of giggles – from which she breaks off, and slowly, achingly folds into his arms with a moan.*)

ROSIE: I can't bear it, I can't bear to think of a *day* without you, let alone the rest of my life. I want you, your children, your old age, your gentleness, your patience, your mind, your forgiveness, your laughter – I'm so angry, Stanton. I *know* you love me, I see it from the way you look at me, and you're denying it. It's crazy, just crazy. It's so wrong of you to deny it. *No* one will forgive you.

(*She's crying, helplessly. He caresses her, soothingly.*)

STANTON: Shush, shush, easy, Rosie, easy.

(*The dawn creeps through closed curtains. They begin to dress.* ROSIE *slips swiftly into a tracksuit.*)

ROSIE: You know when it'll really hit me? In about two weeks from now. (*Pause.*) Stay and fuckin' marry me, Stanton! (*Pause.*) Like talking to a dead horse. What the hell was I doing making love with a dead horse?

STANTON: (*Taking her in his arms*) Come here, four eyes.

ROSIE: Who are you calling 'four eyes'?

(*She snuggles up. Their faces and mood are flat though their humour rolls on.*)

You'll be all right. A little strain at first, but one by one they'll come round. Judy will forgive you. Your friends will look at you with different eyes, a bit of a hero, the one who almost got away. The children will love you as always. Nothing much will change.

STANTON: I know exactly what it'll be like when I get back. *You'll* be all right but *I'll* grieve. You'll meet your friends, make your sunny jokes, pursue your degree studies, hide it all inside. Not me. I'm transparent. That's how the family knew. I came back from the seminar last time and all I did was keep playing your music. Jesus! How could they *not* know. Grieve. Sit shivah. Know what 'shivah' is? After a death the Jews insist on a week in which you do nothing. Everyone who isn't family does it for you. I'll sit shivah. Grieve.

Scene XII

Airport. Departure gate.

ROSIE *in her grey baggy tracksuit trousers, a yellow sweatshirt, sneakers and her grey 1930s astrakhan coat. She's zany and kid-like.*

ROSIE: Hey! Look at the way I walk in sweats.

STANTON: If anyone had ever told me I'd be walking out with a teeny-bopper . . .

ROSIE: If anyone had told me I'd be seen walking out in sweats! Look, as soon as I wear them I walk a certain way. Can't help myself. Look.

(*She pushes* STANTON *ahead so that he can see her; then she walks towards him swaggering like a male athlete. Into his arms. She clings.*)

We did a lot in twelve days.

STANTON: Lived a whole lifetime.

ROSIE: Except we didn't play chess in Washington Square.

STANTON: Damn!

ROSIE: (*Inspecting his face*) How did all those little blood vessels burst on your nose?

STANTON: The effort of it, Rosie, the effort.

ROSIE: I can't *believe* we won't be seeing one another again.

(*She weeps. It's time to part.* ROSIE *and* STANTON *face each other. They kiss. Simply.*)

You take care, now.

STANTON: Study hard, Rosie, promise me?

(*Another simple kiss.*)

ROSIE: Shit! We should've made love in the taxi!

(*He gives her a last simple kiss, turns, and moves towards the door. In that instant his back is turned she flees. He turns for a last wave. She has gone. He is desolate. Slow, slow fade of the light.*)

BLUEY

CHARACTERS

Main roles

HILARY HAWKINS   a High Court judge, aged about fifty-eight

SOPHIE   his wife, aged about fifty-five

MRS HAWKINS   his mother, aged about seventy-eight

RON KIMBLE   a Cockney plumber, young at twenty-five, old at
sixty-five

Secondary roles

MARTIN SEYMOUR SCOTT   wine salesman, aged thirty-two

STRIVEN   a scrap-metal merchant, aged forty-three

YOUNG HILARY   carpenter's mate, aged about eighteen

AUDREY   his girlfriend, young at fifteen, older at forty

TOM VINTERS   a Cockney carpenter, young at twenty, old at sixty

KATIE   Jewish delicatessen shopkeeper, about sixty

Minor roles

COUNSEL FOR THE PLAINTIFF

RADIO ANNOUNCER

FRIEND OF HILARY'S   stockbroker, aged fifty

RORY KELLY   Belfast Irish plumber's mate, about eighteen

MRS MONTGOMERY   a housewife, about thirty-five

MRS MITCHUM   a housewife, about forty-five

Two different actors have to play HILARY as young and old. But I
leave it to the discretion of the director whether two actors are
needed to play the young and old other characters of RON KIMBLE,
AUDREY and TOM VINTERS. My guess is that it would be less
confusing and more of a challenge for the actors if one played both
ages.

A.W.

Bluey, the European Radio Play Commission for 1984, was first transmitted by Cologne Radio on 16 May 1985.

It was subsequently transmitted on BBC Radio 3 on 11 December 1985, when the cast was as follows:

HILARY HAWKINS	Patrick Stewart
SOPHIE	Mary Wimbush
MRS HAWKINS	Anne Dyson
RON KIMBLE	David Swift
MARTIN SEYMOUR SCOTT	Peter Acre
STRIVEN	Joe Melia
YOUNG HILARY	Michael Thomas
AUDREY	Nichola McAuliffe
TOM VINTERS	Norman Jones
KATIE/MRS MONTGOMERY	Mia Souteriou
COUNSEL FOR THE PLAINTIFF	David Garth
FRIEND OF HILARY'S	Garard Green
RORY KELLY	Chris. Dunne
MRS MITCHUM	Gwen Cherrell

Director Margaret Windham

PART ONE
REMEMBERING

Sound of a voice from on high shouting, 'Below.' A second's pause. A thud and immediate cry of great pain.

The cottage – the present.

Sound of rain, of wind. Scratch of pen on paper. JUDGE HILARY HAWKINS, *alone in a country cottage, is writing his diary.*

HILARY: I sit here, as I have sat over the years, listening to the rain, wondering will it ever stop. Though it could happen in no better place, high in these Black Mountains of Wales where, I remember an old aunt warning, it always rains.

We bought it nevertheless and filled it with auction furniture, lively friends, and family memories; a place to which I once needed to retreat in order to sift the lies from the truth and consider my judgments upon the sad men and women who passed through my court carrying the great mess they made of their one and only lives.

Now I sit here, look out across the fields to the hill they call the Tumpa and write my diary. I do not think I could ever pass judgment on anybody again.

(*Sound of a voice from on high shouting, 'Below.' A second's pause. A thud and immediately a cry of great pain. Sound of rain, of wind. Scratch of pen on paper.*)

I *think* I am recovered. We can never be certain, though. The diary worries Sophie.

SOPHIE: (*As in memory*) It's like being in competition with another woman. You tell her things you don't tell me. Why, Hilary? It makes me feel so inadequate. Why her? What's she got I haven't?

HILARY: (*Writing*) 'She' has the virtue of never being confused by my contradictions. A diary cannot answer back. No! I do not mean that. It cannot condemn you. No! Judge you. No! Pity you.

Am I recovered? I feel like a poor ghost returning to complete an unfinished life. Ghosts! When I first began coming to work here I would go up to bed with a thick stick and lay it beside me. I felt nervous crossing the courtyard in the dark from the study to the main house. Had a madman entered while I was at work? There may be no one downstairs but might they be upstairs? Or would I encounter a strange spirit? I moved forward with a careful bravery, muttering to myself not to be stupid, keeping myself company with my own voice, very, very alert.

Night, isolation, howling winds, the crack of trees. The imagination *is* stirred, and a stirred imagination stirs the blood.

(*Swell sound of rain.*)

Rain! The injustice of days without sun! I long for a clear day, a starry night. Some warmth for my old bones.

(*Lower sound of rain.*)

Poor Sophie! I suppose it *is* insulting to talk to a diary rather than a wife.

SOPHIE: (*As in memory*) I'm not insulted, Hilary, I'm worried. I know about privacy but I also know it's not good to be alone. Solitude doesn't incline a man to be fair to himself. Everything will seem like a life among ruins. You'll get lonely, then self-contempt will creep in, then recrimination, then self-pity. I warn you, you'll discover sins you didn't know you had, they'll proliferate like a plague of vermin after the fall . . . (*Fade.*)

HILARY: How vividly she reproaches. She would have made a better counsel than I did. *Why* did she give up? The money was hers for *au pairs*, nannies, *any*one to look after the boys. I teased her that she did it to make me feel guilty; have a hold over me.

SOPHIE: (*As in memory*) Silly boy! I did it because I felt guilty. I couldn't reconcile the two lives. And if I must be honest I preferred the domestic life on balance. Gave me more freedom to do the things I *like* rather than the things I *had* to do for my freedom . . . (*Fade.*)

HILARY: (*Writing*) Clever wife! '. . . sins will proliferate like a plague of vermin after the fall!'

Why do I sit here, then, as I have sat over the years, listening to the rain? What do I imagine I am doing? I wait for the events of my life to assemble, like the film of a smashed vase run backwards, the broken parts fitting together, making a shape I once thought I had seen.

(*Sound of a voice from on high shouting out, 'Below.' A second's pause. A thud and immediately a cry of great pain. Sound of rain, of wind. Scratch of pen on paper.*)

'Below'! What an absurd word. Wherever I went, a stroll, to a shop, a dinner-party – 'below'! Again and again, 'below, below, below'! A conspiracy to unnerve me. What was I being told? Why was my unconscious forcing attention towards this silly, five-lettered boring preposition? It was not a conceptual word, not even an adjective. Had it been 'beware' I would have felt something. Or 'death', I might have understood. Or liar, bigot, blind, scream, fear, money, silence! A word that warned, sounded with portent, rang resonant bells through me – but 'below'!

I sit waiting in this unfinished study with damp walls, listening to the rain, trying to remember when I first began hearing it. 'Below.'

The courtroom – the past.

Fade in COUNSEL FOR PLAINTIFF.

COUNSEL FOR PLAINTIFF: And so, my lord, we have a case before us precisely for which the law was designed. We have heard witness after witness brought by Mr Scott's defence counsel to describe my client, James Striven, as being what the world might regard as an unpleasant personality – mean, avaricious, morbid, sordidly pursuing pornography as a pastime as though to be unlovable is a crime, or more to the point is justification for a crime. But to be unlovable – fortunately for many of us – is not a crime. A man may be as socially unacceptable as he please yet must he enjoy equal protection under the law as those who may not wish, socially, to accept him. My client's property and privacy were invaded and his character besmirched, and all for the Galahad cock-and-bull inventions of Mr Scott. We could be, but we are not, demanding damages for defamation, that would be to give credence to Scott's fantastic allegations. But the law of property is sacrosanct and my client's claim of damages for trespass must be pressed. The sanctity of law must be upheld not only if the strong trespass upon the weak from on high but also, difficult though it may be to contemplate, when the weak clamber up and trespass upon the strong from below.

(*The word 'below' is repeated and echoed like a recurrent tune in the head.*)

The house – the past.
Fade in RADIO ANNOUNCER.
RADIO ANNOUNCER: And now for *Financial Report*. The *Financial Times* share index has dropped below yesterday's spectacular rise to . . .

(*The word 'below' is repeated and echoed like a recurrent tune in the head. Fade in* HILARY's *wife*, SOPHIE. *They are in telephonic contact.*)

SOPHIE: But Hilary, my darling, what does it matter if you're only using the study for your legal work? You have to go back into the house at nights and I don't want you going back into a cold house. What if you want to read a novel in bed? Don't be stingy. Keep the heating on during the day.

HILARY: (*Through the phone*) I *do* keep it on during the day, it's just that I put the thermostat down to 50 degrees. We must save oil, Sophie, it's expensive.

SOPHIE: Fine. Save it! But promise me you won't put the thermostat below 50 degrees . . .

(*The word 'below' is repeated and echoed like a recurrent tune in the head, but this time it ends like a shout from on high. A second's pause. A thud and immediately a cry of great pain.*)

The cottage – present.
Sound of rain, of wind. Scratch of pen on paper.
HILARY: They were not good years for me. Not for anything I did. Years in which confused judgment followed judgment misplaced, misinformed, ill-considered, and all overturned on appeal. How did I ever become a judge, I kept asking myself. What powers had I once revealed that commanded attention and respect but which were now, it seemed, receding. No! draining? No! weakening?

Once in the London house, standing in the middle of my study, a room where I had made love, entertained colleagues, burnt the midnight oil wrestling at a desk laden with a mass of conflicting evidence to arrive at a judgment, I looked at the shelves of books and records, the prints on walls, the hand-picked furniture, the objects which I had long forgotten had come from whom for what reason, and I thought: what has any of this to do with me? I am a stranger in this room. Why am I lingering? And because I could see no setting in which I belonged, no alternative life, I experienced the most extraordinary sense of levitation. No! Floating. No! Disembodiment. No! Discontinuity. No! No! The word should be 'disorientation', but it is not. Not quite. Not precise. I want to understand precisely. Displacement. Better. I was displaced from the life I had so painstakingly assembled. Adrift. Of no fixed address. Bereft. A wealth of a word, that one, bereft. And afraid.

(*Swell sound of rain, briefly.*)

Not good years at all. I lost my nerve, my courage, my appetite for things.

The courtroom – the past.

Fade in voice of MARTIN SEYMOUR SCOTT *giving evidence.*

COUNSEL FOR PLAINTIFF: Please give the court your name and age and nature of employment.

SCOTT: My name is Martin Seymour Scott, I'm aged thirty-two, and I work in Harrods selling wine.

COUNSEL FOR PLAINTIFF: Thank you. Now, will you tell my lord, in your own words, exactly what happened that drew you into Mr Striven's house.

SCOTT: I suppose it began from the first day Striven and his wife moved in next door. He was an angry man, vicious. He seemed never to shave or wash and no one would dare answer him back because he had the look of someone who wouldn't think twice about laying hands on you. And his voice was like a, like a slow knife. I remember he made a fire in the garden. The very first week. A huge fire, which stank. God knows what he was burning, but it stank and made black smoke which blocked out the sun and dropped soot and ashes over all our houses. Every week I had to clean my window ledges, and I watched his flowers die, his grass grow, and his shrubs strangle one another, and I couldn't understand none of it. They weren't poor. He was a wealthy scrap merchant, wasn't he? Employed people. And in the night there was the screaming of his wife. One day I took the afternoon off to come back early and speak with her. She invited me in. It was a neat house, sir, clean, and well stocked. But I could see he beat her. What do you do in a situation like that, your honour? It's not easy to report neighbours to the police, and it's not easy to live near the suffering and remain quiet. Especially for an Englishman. No Englishman likes interfering in other people's lives. But in the end I couldn't bear it. One evening I knocked on the door in the middle of his rantings and asked him to stop it and leave his wife alone. And that voice, that slow knife, it cut back at me.

A street front door – the past.

Fade in voice of STRIVEN *at his front door.*

STRIVEN: Oh, and what shall we do about it? Shall we strike me violently? Shall Sir Galahad apprehend me, report me? Who to? What for? It would give me great pleasure to smash your face into my mantelpiece and stick your head down my lavatory pan, Mr Scott. But that would only land me in deep with the law and give you satisfaction.

Instead, you listen to me and you listen very hard. There's a fence round this house, and everything in it belongs to me. The air, the space, the smells, dirt-bins, every brick, windowsill, drain and all the living creatures within it. Even the overgrown grass I know you hate because I see you mow your lawn like clockwork. Mine! To do with as I please. Which no one inside or outside the law can touch or tell me how to manage. My possessions! Belonging to me! Mine! Now, I have given you five minutes inside these fences. *I've* been generous and *you've* been lucky. You've got thirty seconds to get out or I will do things no law court could deny me the right to do. Fuck off from my territory. And don't forget it *is* my territory. Don't forget . . .

(*The phrase 'don't forget' is repeated and echoed like a recurrent tune in the head.*)

The cottage – the present.

Sound of rain, of wind. Scratch of pen on paper.

HILARY: In his statement which he read out in court, Scott described how he left shaking. He had come face to face with the devil, he declared, and it had made him sick. Quite literally ill. He had to stay away from work to recover, so profound had been the experience. On the last afternoon of his illness he heard a pitiful howling from the stricken house next door. The man, Striven, was at his scrapyard.

The courtroom – the past.
Fade in voice of SCOTT.
SCOTT: I thought of knocking, but each time I contemplated it I was overcome with a feeling of terror. The howling went on. I had to knock. No one let me in. I found a window ajar, eased it open, and entered the house. I looked around. There was no sign of life anywhere. I was terrified but I decided to be systematic, and being systematic helped me cope with my terror.

I started at the top and looked into every room until I reached the cellar. It was divided into three parts. In one was kept coke. In another was lumber. The third was a room. I put my ear to the door. I heard breathing. Strange breathing. As though someone was trying not to breathe but then had to let it out. I opened the door. You must believe me, sir, I opened the door and fainted. I'm not normally a weak man but what I saw made me pass out. His wife was chained up, half naked, and covered in whip lashes and congealed blood, and standing in her own excrement. She must have been there for days.

It seemed I was out for ages, and when I woke my nostrils were full of that smell, that smell of sweat and excretion. I carried it around for weeks. I tried to unchain her but she cried out not to, to leave her. She was pitiful, begging me to leave, and threatening to kill herself if I moved one thing in the room. I was to leave as I came and say nothing, to no one. She made me promise. On my life. 'Don't forget,' she kept saying. 'You've promised, on your life, don't forget, don't forget . . .'

(*The phrase 'don't forget' is repeated and echoed like a recurrent tune in the head.*)

The cottage – the present.
Sound of rain, of wind. Scratch of pen on paper.
HILARY: At which point he conceived his quixotic plan to liberate her and take her to a little cottage he imagined he could buy in the

270

country, though with what I could not ascertain. Poor fool! It was easy for plaintiff's counsel to destroy the credibility of such a man. All the tangible evidence was against him. The cunning neighbour could see he had a noble idiot next door, and he taunted Scott beyond endurance. Scott waited till he judged it the right moment to enter Striven's house and release the chained slave. There was no chained slave, only Striven and a neat, seemingly bewildered wife. They called the police, Scott told his story, the police investigated and – found nothing! Everything had been cleared away. His wife, blooming and immaculately dressed in court, had recovered and denied everything. It was obvious to us all. Striven was lying and Scott had told the truth. But the law had to support the liar because, even had such a torture chamber existed and the lie been discovered, the lie was irrelevant. Striven had turned from the sadistic satisfactions of wife-beating to the thrill of trapping his poor neighbour into trespass for which he now claimed damages. I was powerless.

The courtroom – the past.
Fade in voice of STRIVEN *in court.*
STRIVEN: He's not liked me from the day I first moved in next to him. Kept complaining I blocked out his sunlight. (*Shouting across the courtroom*) I've never once crossed your threshold to do you a bad turn, Scott. Have I? Have I? You scheming bastard, Scott. You interfering scheming bastard.
HILARY: Mr Striven, control yourself in court.
STRIVEN: (*Ignoring him*) You wanted to get me but I've got you.
HILARY: Mr Striven –
STRIVEN: I told you it was my territory, I warned you.
HILARY: Mr Striven, if you don't desist you will be in contempt of court, and I may have to –
STRIVEN: (*Persisting*) Don't forget, I told you, my territory, I said, *my* territory, don't forget, I said don't forget!
(*The phrase 'don't forget' is repeated like a recurrent tune in the head.*)

The cottage – the present.
Sound of rain, of wind. Scratch of pen on paper.

HILARY: I lost control of my court. I could focus on nothing. And now this second phrase, knocking at my memory, persistent like a melody clamouring to be recognized. Everyone seemed to use it: 'Don't forget.' My clerk kept telling me not to forget things. 'Don't forget! Don't forget! Don't forget – below!' I knew it referred to something familiar, but what? What?

And then there was the personality of Striven himself. That venomous dealer in discarded metals had stirred some recess of my mind. Never had I met a man in whose nature was concentrated so much ugliness. No. Bestiality. No. Cruelty. No. Malevolence. His wife insisted upon her husband's kindness, and much evidence was produced of his gifts to charity. But for me he was a bleak landscape whose charitable acts seemed like bribes to heaven's gatekeepers and served only to put his blackness into sharper focus. Winter promises spring but *his* nature was relentlessly dark, a frozen cruelty promising no pity. He offended me, tore at my spirit, sapped my will, hit me at my darkest suspicions, reminding me: it is impossible to overcome man's brutalities. I could not bring myself to let the law win him justice, nor could I bring myself to distort the law which was in his favour. The good man was wrong. The evil one, right. It was a conflict I could neither support nor resolve. Inevitable that I would crack. I did. And through the crack began creeping out all the shames of my past.

Mrs Hawkins's flat – the past.
Key unlocks a front door. Hold.
MRS HAWKINS: Fee fi fo fum I smell the tobacco of my long lost son.
HILARY: (*From end of passageway.*) Not long lost. Just busy, Mother.
   (*Door closes.* HILARY's *voice approaches.*)
   Here, let me bring those carriers in.
MRS HAWKINS: Weighed down by the criminal world, are you?
HILARY: They don't have to be criminals to depress me. (*Beat.*) Good God! You live alone, how come all this shopping?
MRS HAWKINS: I shop once every two weeks for the essentials.
HILARY: I'll unpack them.
MRS HAWKINS: You always loved unpacking the shopping. Nice orderly mind you had.
HILARY: Not so orderly these days.

MRS HAWKINS: Guess who I saw? (*Beat.*) Little Audrey.

HILARY: Audrey.

MRS HAWKINS: Remember? And little Audrey laughed and laughed
. . . (*Fade.*)

Young Hilary's home – the past.

His parents are out. Fade in energetic passage of Rimsky-Korsakov's
Scheherazade. *Voices of* YOUNG HILARY *and a girlfriend,* AUDREY.
Spring Awakenings!

AUDREY: (*Giggling and seductive*) And little Audrey laughed and
laughed and laughed. Stand, Hilary, come, be a good boy and stand
for Audrey.

YOUNG HILARY: Oh Christ, Audrey, but you're incredible. You're so
open and shameless and happy about it.

AUDREY: Why not? It's all natural. You enjoy it, I enjoy it, they enjoy
it. I only wish we could do it more often. But you and your law
studies! You're such an egghead, so difficult to get hold of. (*Pause.*)

YOUNG HILARY: What about these muscles, Audrey, all that holiday
work on building sites? Feel!

AUDREY: Stupid boy! Imagining I care about muscles. It's *who* you are
not what you *feel* like. What do I care about your stupid muscles and
your labouring on building sites? (*Beat.*) Oh, Hilary, aren't you a
little in love with me?

YOUNG HILARY: I think you're unique. Isn't that enough?

AUDREY: I'm in love with you, Hilary. It can't be enough.

YOUNG HILARY: Be my mistress.

AUDREY: I don't want to be your short-term mistress, I want to be
your forever sweetheart with a ring on my finger. Two rings, in fact.
Now, lie there, I'm going to sit on you.

YOUNG HILARY: Oh Christ, Audrey. God in heaven! What are you
doing to me?

AUDREY: I've got all sorts of lovely things in store for you if you
behave yourself.

YOUNG HILARY: Don't you think *you* ought to behave yourself?

AUDREY: Lie still.

YOUNG HILARY: How can I lie still when you're exciting me so?

(*As she moves up and down she sings over* Scheherazade.)

AUDREY: My uncle he was a Spanish Captain.

Went to sea a month ago
First he kissed me then he left me
Bade me always answer 'no'.
Oh, no John, no John, no John, no!

YOUNG HILARY: Ahhhhhhhh! (*Orgasm.*) I want to cry. No! Shout!
No – I don't know what I want to do.

AUDREY: Aren't you a *little* bit in love with me? A little? Just a little,
little, leeetle?

Mrs Hawkins's flat – the past.
As before.

HILARY: We were all a little bit in love with her. Initiated us.

MRS HAWKINS: (*Horrified*) But she wasn't more than fifteen!

HILARY: And we were all older and very, very lusty.

MRS HAWKINS: I don't want to hear about it.

HILARY: It was her pleasure to pleasure us.

MRS HAWKINS: I was too broad-minded with you!

HILARY: Nothing crude. Nothing smutty. Sweet. She was sweet and
good-natured. Consoling when we despaired, reprimanding when
we succumbed to self-pity. The first sunny person I ever knew.

MRS HAWKINS: And she's still got that smile. Lights up the street –
cheeky, mischievous.

HILARY: She would've been happy to wife us all, with a dozen rings on
her fingers and a dozen more on her toes.

MRS HAWKINS: She asked after you. Says she follows all your cases in
the press. Says there's something she wants to talk to you about.
Might ring you.

The house – past.
Fade in voice of AUDREY *in the middle of a phone conversation with*
HILARY.

AUDREY: No, don't panic, Hilary, I'm not going to ask you for a
handout now you've been made a judge. I bet you get a lot of that –
strangers or old school chums asking for handouts, thinking you
must be rich? Not Audrey. Wouldn't even if I needed it. But I'll
come to the point, musn't waste your time listening to my nonsense. On the other hand – I'm going to contradict myself now – on
the other hand I would like you to give a little time up for me. You

see, I'm not well. No! Don't say anything. Just listen a little. Doctors don't know what's wrong, they never do, do they? And I'm feeling a little low. I'd perfectly understand if you couldn't. Honestly I would. But every so often, when I go shopping in Finsbury Park, I see your mother, and she tells me about you and so I've got this urge, for old time's sake, just to natter, go over the past, gossip a bit. Would you? I've got no right to ask, really. We drifted apart. I know that. And it's always difficult meeting old friends. Never know what you'll find. But would you? Come and see me? I'm a bit fatter, not as pretty as I was, and I don't laugh so much these days . . .

(*Fade in voice of* MRS HAWKINS.)

MRS HAWKINS: The doctors knew all right, son. Cancer! I met her in Finsbury Park out shopping, took one look at her and knew. Cancer! As sure as eggs is eggs.

HILARY: I told her I'd ring to make a date as soon as the case was over.

MRS HAWKINS: See her, Hilary. I think you should. She always asks about you, and she was a good friend. Even I liked her, and I didn't like many of your friends.

(*Sound of phone ringing at the other end.*)

AUDREY: (*Through phone*) Hello, Mountview 3105.

HILARY: Audrey?

AUDREY: Speaking?

HILARY: It's Hilary.

AUDREY: Hilary!

HILARY: I'm ringing to make that date.

AUDREY: Oh, no! I'm all embarrassed now. Don't know what to say.

HILARY: I want to know what this nonsense is about being ill.

AUDREY: I wish it was nonsense. I prefer talking nonsense. Never did like being serious. Remember?

HILARY: I remember a lot of things, Audrey.

AUDREY: Ah! Naughty! No naughty reminiscences.

HILARY: I thought that's what you *wanted* to do – reminisce.

AUDREY: There's reminisce and reminisce.

HILARY: How are you?

AUDREY: What can I tell you? I'm not a well person.

HILARY: I'm coming to see you.

AUDREY: You're a good boy, Hilary.

HILARY: No longer a boy, Audrey, I've got three young teenagers.

AUDREY: Oh, how I'd love to see you.

HILARY: You will, you will. You'll come with your husband to dinner.

AUDREY: You won't like my husband, Hilary. He's not your sort. A bit rough, Jack. Not bad at heart but – rough, impatient with the world, full of opinions but no thought. What *you* would call a reactionary.

HILARY: Will he approve of me coming to see you?

AUDREY: Come when he's at work. What the eye don't see . . . (*Fade.*)

(*Sound of phone ringing in the house. It is answered.*)

(*Through the phone*) I'm sorry, Hilary. I must cancel our date. I'm too ill. I look awful. I don't want you to see me looking awful. Vain of me I know, at my age, but that's how it is. Wait a little, will you? Till I'm better? I'll be better soon, and I *would* like to see you. Honest. It's been so long. Where's the time gone? What've I done with it? The doctors say this'll pass. Ring me in a couple of weeks, will you? Please? *You* ring *me*, that way I'll know it's not *me* nagging but *you* wanting. Promise? Two weeks' time. The doctors have this new drug . . . (*Fade.*)

The cottage – present.

Sound of rain, of wind. Scratch of pen on paper.

HILARY: I did not ring. I made no contact at all. She had been so pretty, such a sweet and generous soul, I just could not face her dying. That bloated skin hairy from the drugs, I would have wept and she would have seen her dying in my eyes. I was not strong enough for the pain of that. Something had snapped and I was beginning to turn away from disaster stories in the press, to weep at the sight of a starving child on television, rage if I saw rudeness or insensitivity in my children. No matter how ashamed I was to be incapable of that comfort some have and can hand to others – there it was! I could not go. Audrey would have come to *my* deathbed. With all her lack of sophistication, her absence of what is called 'good taste' *she* would have found the right tone of voice, pitched her sunniness at the right angle, not too high and bright and hot in the sky, but a cool summer's evening full of drunk bees and trivia.

(*Fade in* MRS HAWKINS.)

MRS HAWKINS: (*In memory*) I saw her. It was good you didn't go, son. You'd have been very upset. It's better this way. You'll remember her as she was. I think she really wanted that, that's why she cancelled your first date. She wanted to see you but she didn't want *you* to see *her*. She'd have gone on cancelling dates.

(*Sound of rain and wind swells.*)

HILARY: Forgive me, Audrey. I hope you had around you those you loved. I hope you were cared for and cherished. Forgive me. You were never forgotten.

(*Scratching of pen on paper ceases. He weeps, talks to himself.*)

Oh Christ, Audrey, you wouldn't approve of these tears, would you?

(*Pause. Scratch of pen on paper.*)

I sit here, as I have sat over the years, listening to the rain, remembering these things. They were not good years for me. Cracked years, and through the cracks have crept out all the shames of my past.

The house – the past.

Fade in voice of HILARY.

HILARY: God help me, Sophie! Another letter from the past.

SOPHIE: Read it. Might be someone you liked.

HILARY: (*Reading*) 'Dear comrade of long ago. Before you look at the signature at the end of the letter please can I ask you not to.'

SOPHIE: Sounds intriguing.

HILARY: I hate guessing games.

SOPHIE: Might be an old girlfriend.

HILARY: Girlfriends don't call one 'comrade'.

SOPHIE: Don't snap at me, darling.

HILARY: I'm too busy for guessing games. I have to face this man Striven every day in court and he's the most deeply unpleasant and distressing personality I've ever had to cope with.

SOPHIE: Sometimes voices from the past can be soothing. Read it.

(*Fade in voice of* FRIEND.)

FRIEND: Dear comrade of long ago. Before you look at the signature at the end of the letter please can I ask you not to. It is important that I try to remind you of the things that we experienced together and of course perhaps also finding out what things you remember me by.

Let me give you clues. It was the days of conscription. I was clever and spoiled, destined to become an officer; you were struggling against the fates, the Finsbury Park Fates as your mother once sardonically described them.

We square-bashed together, me hating it, you being philosophical. It was you got me through those eight absurd weeks of basic training. Made me feel very humble. I thought we'd never meet again. But coincidence! Coincidence! We did! Studied law together. Are you remembering me yet?

Law was too demanding for my kind of butterfly brilliance. Only stuck it for two years.

You must remember me by now. Or perhaps I'm very forgettable. Why do I write? I don't know, really. Yes, I do!

You see, I was fifty, four months ago. My children are grown up and gone away and I'm left with those Sundays in which husbands face boring wives who find their husbands boring. But I'm not writing out of boredom.

Let me be blunt. I'm frightened. I've lost that still centre. I wake up not understanding where I am or what I'm supposed to be doing. With all my cleverness I've placed myself among people who neither touch me nor make sense. I don't see the point of their existence, not in relationship to me anyway. And my memory of you is of a being with a very still centre. All things had their place when you were around. And so I wondered, could we meet, have a drink together, share a meal?

I know it's a long time. But please would you bear it, for old time's sake? Best wishes, your friend of long ago. PS. Do you ever get the feeling you want to climb a roof and shout out? I don't know what, but something, just simply to – shout out.

(*The phrase 'shout out' is repeated and echoed like a recurrent tune in the head.*)

The cottage – the present.

Sound of rain, of wind. Scratch of pen on paper.

HILARY: I had no idea who was writing until I reached the signature. Indeed I remembered him. Even with affection. He was the first person from the upper classes I had ever encountered. Oddly, like Audrey, he was also sunny. And endowed with cleverness. Unlike me. I had to force my brain to function. We walked a lot together and he used to tease me for working so hard. Now he had been afflicted with a darkness like a virus. I feared its contagion.

I began to reply. It took me an hour to write thirty-three lines. Then I abandoned it. I dreaded the encounter. He would be maudlin, become drunk, ask my opinions on all the big issues in the world, look for wise judgements, have unbearable expectations. I had nothing to offer and had no wish to be brought face to face with that fact. Like him I wanted to shout out from a roof-top but could make no sound nor knew about what I had to shout.

(*Sound of rain and wind swells and falls.*)

Not good, those years. No pleasure in them, and full of things left undone, too late, neglected.

Mrs Hawkins's flat – the past.

Key unlocking a front door. Door closes. Footsteps in the passageway.

HILARY: Mother? Mother, where are you?

(*Doors open and shut.*)

Mother! You're in bed.

MRS HAWKINS: I heard you telephoning. I knew you'd come.

HILARY: What is it?

MRS HAWKINS: I'm ill, that's what it is.

HILARY: Why didn't you phone back?

MRS HAWKINS: I couldn't move.

HILARY: Call for a neighbour?

MRS HAWKINS: Too weak even to shout out . . .

(*The phrase 'shout out' is repeated and echoed like a recurrent tune in the head.*)

HILARY: You should be living with us.

MRS HAWKINS: Mothers can't live with daughters-in-law. It's not fair to either of them. Especially strong personalities like Sophie and I.

HILARY: Sophie and me.

MRS HAWKINS: Sophie and me. I love it when you correct my grammar.

HILARY: That's the only reason I do it. What do I care how you speak!

MRS HAWKINS: Reminds me I've got an educated son.

HILARY: You should live nearer. Loneliness is a killer.

MRS HAWKINS: Oh, it's not so bad. It's bad, but it's not *so* bad. I shop, I read my paper, clean a bit each day, keep an eye on my neighbours. I even go to the cinema now and then, riding around on the top of buses. Lovely! Everything's cheap for old-age pensioners, you know.

HILARY: The old shouldn't be left alone.

MRS HAWKINS: Old is old and there it is.

HILARY: A house and children need grandparents.

MRS HAWKINS: I like sleeping late, I like listening to my favourite radio programme. I like windows open.

HILARY: The old, the young, Sophie and I in the middle.

MRS HAWKINS: Sophie and me!

HILARY: Sophie and me!

MRS HAWKINS: I'd be in the middle, silly boy. Where's your head? Clients going to law need a hard head. Forget me and build your practice.

HILARY: My practice is big enough.

MRS HAWKINS: It can never be big enough. Forget me, build your practice and make your head harder.

HILARY: You're not short, are you?

MRS HAWKINS: Keep your money, Hilary.

HILARY: You wouldn't deny me *that* pleasure, would you?

MRS HAWKINS: You have a bank overdraft, a wife who doesn't understand how money works, and children who don't *care* how money works. Forget me, build your practice, make your head harder. I have sufficient.

HILARY: If we found the money to buy a flat nearer us, would you move?

MRS HAWKINS: You're a real nag, Hilary.

HILARY: Would you?

MRS HAWKINS: I've moved enough! I'm tired of getting used to new things.

HILARY: You'd be able to pop in and out.

MRS HAWKINS: And get on Sophie's nerves.

HILARY: She's very fond of you.

MRS HAWKINS: So she should be. I'm a very nice person. I've kept my distance.

HILARY: Is that what being a very nice person is?

MRS HAWKINS: It helps, Hilary. It helps.

HILARY: *You* feel more than *she* asks for.

MRS HAWKINS: I feel what I feel.

HILARY: You could have died!

MRS HAWKINS: So? Bad thing! Old is old! What can you do? Besides, I never wanted to grow into decrepitry.

HILARY: Decrepitude.

MRS HAWKINS: See! A lower-middle-class life shows through. Decrepitude. I always hoped that when it was time to go I'd be tired and *want* to go. Well, I'm getting tired, my child.

HILARY: No longer 'child', Mother.

MRS HAWKINS: You'll be a child till I'm dead. And when I'm dead you'll be nobody's child.

HILARY: I'll get my secretary to contact local estate agents, we'll start looking at once, I'll call the bank.

MRS HAWKINS: Old is old.

HILARY: Somehow or other we'll have you as near as dammit.

MRS HAWKINS: Old is old and that's it. That's it and there it is. (*Fade.*)

The cottage – the present.
Sound of rain, of wind. Scratch of pen on paper.

HILARY: But we never did. It never happened. Oh, we looked at a dozen flats but none of them good enough. And she resisted, and Sophie *was* reluctant, and work *was* pressing, and the money never really looked as if it was there, and so she died one day, a long way from us, and I was not there to comfort her. And she was right – suddenly I was no one's son any more.

I sit here as I have sat over the years, listening to the rain, remembering these things, hearing voices . . . .
(*Sound of rain and wind swells. Fade in voice of* STRIVEN.)

STRIVEN: (*As in memory*) I don't want you to do me the favour of loving me, Mr Scott. I'm unlovable, and very pleased to be that way. Imagine! All that *you* love and admire I hate and despise. The beautiful, the clever, playful children, crying babies, music, lovers, music-lovers, spring, animals, God-believers, Christ-followers, good-cause-collectors-at-the-door – contempt for them all! Except one, Help The Aged. The old and forgotten are the ones I care about. For the rest – weepers and whiners. The bleeding hearts of the world who imagine they know what's wrong with my life. But I have a fence round my house and everything within that fence is mine. Untouchable. Don't you forget that, ever, don't you forget, don't forget . . .

(*The phrase 'don't forget' is repeated and echoed like a recurrent tune in the head. More voices, more clues assemble. Overlapping 'don't forget, don't forget' comes the voice of* SCOTT.)

SCOTT: He had the look of someone who wouldn't think twice about laying hands on you . . . And his voice was like a slow knife . . . They weren't poor . . . He was a wealthy scrap-metal merchant, wasn't he . . . ?

(*Repeat and echo 'scrap-metal merchant, scrap-metal merchant, scrap-metal merchant'.*)

HILARY: My clerk kept telling me not to forget things. Don't forget! Don't forget! Don't forget! I knew it referred to something familiar but what? *What?* And then there was the personality of Striven himself. That venomous dealer in discarded metals . . .

(*Repeat and echo 'discarded metals, discarded metals, discarded metals'. Over it the word 'below' is repeated and echoed, but this time it ends like a shout from on high. A second's pause. A thud and immediately a cry of great pain.*
Sound of rain, of wind, Scratch of pen on paper.)

I had turned my back on a dying friend, remained silent before the plea of an erstwhile chum, and had left my mother to live alone.

I sit here, as I have sat over the years, listening to the rain, remembering. They were not good years for me, and through them, like a tumour in the head, I am obsessed with those words 'below . . . don't forget . . . shout out . . .' and I watch the times move, stupefied by civil wars and revenge, assassinations and rhetoric, the arms race and famine, and I know he has touched me, that man, Striven, in my darkest suspicions. And to my horror I find myself envying his capacity to hate as one envies a talent to sing. Not good years at all . . . (*Fade.*)

(*Echoes as if coming to him in sleep:*

282

'Below, below, below'; 'Don't forget, don't forget, don't forget';
'Shout out, shout out, shout out'. With a cry HILARY unhappily
awakes from sleep.)
(*Slowly remembering*) Don't forget, shout out, 'Below.'
(*Fade out wind and rain.*)

PART TWO
THE STORY

An old factory – the past.

TOM: You what they've sent me?

YOUNG HILARY: Afraid so.

TOM: 'Fraid so, are you? Well let's 'ope I ain't afraid so. You done this before?*

YOUNG HILARY: Not carpenter's mate but building sites plenty.

TOM: You a student?

YOUNG HILARY: Afraid so.

TOM: 'Fraid so, 'fraid so! You better not be 'afraid so' of too many things or you'll be no good to me, cocker. You climb ladders, swing on roofs, rock in cradles and slide along 'igh rafters in this job. I don't want no crying and no jelly livers and no 'fraid sos alongside me. You got that?

YOUNG HILARY: You won't have to worry on my account, Mr –

TOM: You can call me Tom, but that don't mean you can take liberties. I may look only a little older than you and I can see you've got bleedin' clever eyes and I can 'ear your mouth is full of clever books but I'm the chippie on the job and I've got the know-'ow and you see these 'ands? They've got nearly ten years' carpentry in them so what I say goes and that's a thing you and me better get clear from the start. Got that, Mr er –

YOUNG HILARY: I think so. And you can call me Hilary. (*Fade.*)

(*Rustle of sandwich paper.*)

TOM: Says we can call 'im 'Ilary. This 'ere's Ron Kimble, plumber on the job and the 'andsomest plumber this side of the Atlantic which

---

* Cockney dialect is very familiar to actors. I've only hinted at it for Tom by dropping the aitches. It would make tiresome reading to make 'things' 'fings' and 'thoughts' 'fawts', etc.

you'll 'ave proof of cos you'll see the way girls and women look at 'im but, I'll say this for 'im, it don't spoil im, do it, china? 'E turns 'is 'ead and gets on with the job and 'e's a pleasure to work with. And this 'ere is Rory, 'is mate. Be careful of Rory, 'e makes mistakes.

RON: Don't ever do nothing right do yer, matey?

RORY: He's right! He's right! There's nothing I do isn't a balls-up. (*To* YOUNG HILARY) I'll swap half a cheese and chutney for one of your boiled eggs.

YOUNG HILARY: Done!

RORY: But I try. I do try, don't I, Ron? Can't say I don't try. I know what has to be done, I've seen you do it a hundred times but the minute I put my hand to a job – smash! It's a jinx, like night-blindness which me brother suffers from. But God knows I do try.

TOM: Well, there better be no jinx this time cos the job we're doing is clearing the roof of bluey.

(*Pause.*)

RON: He knows what bluey is, don't he?

TOM: You know what bluey is, don't you?

YOUNG HILARY: Lead.

TOM: 'E knows what bluey is.

RON: Does he know the score?

TOM: 'E's only just been sent by the yard, leave off!

RORY: Is he a good boy, that's what we need to know. Is he a good and upright lad?

TOM: Leave 'im 'ave 'is lunch in peace. 'E's not yet lifted a tool in 'is 'and. Right, now, Master 'Ilary, lunch is thirty minutes but you take your time. The trick is not to do too much too fast or they'll expect you to do more, faster. (*Fade.*)

(*Knock of hammers on lead, a dull thudding.*)

Too old and dry and cracked to save this lot. But old and cracked and dry though it is, it's gold dust, like bleeding gold dust. Now, we cut it in strips and we roll and we knock it as flat as we can. Got that?

YOUNG HILARY: Got that.

(*Pause knocking.*)

TOM: Law a difficult thing to study?

YOUNG HILARY: For me it is.

TOM: Bit dim, are you?

285

YOUNG HILARY: Afraid so.

TOM: You mustn't be afraid of so much. You go on and on being afraid you'll fail at everything.

(*Pause knocking.*)

What made you choose law, then?

YOUNG HILARY: My mother. She wanted a lawyer in the family.

TOM: Wanted an honest man about the 'ouse?

YOUNG HILARY: A rich and successful one, I think.

TOM: Ain't your family rich then?

YOUNG HILARY: Now Tom, would I be working in my holidays if I were rich?

TOM: Oh, so your family ain't rich then. Oh! Well, I wasn't supposed to know, was I? I mean in my book all clever people is rich, ain't they? (*Fade.*)

(*Rustle of sandwich paper.*)

RORY: I'll swap half a pickle and ham for half a cheese and tomato.

YOUNG HILARY: Done.

RON: Glad we're not clearing this lead in wintertime.

TOM: Yard'll make a packet out of this lot.

RON: I love working lead.

TOM: Gold dust. Like bleedin' gold dust!

RON: They die mining it but I love handling it.

TOM: Bleedin' better'n gold dust in fact.

RON: You can make lead go round things, mould it how you want. It's solid but pliable. Makes me wish I'd been a sculptor.

TOM: A lunch bag each of this and we'll all 'ave a couple of quid in 'and.

RON: Now then! Putting criminal thoughts in the head of a judge what's to be!

TOM: 'E's not a judge yet and from what 'e tells me 'e could do with a couple of quid in 'is pocket.

RORY: I don't think you should go corrupting your mate, Chippie. That's no way to start a young man off in life – a young man with such clever eyes. I'll swap half an apple for half a pear.

YOUNG HILARY: Done. (*Fade.*)

(*Knock of hammers on lead, a dull thud.*)

TOM: Cor! There's a lot of beams and rafters going to need replacing when we've shifted this lot.

YOUNG HILARY: How long do you think this lead's lain here, Tom?

TOM: Gawd knows! A lot more years than you and me'll ever see.
  (*Pause knocking.*)

YOUNG HILARY: Tom.

TOM: Yes, China?

YOUNG HILARY: I think I *know* what you're all doing.

TOM: What's that then, China?

YOUNG HILARY: Behind that sheet of corrugated iron, those lumps of bluey you're stacking away – you're going to sell them, aren't you?

TOM: We was gonna cut you in.

YOUNG HILARY: I wasn't looking for a cut. I just wanted you to know I knew. Save you having to be embarrassed.

TOM: Embarrassed?

YOUNG HILARY: Crafty.

TOM: Crafty?

YOUNG HILARY: Circumspect!

TOM: Oh, I do like *that* word. Oh yes. That's a wealth of a word that one. It tells you what it means straightaway, don't it? Circumspect! So, you ain't aiming to tell no one?

YOUNG HILARY: Do I look the treacherous kind?

TOM: No lectures on thievery and rogues and wrong-doing and pure living and conscience and things? (*Pause.*) That's my old China. Liked your face from the start. Those bleedin' clever eyes . . . (*Fade.*)

Street beside the old factory – the past.
  Evening sounds, voices in whisper.

TOM: Now 'ere's the plan. We've got to be very 'circumspect'. Rory takes up watch. Ron stands by with our four packs. 'Ilary and me – up inside the window which was conveniently left open by yours truly, and up the ladder also left conveniently in place by yours truly. 'Ilary shifts the bluey from under the corrugated sheet to the ledge. I'll whistle once to make sure Ron's in place, and then Ron – that 'andsomest of plumbers – will whistle back. I yell 'below', count three, drop, whistle. Yell 'below', count three, drop, whistle, and so on. Got it?

RORY: It's very clever of you to put me on look-out. Can't do anything wrong just looking out, can I? I mean, I just stand around and look out. Simple!

RON: You *could* fall asleep!

TOM: Right, we're off.

(*Footsteps. Window opening. Grunting.* HILARY *drops down. Grunting.* TOM *drops down. Feet climbing ladder. Stumble.*)

Jesus Christ! This ladder's not secure. Rope's loose. Must fix that. Now mind you don't fall. Everything's different in the dark. Right, off you go. One at a time. And don't slip.

(TOM *whistles.* RON *returns the whistle.*)

(*Whispered shout*) Below! (*To himself*) One, two, three, over she goes.

(*Dull thud of lead landing. Pause. Shuffling.*)

(RON *whistles.*)

Below! One, two, three, over she goes.

(*Dull thud of lead landing. Pause. Shuffling.*)

(RON *whistles.*)

Below! One, two, three, over she goes.

(*Dull thud of lead landing. Pause. Shuffling. Pause.*)

What's 'olding 'im? Ron! You all right?

RON: The last lump's too big. I'm cutting it into smaller pieces. You'll have to hang on a bit.

TOM: 'Ilary. You can throw the next one. I'm going to tighten the rope on the ladder. Wait for Ron's whistle, and don't forget, shout out 'below', count three, and 'eave over.

(*Shuffling along roof ledge.* TOM'*s puffing as he reties rope.*)

'E whistled yet?

YOUNG HILARY: Not yet.

TOM: You're so cool about it. Like you lifted bluey every day of the week. You sure you ain't never stolen anything before?

YOUNG HILARY: I used to steal sweets from Woolworth's as a kid. Creep around picking them out between the glass joins.

TOM: Wicked!

YOUNG HILARY: I kept a book from the library and said I'd lost it.

TOM: Wicked! Wicked!

YOUNG HILARY: I once pinched pennies from my mother's bag.

TOM: Wicked! Wicked! Wicked!

(RON *whistles. The rest happens with speed and panic.*)

YOUNG HILARY: (*To himself*) Over she goes.

TOM: (*Urgently*) Did you yell 'below'?

YOUNG HILARY: Christ! Below!

(*The voice from on high is followed by a second's pause. A thud and immediate cry of great pain.*)

The cottage – the present.

Over the cry of pain HILARY *having woken from sleep in distress.*

HILARY: I didn't shout 'below'. I forgot to shout 'below'. I forgot it! I forgot it! Oh, God help me, I forgot to shout 'BELOW'.

(*Long pause. Sound of rain, of wind. Scratch of pen on paper.*)

And when I did, he looked up just in time to see the jagged lump that was about to hit him. What happened next? I have forgotten what happened next. Did we call an ambulance? Did Tom walk him to a hospital? As I write, I remember he said, 'Clear away the bluey before anyone comes.' Did I hear him say that or do I remember being *told* that is what he said? (*Beat.*) There was a conversation.

(*Fade low sounds of rain, wind and pen.*)

TOM: (*In memory*) I been to see 'im. Not pretty. Ward sister tell me 'e'll be all right but not for a while yet. Concussion. Bloody 'ell! Lucky 'e wasn't killed, lump of lead like that. Lucky for you too, cocker . . . (*Pause.*) Course 'e didn't *say* it was a lump of lead. 'E was very circumspect about it. Said it was some slates and bricks the wind blew off a building site coming 'ome from the pub. (*Beat.*) I tell 'im we couldn't sell the stuff after that. (*Beat.*) I tell 'im we took it back to the yard. (*Beat.*) Poor sod! Don't think 'e took much in. Or really cared. (*Beat.*) Only 'ave to split the money three ways now.

(*Fade back sounds of rain, wind and pen.*)

HILARY: I was furious and raged at him for his tawdriness, his lies, his cheating! He *could* split it three ways, I told him, but not to include me. And I feebly imagined that to decline a share in the loot absolved me of guilt. But I can recall nothing more of the incident itself. In what state did I climb down off the roof? What did I say to Ron Kimble? Was I involved in confirming the lies told at the yard? Did I check that Tom *had* shared the money with the plumber? Why can I not remember? Nothing more comes to me. I cannot see images. I cannot see settings. I cannot see his face. Dear God! I cannot even remember visiting him in hospital.

I sit here, as I have sat over the years, listening to the rain, grateful to have unlocked part of memory, relieved the words have fallen into place, but – did I want to remember? I am tormented by new thoughts. Whatever happened to the man? A scarred face haunts me now.

(*Fade out sounds of rain, wind and pen.*)

The house – the present.
Weeks later.

SOPHIE: (*Impatiently*) You look dreadful, Hilary. Your face is drawn and thin and you have dark rings round your eyes. Dreadful! This is no way to recover. You've solved the riddle of the disjointed phrases, the doctor has passed you fit, what more do you want? I'm not being unsympathetic but you don't eat adequately or regularly, and you're indulging yourself in morbid introspection, and to be frank you're a brooding and unhappy presence in the house. Most men would be thrilled with early retirement, catch up on books, hobbies, travel. You? You look haunted, hunted and dreadful. (*Fade.*)

(*Days later.*)

(*More tenderly*) Hilary, this is not you. To be brought down by the past? You've seen too many skeletons paraded out of other people's cupboards, why should *you* be different? Talk with your friends, ask them to share a guilt or two. Don't be so harsh on yourself, as though the world wasn't harsh enough! Was it *such* an awful crime? A petty thing in which you took no share, and for the rest – an accident. Believe me, darling, if mankind boasted no more wickedness than that, oh what a lovely world to be alive in! But it's not lovely, it's bewildering, and in it *you* bewilder *me*. You do, my darling, you do bewilder me. Very much.

The cottage – the present.
A week later.

SOPHIE: (*Through the phone; now angry*) You shouldn't have gone back to Wales. I begged you. Solitude is unnatural, I don't care what ascetics say. There's no health in those hills if your heart's heavy and your mind's tormented. Do you eat? You don't even feed yourself. And you're making *me* sick with worry. I've lived your nervous breakdown with you but now it'll happen to me. Have you thought about that? The anxieties you're passing on to me? What do you *do* there? You've no cases to consider. You tell me you can't concentrate on books. You're too lethargic to take walks. You've no heart to work in the garden. Don't you know what an exterminating angel loneliness is? Listen to me. You can't reflect in isolation. (*Beat.*) Thought eats thought. (*Beat.*) Self-hatred feeds upon itself. (*Beat.*) You won't lay old ghosts, you'll simply conjure up new ones. Hilary, listen to me. Come back. Be among people.

(*Sound of rain and wind. Scratch of pen on paper.*)

HILARY: (*His voice weaker*) My wife is wrong. I do not conjure up new ghosts. The old ones simply become more vivid. She doesn't understand. I have accumulated too many sins of omission. Clogged up the arteries with rusty old errors. Calcified the heart with small deceits. And the Strivens of this world make me unfit for the company of wives. Ashamed.

RON: (*As in memory*) I love working lead.

HILARY: Ashamed. I'm so ashamed.

RON: They die mining it but I love handling it.

HILARY: It was cowardly not to visit you.

RON: You can make lead go round things, mould it how you want. It's solid but pliable. Makes me wish I'd been a sculptor.

HILARY: I hid myself away from the event and then hid the event from myself. But there it lay, biding its time to rise and strike. You forget nothing. I have lived all my life not knowing how a man I had damaged lived his. I cannot bear that thought. I cannot.

I sit here, as I have sat over the years listening to the rain, and wonder at the rain, and the years, and myself in them. There was a time I felt capable of identifying wrong, and was certain of the redemptive power of punishment. I could carry the law, the land and my loved ones like a featherweight of flowers. Easy! Now I know there are crimes no law can touch and no punishment redeem. Sad.

(*Scratching stops. Diary book is closed. Chair is pushed back as* HILARY *stands, stretches.*)

(*Talking to himself*) Sat too long. I'm too old to sit too long a stretch. Wish I could give up writing this diary. Who do I write for?

(*Begins to sing.*) 'My uncle he was a Spanish Captain . . .' (*Stumbles.*) Oh! Legs gave way. Think I better sit again. What was I singing for? Don't usually sing to myself. How strange I feel. Floating. Dizzy. Weak. Haven't eaten. Three days without food. Penance! I'm doing penance for you, Ron Kimble. Don't feel ill, though, just – high. Bit delirious perhaps. Quite pleasant, actually. Not much of a penance to be pleasantly high.

(*A very ghostly voice is heard, mixed with the wind. It seems to be whispering, 'Look for me, look for me, look for me.' Door opens. Wind howls. Voice is louder, blasting him.*)

(*Talks to himself loudly, as though to drown out the wind and voice.*) Do you wonder about me as I wonder about you, Ron Kimble? Are you philosophical, bitter, did you marry, did you have children, were you scarred for life, did you become ugly, live alone, full of hatred? I have so many questions to ask you, so much I need to know.

(*The voice grows insistent in its demand.* HILARY *has made it across the courtyard, unlocked the front door, entered. On closing it the wind and the voice are fainter: 'Look for me, look for me, look for me.' Fade out.*)

PART THREE
THE QUEST

All in the present.
At Tom's front door.

TOM: (*Very old now*) I don't believe it. I don't believe it. You don't 'ave to tell me 'oo you are. I know 'oo you are. I'd know 'oo you are anywhere, anytime, any age. Those bleedin' clever eyes and a mouthful of clever books. Come in, come in! Well! This is an honour your honour. (*Fade.*)

. . . and you've got to believe that. I *did* give 'im 'is share of the money cos you put the fear of God up me, straight! Even then. Cor! I shouldn't like to be before you as a judge now. Anyway, I did see 'im once or twice after . . . (*Fade.*)

Now follows a series of encounters with two East End house occupants and a shopkeeper.
A front door.

MRS MONTGOMERY: No, no one name of Kimble lives here. No one name of Kimble lived here *before* us. Name of Montgomery lives here now, and the name of Mitchum lived here before us. I can tell you where the Mitchums live if you want to know because the Mitchums live round the corner in a bigger house. That's why they moved from here. They kept having children and so this house got too small for them and they moved to number 83 Larchmont Road. I know they moved there cos we helped them move . . . (*Fade.*)

A front door.

MRS MITCHUM: Kimble? Kimble? No, no one by that name lived in Kings Street when *we* moved in there. Their name was Morgan, and the Morgans didn't move anywhere because they got killed poor things in a car crash which was funny old fate if you think

293

about it since he built his own car. With his own hands! Took eighteen months to construct his own coffin, you might say. Funny old life . . . (*Fade.*)

Katie's delicatessen.

KATIE: (*Jewish*) Come in, sir, come in. We got lots more goodies inside, so keep looking. Only Jewish delicatessen shop left this side of the East End but they come from miles around to old Katie's because old Katie was featured in *The Sunday Times* colour supplement. See? Nice picture, eh? Keep looking! Keep looking! What can I serve you? You're not a Jewish gent so perhaps I'll explain what's what. Well, you'll have heard of matzos, Jewish or not, everybody eats matzos. Unleavened bread, supposed to be eaten only at Passover to remind us of our time in the wilderness, though who says we're not still in the wilderness, eh? You tell me! Cream cheese? Chopped liver? Chopped herrings? Pickled cucumbers I pickle myself with a special recipe my old mother handed on to me from Poland? Salami? With garlic or without? Without! Very good, sir. Keep looking, keep looking. Cream cheese? With chives or without? With! No problem. Keep looking, keep looking. Those? those are bagels – sour dough rolls with the middle missing. Dozen of those? You sure? A whole dozen? You got a party or something? My pleasure. Keep looking, it's all fresh and tasty, keep looking, keep looking . . . (*Fade.*)

The house.
Sound of carrier bag.

SOPHIE: Hilary! Have you gone mad? What have you bought all this food for? When will we eat it? And since when do you like spicy pickled cucumber? From one extreme to another – penitence to gluttony. Stop this! It's not fair of you to frighten me, to be so strange. I will be the one to go under. You'll end up driving me to a nervous breakdown. And I won't recover. (*Fade.*)

The cottage.
Sound of rain, of wind. Scratch of pen on paper.

HILARY: Nobody who is unhappy should assume responsibility of any kind. Neither to teach nor judge nor to entertain nor place oneself among friends. Unhappy people should not advise nor comment nor create nor be lovers nor have children. Unhappiness is like cancer, it eats the goodness from life, drains away all energy. (*Pause; desperate*) I have a ghost I cannot exorcize.

(*Scratch of pen stops. The voice of* HILARY *enters dreamland. He is asleep, restlessly dreaming against the sound of his sighing and moaning:*)

I have a ghost I cannot exorcize. I have a ghost I cannot exorcize. I have a ghost I cannot exorcize.

(*Superimposed upon this, like two other instruments entering an orchestration:*)

RON: Look for me, look for me, look for me.

KATIE: Keep looking! Keep looking! Keep looking!

(*It's* KATIE'S *insistent order which grows above and drowns out the others like a final command.*)

Keep looking!

(HILARY *wakes with a start.*)

Katie's delicatessen.

HILARY *has returned.*

KATIE: Yes, of course I remember you, sir. And you've come to the right person because Katie remembers all her customers. So I remember you and I remember Mr Kimble. You don't forget the Mr Kimbles of this world, struck by the hand of God to carry his message about the world telling us never to be sure of anything. God's like that, you know. Sometimes he does things too well and then regrets it. And Ron Kimble walks around as the living proof. He was too handsome. The right side you fall in love with, the left – well, you'll see, like a huge beast had scratched him. Deep scars. Angry. So you were right to think of Katie. She does special dishes for Ron Kimble. Now, you go out of here and you first turn left, then by a pub called The Mason's Arms . . . (*Fade.*)

Standing on the street corner, watching the front door of Ron Kimble's house, HILARY *imagines three encounters with him:*

FIRST RON: You? I forget your name but – you? Well, strike me dead! (*Laughs.*) You nearly did, didn't you? Ha! That's a joke. Strike me dead! You!

You're a judge, ain't you? Remember the first time I see your photo in the paper I said I know that face. It was the eyes. Young Tom used to call you 'bleedin' clever eyes'. There's a lot of water passed under the bridge since then, eh?

Come to see old scarface? Come to see how the handsomest of plumbers survived? Well, I can't grumble. I was scarred but I wasn't maimed. Could've lost a hand on a blow lamp in our trade, couldn't we, or fallen off a ladder and broke me back? I'm a bit of a sight to look at, and age don't help, but I've got me health, and as you can see from me flat I ain't bad off. Blimey! You do look pale.

Tell you what. It's only the afternoon, I know, but how about a spot of whisky? What'll your blood say to that? Bring a bit of colour to your cheeks this will. The best. Glenmorange. Spoil meself. We don't want to go remembering rotten old times. I didn't have a full life, not a full family life like others but it was a sort of life. Even travelled a bit. Plumbed on liners to sunny places. And I've seen poverty and misery makes *my* life seem like it was spent in heaven.

(HILARY *is crying.*)

FIRST RON: You crying? You mustn't cry. That's not a manly thing to do, your honour, not for someone in your position. And what for? I didn't much cry for meself so I don't have no need of your tears. (*Fade.*)

SECOND RON: (*Cry of rage*) *Out!* Get out! You value your life you'll get out. Out! Out! You won't? Right! See this wire brush, see it? If you're not out by the time I count three, I'll have this down the left side of your face. One. Two. Three. *Out!* Get out!

(*His rage subsiding*) You knew, didn't you? You cocky bastard, clever eyes, you knew I couldn't do it. Though God knows how you knew cos there's many a time I imagined meeting you or looking you up and it was only with murder in my heart, I promise you.

What've you come for? Say sorry? Offer me compensation now you're a rich and famous judge? Why now? Why not when I was in torment cos I knew I'd never find a wife and never have a family and me friends were gone and me spirit and me hope for things?

And how did you find me? Eh? Of course! The Lords of the land have access to all things. You can look up your files and ask friends in high places.

No. It was Katie wasn't it? But how did you get to *her*? Oh well, it don't matter, do it? Not any of it. Life's over. When you retire life's over anyway.

(HILARY *is crying.*)

SECOND RON: No good *you* crying, mate. It's me got things to cry for. Ha! Listen to him. *He's* crying . . . (*Fade.*)

THIRD RON: Can't say I can see you properly. Lost me sight, see. Had an accident made everything blurred. That's why the place is in such a mess so you'll have to excuse it. Can you find somewhere to sit in all this rubbish? I have someone come in and clean up once a week but I can't see what she does. As long as the main things are in place so's I can find me way around and there's a smell of lavender polish, I don't mind. Lavender polish! Must have the smell of lavender polish about the place.

Hilary Hawkins you say your name is? Can't honestly say I remember a Hilary Hawkins. Can't honestly say I remember anything much. Work in the legal profession, do you? What you come and see me for? I done something wrong? Funny thing, that. I tell you what I do wrong, mister, I go on living, that's what I do wrong. I go on and on and on and on, much as I'd like not to. I mean would *you* want to go on living like this?

Some old people round here I meet them sometimes and they tell me, they tell me they wake up in the mornings and they say, 'Well, thank God I made it to another day.' Not me. I wake up from darkness into semi-darkness and I say, 'Oh Hell!' I say, 'Not another day.' I wake up and I say, 'God help me, I've got to go through this lot again.' I wake up and I say, 'Bloody Christ! The dream's over.' Every day for forty years the dream's been over for me.

(HILARY *is crying.*)

THIRD RON: What's that whimpering? You hear whimpering? Where's it coming from, I wonder? Can you hear it? Sounds like a child's crying in a corner, done something wrong and gone into a corner to get out the way of punishment. Open that door. See if you can see someone. Here, sonny! Here, little boy! Don't cry! You can't go through life expecting never to do anything wrong. Come here to old scarface. I've got some chocolate here. You come an' tell old scarface about it, he'll put it right. He'll tell you about the world and things. Once upon a time there was the most handsomest plumber this side of the Atlantic . . .

The cottage.
Sound of rain and wind. Scratch of pen on paper.
HILARY: I sit here as I have sat over the years listening to the rain, wondering will it ever stop, writing my diary, glueing together a cracked life. I did not visit the handsomest plumber this side of the Atlantic. I just watched him from afar, shopping at Katie's, and followed him home. And at his door he stood, looked out into the street as though for the last time and then turned back into his world. A destroyed life. Ghosts like that can never be laid. Nothing will assuage the reproach. No, the remorse. No, the pain.

I sit here as I have sat over the years . . . (*Fade.*)
(*Sound of rain and wind. Scratch of pen on paper. Fade.*)